"AN EVER CLOSER UNION"

European Integration and its Implications for the Future of U.S. - European Relations

JAMES B. STEINBERG

Prepared for the United States Army

RAND

R-4177-A

PREFACE

Spurred on by the Single European Act of 1987 and by the plan to complete the Single Market by January 1, 1993, European integration has grown in scope and ambition with the profound changes in Europe's political and security landscape over the past several years. The Maastricht Treaty, agreed to at a meeting of the European heads of state and government on December 9–10, 1991, was a further step in the evolution of the European Community that in turn triggered a far-reaching debate on the future of European integration. This Report examines how the process of European integration has shaped and will shape the future European economic, political, and security environment and assesses the implications of these developments for U.S. policy. It covers developments up to the European Community summit in Edinburgh on December 11–12, 1992.

It contributes to a larger project on the future U.S. role in Europe and implications for the Army, conducted within the Strategy and Doctrine Program of RAND's Arroyo Center. The broader project examines Europe's evolution since the end of the bloc-to-bloc system and the future U.S. and U.S. Army role in and contribution to European security. It is jointly sponsored by the U.S. Army, Office, Deputy Chief of Staff for Operations and Plans, and the Training and Doctrine Command, Fort Monroe.

The Report should be of interest to military planners, government officials, and analysts working on European economic, political, and security issues.

THE ARROYO CENTER

The Arroyo Center is the U.S. Army's federally funded research and development center (FFRDC) for studies and analysis operated by RAND. The Arroyo Center provides the Army with objective, independent analytic research on major policy and organizational concerns, emphasizing mid- and long-term problems. Its research is carried out in four programs: Strategy and Doctrine; Force Development and Technology; Military Logistics; and Manpower and Training.

Army Regulation 5-21 contains basic policy for the conduct of the Arroyo Center. The Army provides continuing guidance and oversight through the Arroyo Center Policy Committee (ACPC), which is co-chaired by the Vice Chief of Staff and by the Assistant Secretary for Research, Development, and Acquisition. Arroyo Center work is performed under contract MDA903-91-C-0006.

The Arroyo Center is housed in RAND's Army Research Division. RAND is a private, nonprofit institution that conducts analytic research on a wide range of public policy matters affecting the nation's security and welfare.

Lynn E. Davis is Vice President for the Army Research Division and Director of the Arroyo Center. Those interested in further information about the Arroyo Center should contact her office directly:

Lynn E. Davis
RAND
1700 Main Street
P.O. Box 2138
Santa Monica, CA 90407–2138

SUMMARY

INTRODUCTION

The Europe of the Cold War is gone, but what will take its place? The answer to this question will shape the future of U.S. relations with Europe. The European Community (EC) nations are among the United States' most important political allies and trading partners. Our relations with Western Europe have formed the cornerstone of U.S. policy throughout the post-World War II era. The institutions we have built with West Europeans—from the North Atlantic Treaty Organization (NATO) to the General Agreement on Tariffs and Trade (GATT) to the G-7—are fundamental to our security and prosperity.

This Report examines how the process of European integration since the Single European Act of 1987, especially the recently signed Maastricht Treaty and the debate over ratifying the Treaty, will shape the European economic, political, and security environment and assesses the implications of these developments for U.S. policy toward Europe.

THE MOVEMENT TOWARD "EVER CLOSER UNION"

The debate over four recurring issues has shaped, and continues to shape, Europe's efforts to achieve greater political and economic integration:

- *The goal of integration:* a "political union," including foreign policy and defense, versus a free trade association;
- *The process of collective decisionmaking:* supranational institutions versus intergovernmental arrangements;
- *Economic philosophy:* deregulation and neo-liberalism versus interventionist economic policy;
- *Geographic scope:* a small, homogeneous community versus a broad association of European nations.

Table S.1 shows that, although debates within the Community have led to shifting alliances, Western Europe's post-war history reveals that most of the major nations have adopted relatively consistent approaches when dealing with these four key issues.

Table S.1

European Attitudes on Political and Economic Integration Prior to the Maastricht Treaty

	Security Included	Supranational	Economic Activism	Broadened Membership
Belgium	Yes	Yes	Yes	No
Denmark	No	No	No	Yes
France	Yes	No	Yes	No
Germany	Yes	Yes	No	Yes
Greece	Yes	Yes	Yes	No
Ireland	No	Yes	Yes	No
Italy	Yes	Yes	Yes	Yes
Luxembourg	Yes	Yes	No	No
Netherlands	No	Yes	No	Yes
Portugal	No	Yes	Yes	No
Spain	Yes	Yes	Yes	No
United Kingdom	No	No	No	Yes

In the end, the future of European integration will turn to a large degree on the resilience of the nation-state as the organizing principle in modern Europe. The intense public debate over ratifying the Maastricht Treaty has demonstrated the extent of European discomfort over transferring sovereignty to a "technocratic" government in Brussels.

On the whole, EC member-states with the longest tradition of nationhood and with more homogeneous populations have tended to favor intergovernmental solutions that preserve a strong sense of national identity. Countries for which nationhood is a relatively new development—notably Germany, Italy, and Belgium as well as the Netherlands—seem less wedded to preserving national prerogatives. This division also reflects differences between states with highly centralized governments (France, the United Kingdom) and those that share power with local or regional entities (Germany, Belgium, Spain).

TO MAASTRICHT AND BEYOND: THE ELEMENTS OF EUROPEAN INTEGRATION

At its core, the dynamic leading to Maastricht stemmed from a broad Franco-German bargain on both economic and political issues: Germany would support the move toward European Economic and Monetary Union (EMU) and an expanded security role for the Community as part of an Intergovernmental Conference (IGC) that would also address EC institutional reform; France would accept strengthening the supranational character of the Community to get EMU and European defense.

Each of the 12 EC leaders left Maastricht claiming victory for his objectives, with a shared belief that only technical work was needed to convert the Maastricht agreement to the new constitutional framework for Europe. But storm clouds were gathering even before the ink was dry: German public opinion began to question the wisdom of abandoning the sacred deutschemark. Denmark narrowly rejected the Treaty in a referendum, while French voters approved, but by a slim margin. The Treaty was attacked by both left and right in the United Kingdom.

Despite these serious difficulties, the odds remain favorable that the Community will ratify the Maastricht Treaty, with suitable accompanying declarations to address continuing public concerns. But the contentious post-signing debate has raised an important question. Is Maastricht yet another step on the road to "ever closer union"? Or will it in fact represent the last, rather limited achievement of the Eurofederalists in the face of pressures to retain the nation-state as the dominant actor in a loosely confederal Europe from Brest to Brest (or beyond)?

Although the Treaty may look like a jumble of horse trading, compromise, and ambiguity among 12 states with differing views and interests across the four principal dimensions of the long-running EC debate, some general themes emerge that are likely to guide the Community's future development.

- The Franco-German partnership will continue as the locomotive of Community construction and will remain an effective engine to the extent that France's and Germany's objectives coincide.
- Germany will exert increasing influence in Community affairs (the "conductor" of the locomotive).
- The timing and extent of Community enlargement will help determine the future of European integration.
- Economics remains the focus of European integration and the area of greatest consensus, although moving to a single currency will prove much more difficult than EC leaders anticipated.
- While economic protectionism remains a concern, Maastricht reinforced the likelihood that the Community on the whole will pursue a noninterventionist and relatively free trade approach.

- The EC will expand its ties with Japan, but these ties will remain overshadowed by the U.S.-European relationship.
- A truly "communitarian" foreign and security policy and a defense role for the Community remain a highly uncertain prospect.
- Equity issues between richer and poorer EC states are likely to plague Community consensus.
- There is a growing tendency toward a "multiple-speed" Europe—that is, varying membership for different Community activities (such as EMU, social policy, and defense).
- The process of integration is threatened by deep public dissatisfaction with mainstream political parties.
- The nation-state will remain the principal locus for political decisionmaking in Europe.

Given these trends, the Community at 2000 will likely be larger by two to five states; will be more integrated in its economic activities, with some (but not all) countries sharing a single currency; and will be more institutionalized in terms of foreign policy cooperation, yet will retain a strong intergovernmental flavor and still flirt with, but not act on, real defense integration. In other words, it will be a Community that continues to follow the course of its first 40 years—ever closer, but not union.

IMPLICATIONS OF EUROPEAN INTEGRATION FOR U.S.-EUROPEAN RELATIONS

This portrait of the Community's likely evolution suggests that the course of U.S.-EC relations is likely to change, but not radically. Overall, there will be shifts in the balance of power as Europe comes to speak somewhat more frequently with one voice in economic and political affairs. Yet the prospects for generally positive relations remain good.

Economic Implications

European integration will have significant consequences for the evolution of U.S.-European economic relations, although the ultimate direction depends on a number of other factors, including the overall world economic situation and unpredictable economic events.

Three broad conclusions in the economic dimension stand out:

- U.S. leverage over European economic policy decisions will decline, especially in macroeconomic policy, if the EC actually moves to EMU.
- Europe will not become broadly protectionist, but serious disputes will develop or continue in a number of key sectors.
- European growth, spurred on by the Single Market and EMU, will produce further conflicts with the United States over interest and exchange rates and access to capital.

Foreign Policy and Security Implications

For the most part, maintaining close foreign policy and security ties and a cooperative relationship between the United States and the EC countries will turn on the continued perception of shared interests and objectives rather than on the organizational structure through which Europe arranges its affairs. Shared interests have knit the Alliance together through difficult times in the past and have helped contain differences in policy approaches. It is difficult to predict whether a more integrated Europe will cause these common interests to diverge—whether Europe will become more Eurocentric or, as its power grows, will assume greater global responsibilities. But the common commitment to democracy, economic growth, and human rights ensures that on many important international issues Europe and the United States will see reasonably eye-to-eye.

Still, the organizational structures through which Europe arranges its affairs can have some impact. In particular, growing European foreign policy and security integration will have five important consequences:

- An expanded EC foreign policy and defense role will reduce but not eliminate NATO's importance as a forum for transatlantic dialogue.
- European foreign policy will become less disposed to accommodate the American view.
- The importance of "special relationships" will diminish but will not be eliminated completely.
- Europe will become increasingly independent on foreign policy matters that directly touch on European interests but will continue to look to the United States for leadership in many important aspects of global affairs.

- Europe will make some progress toward an independent defense capability distinct from NATO. But most EC members will remain committed to a (reformed) NATO-integrated military command, and NATO will remain (for some time to come) the primary forum both for consultation on major security questions and for implementing decisions requiring the use of military forces.

POLICY RECOMMENDATIONS FOR THE UNITED STATES

In light of these economic, foreign policy, and security implications of European integration, the United States should take the following steps:

- The United States should continue its long-standing policy of supporting European integration because such integration will serve a number of key U.S. interests. Specifically, a politically integrated Europe will enhance European political stability, an integrated European market will help promote world economic growth and financial stability, and a more concerted European foreign and security policy can offer an alternative to U.S. involvement when such involvement is not desired.
- The United States should champion the cause of a broader European Community. Although an enlarged EC poses potential risks for the United States (e.g., a decrease in cohesion, leading to the revival of intra-European feuds), extending EC membership to Central and Eastern Europe's developing democracies is critical to promoting their economic growth, easing the transition to free markets, solidifying democratic governments, containing ethnic conflicts and separatist movements, and providing a measure of enhanced security.
- The United States should support NATO reforms that promote the complementarity of NATO and the EC/Western Economic Union (WEU). Although the movement toward a European defense identity is likely to be slow and limited (and to produce some problems for the United States), the United States has a stake in the orderly development of European capabilities because it enhances the European contribution to NATO, provides a more effective partner for joint security operations outside NATO, and creates an option for military response in situations where the United States chooses not to act.
- The United States should focus its bilateral diplomacy on nations that are the most influential in the European Community, especially Germany and, if possible, France, as well as the traditional

ally of the United States, the United Kingdom, although this may prove difficult because the problems in the Franco-American relationship stem from real differences in strategic perspective.

- The United States should strengthen its bilateral relationship with the EC in economic and security policy. In security policy, this means closer links with European Political Cooperation (EPC) or its successor, the Common Foreign and Security Policy (CFSP), if CFSP is adopted, and similar links with the WEU as its coordinating and planning role grows. In the economic area, the most important new link to forge is with the emerging EC macroeconomic policy process.

ACKNOWLEDGMENTS

The author would like to thank Peter Goldstone, Michael Shires, and Denise Quigley for their valuable research assistance. RAND colleagues Nanette Gantz and Marten van Heuven and Dr. Gregory F. Treverton of the Council on Foreign Relations provided insightful comments and suggestions on earlier drafts, and Doris Siegel brought all the pieces together.

CONTENTS

FIGURE

TABLES

ACRONYMS

BRITE	Basic Research in Industrial Technologies for Europe
CAP	Common Agricultural Policy
CDU	Christliche Demokratische Union (Christian Democratic Union)
CET	Common External Tariff
CFSP	Common Foreign and Security Policy
CMEA	Council for Mutual Economic Assistance
CSCE	Conference on Security and Cooperation in Europe
CSU	Christliche Soziale Union (Christian Social Union)
EAGGF	European Agricultural Guidance and Guarantee Fund
EC	European Community
ECB	European Central Bank
ECJ	European Court of Justice
ECSC	European Coal and Steel Community
EDC	European Defence Community
EEA	European Economic Area
EEC	European Economic Community
EFTA	European Free Trade Association
EMI	European Monetary Institute
EMS	European Monetary System
EMU	Economic and Monetary Union
EP	European Parliament
EPC	European Political Cooperation
EPP	European People's Party
EPU	European Political Union

ERDF	European Regional Development Fund
ERM	Exchange Rate Mechanism
ESA	European Space Agency
ESCB	European System of Central Banks
ESF	European Social Fund
ESPRIT	European Strategic Program for Research in Industrial Technology
Euratom	European Atomic Energy Community
FDP	Freie Demokratische Partei (Free Democratic Party)
GATT	General Agreement on Tariffs and Trade
IEPG	Independent European Program Group
IGC	Intergovernmental Conference
JESSI	Joint European Submicron Silicon Initiative
MEP	Member of the European Parliament
NAC	North Atlantic Council
NACC	North Atlantic Cooperation Council
NAFTA	North American Free Trade Agreement
NATO	North Atlantic Treaty Organization
OECD	Organization for Economic Cooperation and Development
OEEC	Organization of European Economic Cooperation
RACE	Research in Advanced Communications Technology in Europe
RPR	Rassemblement pour la Républic (Rally for the Republic)
RRC	(NATO) Rapid Reaction Corps
SACEUR	Supreme Allied Commander, Europe
SEA	Single European Act
SHAPE	Supreme Headquarters, Allied Powers Europe

SPD	Sozialdemokratische Partei Deutschlands (Social Democratic Party of Germany)
UDF	Union pour la Democratie Française (French Democratic Union)
VAT	Value-added taxes
WEU	Western European Union

PART 1

THE DYNAMICS OF EUROPEAN INTEGRATION

1. INTRODUCTION

BACKGROUND AND OBJECTIVES

The past half decade has witnessed a dramatic reshaping of the process of European integration. This new era of Europe building, initially spurred on by the Single European Act (SEA) of 1987 and the drive to complete the Single Market by January 1, 1993, has grown in scope and ambition with the profound changes in Europe's political and security landscape over the past two years. The collapse of communism in Central and Eastern Europe, the disintegration of the Soviet Union, German unification, and the challenge posed by crises in the Persian Gulf and in Yugoslavia have transformed the debate over European integration from economic efficiency to high politics. The Europe of the Cold War is gone, but what will take its place?

The answer to this question will shape the future of U.S. relations with Europe. The European Community (EC) nations are among the United States' most important political allies and trading partners. Our relations with Western Europe have formed the cornerstone of U.S. policy throughout the post-World War II era. The institutions we have built with West Europeans—from the North Atlantic Treaty Organization (NATO) to the General Agreement on Tariffs and Trade (GATT) to the G-7—are fundamental to our security and prosperity.

The purpose of this Report is to examine how the process of European integration since the Single Act, especially the recently signed Maastricht Treaty and the debate over ratifying the Treaty, will shape the future European economic, political, and security environment and to assess the implications of these developments for U.S. policy toward Europe.

ORGANIZATION OF THIS REPORT

Part 1 of this Report begins with a short historical review of the European Community's evolution through the Single European Act (Section 2), then turns to an overview of the key elements of the debate that led to the Maastricht Treaty and the ensuing debate over ratification (Section 3). Part 2 reviews in detail the main dimensions of the integration process: institutional reform (Section 4), foreign and security policy (Section 5), economic policy (Section 6), and enlargement (Section 7). Finally, Part 3 discusses the implications of the integration process for Europe (Section 8) and for U.S. relations with Europe (Section 9).

2. THE MOVEMENT TOWARD "EVER CLOSER UNION": EUROPEAN INTEGRATION FROM THE END OF THE SECOND WORLD WAR TO THE 1991 INTERGOVERNMENTAL CONFERENCES ON ECONOMIC AND POLITICAL UNION

THE FOUNDING ERA

During the first years after World War II, European visionaries such as Jean Monnet and French Foreign Minister Robert Schuman began to sketch out a plan for a politically united Western Europe.[1] Early efforts included creating the Organization of European Economic Cooperation (OEEC)[2] and, in 1949, the Council of Europe (an intergovernmental consultative body).[3] In the security sphere, Western European cooperation centered around the Treaty of Brussels (1948), a mutual defense pact among France, the United Kingdom, and the Benelux countries.[4]

---

[1]Some would argue that Winston Churchill qualifies as the first post-war "father" of European integration, based on his Zurich speech in September 1946, in which he called for a "United States of Europe." Monnet's vision was distinctly supranational; his motto was "We are not joining together states, we are uniting people." Other early advocates for a supranational Europe included Luigi Einaudi, who was Italy's President from 1948 to 1955. ("Italy must be ready to sacrifice part of its sovereignty for this Europe," as quoted in the *Financial Times,* August 20, 1990.) The roots of European integration lie even earlier in the pre-World War II era, with advocates such as Richard Coudenhove Kalergi, or even earlier, Victor Hugo.

[2]The OEEC was created in 1947 to foster European reconstruction in connection with the Marshall Plan. In 1960, the members of the OEEC, together with the United States and Canada, agreed to extend the organization's role to development assistance outside of Europe. They renamed the organization the Organization for Economic Cooperation and Development (OECD).

[3]The Council of Europe's original 10 founding members were Belgium, Britain, Denmark, France, Ireland, Italy, Luxembourg, the Netherlands, Norway, and Sweden. As of August 1, 1992, there were 27 member-states. While the Council of Europe's activities include economic, social, and cultural aspects of European cooperation, it is perhaps best known for the European Convention for the Protection of Human Rights and Fundamental Freedoms (1950) and the associated European Commission for Human Rights and European Court of Human Rights.

The Council of Europe is governed by a Council of Ministers from the member-states, which requires unanimity for decision. It has no supranational authority (implementing decisions requires legislation by national parliaments). There is an advisory Parliamentary Assembly attached to the Council.

[4]In a move that foreshadowed the European Economic Community, the Benelux countries formed a customs union in 1948.

In May 1950, Schuman put forward a plan for common operation of, and a common market in, coal and steel for Western Europe. His proposal culminated in the Treaty of Paris,[5] establishing the European Coal and Steel Community (ECSC). The ECSC, which included France, Germany, Italy, and the Benelux countries,[6] was designed to facilitate the economic recovery of this key sector and to reassure Germany's neighbors that a revitalized, self-sufficient German coal and steel industry could not become the basis for a new security threat.[7] The ECSC was run by the High Authority, a supranational body with considerable independence from the Council of Ministers that represented the participating states.[8]

During this same period, the growing perception of a Soviet threat to Western Europe following the outbreak of the Korean War led to renewed interest in fostering German rearmament. European and American leaders drew on the ECSC model as a way to permit German rearmament without awaking fears of a militarily revitalized Germany and proposed creating a European Defence Community (EDC).[9] Although a treaty was eventually drafted to establish a supranational approach to Western European defense, the effort foundered when the French National Assembly refused to ratify.[10] In

---

[5]The Treaty was signed on April 18, 1951, and entered into force on July 23, 1952.

[6]The United Kingdom was invited to join but declined; it became an "associate" member.

[7]The strategy of using economic integration to achieve broader geopolitical goals is clear from the preamble to the ECSC Treaty: "to substitute for age-old rivalries the merging of their essential interests; to create, by establishing an economic community, the basis for a broader and deeper community among peoples long divided by bloody conflicts; and to lay the foundations for institutions which will give direction to a destiny henceforward shared; . . . recognizing that Europe can be built only through practical achievements which will first of all create real solidarity, and through the establishment of common bases for economic development."

The strategy behind the ECSC represented a dramatic turnaround for French policy, which, in the immediate post-World War II years, had focused on weakening Germany through neutralizing the Ruhr, establishing French control of the economy in the Saar, and promoting a Germany of regions. See François Duchêne, "Less or More Than Europe? European Integration in Retrospect," in C. Crouch and D. Marquand, eds., *The Politics of 1992* (Blackwell, 1990), pp. 9–22.

[8]The ECSC also included a Court of Justice and an advisory Parliamentary Assembly.

[9]The EDC was to be accompanied by a European Political Community (EPC) to develop a common European foreign policy. The proposal is often referred to as the Pleven plan, after René Pleven, the French Prime Minister. The EDC Treaty was signed by the six ECSC countries on May 27, 1952.

[10]The French National Assembly finally rejected the Treaty on August 30, 1954. A frequently overlooked feature of the EDC debate, relevant to contemporary discussions of a new European security identity, was the thorny issue of the EDC's relationship to NATO. In 1952, Chancellor Adenauer proposed "corporate" EDC membership in

its place, seven European nations (France, Germany, the United Kingdom, Italy, and the Benelux countries) created a weaker intergovernmental structure, the Western European Union (WEU), in 1954.[11] But with the EDC's defeat, the focus of defense cooperation shifted decidedly toward the transatlantic NATO, where it remained until the early 1990s.

With the collapse of the EDC in 1954 and the consolidation of NATO, Europe's builders once more turned their attention to economic institutions. In 1955, the ECSC's six member-nations appointed a committee, chaired by Belgian Foreign Minister Paul-Henri Spaak, to consider further steps toward economic integration. The Spaak Report, issued in April 1956, culminated in the Treaty of Rome the next year.[12] The Rome Treaty created two new institutions: the European Economic Community (EEC) and the European Atomic Energy Community (Euratom).[13]

The structure of these two new Communities was less supranational than that of the ECSC, giving a greater role to the intergovernmental Council of Ministers,[14] which had a more dependent executive arm,

---

NATO, a proposal roundly rejected by the other nations. See Peter Ludlow, *Beyond 1992* (CEPS, 1989), p. 8.

[11]The WEU remained a relatively dormant organization until the mid-1980s. Spain and Portugal signed a protocol of accession to the WEU in November 1988, and Greece was accepted as a full member at the end of 1992. See Section 5, below.

[12]The Rome Treaty was signed on March 25, 1957, and ratified the same year. It entered into force on January 1, 1958.

[13]The six countries created Euratom out of a conviction that atomic energy would prove the cornerstone of Europe's energy future and that, for economic and political reasons, a coordinated approach was essential. In practice, Euratom has remained a relatively minor component of the integration effort.

[14]The Council of Ministers is composed of ministerial-level representatives from the member-states. It is the European Community's principal legislative body with final say, shared to a limited extent on certain issues with the European Parliament. The Presidency of the Council rotates every six months among the member-states in alphabetical order. The Council of Ministers decides issues by consensus, except in instances where "qualified majority voting" (see below, n. 33) is specifically authorized. The debate over extending qualified majority voting in the Council is discussed in later sections of this Report.

In the EC's early years, Foreign Ministers represented their governments on the Council. As the work of the EC became more complex, the need for other ministers to participate became apparent. Today, there are several "Councils": a General Affairs Council, comprising Foreign Ministers who consider broad policy questions; the ECOFIN Council, comprising Treasury/Finance Ministers who consider economic and financial issues; an Agricultural Council; and several more specialized groupings.

the European Commission.[15] The role of the ECSC Court of Justice and Parliamentary Assembly was extended to apply to the two new Communities as well.

The EEC was designed to be a customs union with a common external tariff, but it also included important integrationist features, most notably in developing common agricultural and external trade policies. Moreover, the Treaty left open further expansion of the Community's role by authorizing the development of policies in any area necessary to achieve the general objectives of the Treaty.[16] Defense and foreign policy issues were, however, reserved for the member-states.

The two new Communities initially included the original six members of the ECSC. British opposition to the concept of a customs union (the United Kingdom preferred a free trade area, with nations retaining their own external tariff policies) and general distrust of common economic and social policies led to the creation in 1960 of the European Free Trade Association (EFTA), comprising the United Kingdom, Austria, Denmark, Iceland, Norway, Portugal, Sweden, and Switzerland (Finland was an associate member). In 1961, Britain reversed field, applying for EEC membership, but in 1963, France blocked its application.[17]

---

[15]The European Commission, in its present form, consists of 17 Commissioners appointed by the member-states for four-year terms (two Commissioners each from the United Kingdom, France, Germany, Spain, and Italy; one from each of the remaining countries). It is headed by a President appointed by consensus by the member-states for a renewable two-year term. The Commission acts collegially; each member has one vote, although each individual Commissioner holds special responsibility for one area of the Commission's work (e.g., external affairs, agriculture, competition, etc.). Under the Rome Treaty, the European Parliament has no say over the appointment of the President or other Commissioners. It may, through a vote of no confidence, dismiss the entire Commission, though this drastic power has never been used.

The Commission's principal power stems from its sole right to initiate proposals for the Community (which can be altered or rejected by the Council) as well as from the technical expertise of its staff and day-to-day responsibilities for implementing Community law and negotiating on behalf of the Community with third countries and in multilateral fora such as GATT. It also has the power to initiate enforcement proceedings against governments for alleged violations of EC laws.

[16]Article 235 resembles in some ways the "necessary and proper" clause of the U.S. Constitution, which has proved a flexible means of expanding the scope of the federal government at the expense of the states. "If action by the Community should prove necessary to attain, in the course of the operation of the common market, one of the objectives of the Community and this Treaty has not provided the necessary powers, the Council shall, acting unanimously on a proposal from the Commission and after consulting the Assembly [European Parliament] take the appropriate measures." (Change in brackets made in the Maastricht Treaty.)

[17]Ireland and Denmark also applied for membership in 1961 and Norway followed in 1962, but negotiations with these three ended with France's veto of Britain's application. Greece received "associate state" status in 1961 (which was frozen during the period of the Greek Junta) as did Turkey in 1963.

Negotiations on association with Spain and Portugal began in 1962.

In 1960, General Charles de Gaulle launched a new initiative to introduce a foreign policy and defense dimension to the common European effort. The so-called Fouchet plans proposed a political union, embracing both economic and security issues. The proposed framework was much more intergovernmental in character than even the EEC, reflecting de Gaulle's mistrust of supranational institutions. But the five other EEC nations rejected the plans because they (especially the smaller Benelux countries) disagreed with the movement away from a supranational approach. They also feared the union's impact on NATO, particularly since the United Kingdom was excluded from the proposed union. With the failure of the Fouchet plans, France and West Germany settled for a more modest bilateral agreement to cooperate on defense and security, the Elysée Treaty of 1963. But friction between Chancellor Erhard's strong Atlanticism and de Gaulle's search for a third way between the superpowers blocked any effective implementation of the Elysée Treaty.

The conflict between France's intergovernmental approach and the other Community members' supranational preferences came to a head in 1965–66, when the European Commission proposed to give the Community its own source of revenues and enhance the European Parliament's (EP) role in budgetary affairs, ideas vehemently opposed by France.[18] The "Luxembourg compromise" of 1966 restored an uneasy peace by confirming the role of the Commission but retaining a strong de facto national veto in the Council of Ministers.[19]

With the Luxembourg compromise, the Community was able to turn its attention to several critical economic tasks: completing the common market, implementing the Common External Tariff (CET), and developing the Common Agricultural Policy (CAP).[20] It also led to merging the executive arms of the three Communities into a single Commission in 1967.

A new phase in the EC's construction began with the Hague Agreement of 1969 (following the departure of de Gaulle), which focused on what has become known as both "deepening" and

---

[18]France actually boycotted the Community (the "empty chair policy") for seven months prior to the Luxembourg compromise.

[19]Prior to the 1965–66 crisis, there had been some majority voting in the Council of Ministers, as envisioned in the Rome Treaty. The Luxembourg compromise did not totally preclude majority voting, except in instances where a nation invoked its "vital interests." But de facto unanimity is required, since states are free to define for themselves what constitutes a matter of vital national interest.

[20]The six finally eliminated all intra-EC tariffs in 1968, one year ahead of the schedule laid out in the Rome Treaty.

"broadening" European integration. The Hague Agreement proposed to deepen the Community by committing the member-states to the twin goals of political and economic/monetary union.[21] It also led to creating a mechanism for consultation on foreign policy issues, European Political Cooperation (EPC), with a view to greater harmonizing of member-states' policies.[22] The move toward broadening began by opening membership negotiations with the United Kingdom, Ireland, Denmark, and Norway, with the former three countries joining the Community on January 1, 1973.[23]

The ambitions of the Hague Agreement soon came face-to-face with political and economic realities in the early 1970s. Divergent national interests, the energy crisis, and the economic recession following the Arab-Israeli war in 1973 led to a period of relative stagnation. The most notable structural developments of the 1970s included creating the European Council (regular meetings of the leaders of the member-states);[24] opening membership negotiations with Greece (1975), Spain, and Portugal (1977);[25] deciding to hold direct elections for the European Parliament (EP) (the first election was finally held in June 1979);[26] and creating the European Monetary System (EMS) (1979). The Community's problems were compounded by recession in the early 1980s. Member-states became disillusioned with the EC's effi-

[21]The Hague summit led to the preparation of two reports: the Davignon Report on Political Cooperation (approved by the member-states on October 27, 1970) and the Werner Plan for Economic and Monetary Union. The European Council agreed to implement the Werner Plan in early 1971, with the goal of full economic and monetary union by 1980, but the international financial crisis of 1971, including the U.S. decision to suspend convertibility of the dollar into gold, derailed the Werner Plan in its first stage.

[22]The evolution of EPC is discussed in conjunction with the debate on the EC's role in foreign and security policy in Section 5.

[23]Norway rejected membership in a referendum. Norway, along with Austria, Finland, Sweden, Switzerland, and Iceland, remained members of EFTA, which subsequently reached a series of bilateral agreements establishing free trade between the EC and the EFTA countries.

[24]Prior to the Paris Agreement of December 1974, heads of states and government met irregularly in what were known as European summits. The Stuttgart Declaration of 1983 (otherwise known as the Solemn Declaration on European Union) set forth the responsibilities of the European Council: to give a general political impulse to the construction of Europe; provide general political guidelines to the EC and EPC; maintain the coherence of the diverse aspects of the Community's activities; define new sectors of activity; and develop common positions on external relations. The European Council did not achieve formal Treaty status until the SEA (see below).

[25]Greece joined the Community on January 1, 1981; Spain and Portugal on January 1, 1986.

[26]Direct elections to the European Parliament are held every five years.

cacy and began to renationalize aspects of economic policy.[27] This period has become known as the era of "Eurosclerosis."[28]

The movement toward greater integration was "relaunched" in 1985 with the preparation of a "White Paper" entitled the "Programme for the Completion of the Internal Market," which set as the Community's goal eliminating the barriers to free movement of people, goods, services, and capital by 1992.[29] This broad action program not only launched the Community on its most ambitious effort to realize the goal of the "four freedoms" of the Common Market (freedom of movement of people, goods, services, and capital) but also led the way to a more far-ranging revision of the Community's institutional structure in the Single European Act.

---

[27]In its own history of the Community's evolution, the Commission, commenting on the situation in 1982, wrote: "The governments of the Member-states are now so concerned with national problems that they display little interest in making progress on Europe. The manifest inability of Community policies to curb the steady rise in unemployment damages the Community's public image. Disputes occur daily and the most the Community can hope to do is preserve what it has already achieved." Commission of the European Community, *Steps to European Unity* (Luxembourg Office for Official Publications of the European Communities, 1987), p. 72.

[28]"Eurosclerosis" refers to the lack of growth during this time and the perception that Europe was incapable of revitalizing itself. This sense of pessimism can be seen in a report authored by a number of leading European political analysts in 1983. In their introduction, entitled "Why This Report?" they observed: "This report is born out of a sense of alarm and urgency. The authors, with their different backgrounds as citizens of large or small member-states of the European Community, coming from the north or the south, all share the conviction that Europe is drifting, that the existence of the European Community is under serious threat. In sharp contrast with only a decade ago, the position of Western Europe seems to be challenged from all sides. If nothing is done, we are faced with the disintegration of the most important European achievement since World War II." K. Kaiser, C. Merlini, T. de Montbrial, E. Wellenstein, and W. Wallace, *The European Community: Progress or Decline?* (Royal Institute of International Affairs, 1983), p. 1.

[29]The White Paper is sometimes referred to as the Cockfield White Paper, after Lord Cockfield, the Vice President of the EC from 1985–88 and a driving force behind the 1992 project. The White Paper identified approximately 280 remaining barriers to achieving the four freedoms. These became the basis of the EC's action program, often referred to as the "Single Market Program" or the "1992 project." See SEA, Article 13. Some of the impetus for the Single Market Program came from European business leaders, through groups such as the European Round Table, founded in 1979. See William Wallace, *The Transformation of Western Europe* (New York: Royal Institute of International Affairs/Council on Foreign Relations Press, 1990), pp. 87–91.

THE SINGLE EUROPEAN ACT AND THE MARCH TOWARD ECONOMIC AND POLITICAL UNION

The Single European Act (SEA)[30] was the first major amendment to the Rome Treaty. Its purpose was threefold—to provide the institutional mechanisms needed to complete the internal market, to reform the Community's "political" (foreign policy) component, and to broaden the EC's jurisdiction in several sectors.[31]

The complexity of the task set out by the Commission's 1985 White Paper convinced member governments that the Community required special, more streamlined procedures to overcome the myriad political and bureaucratic obstacles to adopting needed legislation.[32] The SEA's solution had two elements. It allowed the Council of Ministers to adopt most directives relating to the 1992 program (other than those concerning tax harmonization, free movement of persons, and workers' rights) by "qualified majority voting" rather than unanimity.[33] It also enhanced the role of the European Parliament

---

[30]The text of the SEA was agreed to by heads of government at the Luxembourg summit in December 1985 and signed in Luxembourg on February 17, 1986, and in The Hague on February 28, 1986. Ratification was not completed until July 1987, the delay due in large measure to the decision of the Danish Parliament to reject the Treaty (that decision was overturned in a national referendum in February 1986) and a challenge to the legality of Ireland's adherence to the Act.

[31]The SEA arose out of an Intergovernmental Conference (IGC), convened by the European summit in Milan in June 1985, over the objections of Britain, Denmark, and Greece. Under Article 236 of the Rome Treaty, a majority of member-states can convene an Intergovernmental Conference to consider treaty amendments (though unanimity is required to adopt amendments at the conference). For a history and analysis of the factors leading to the SEA, see Andrew Moravcsik, "Negotiating the Single European Act: National Interests and Conventional Statecraft in the European Community," *International Organizations,* Winter 1991, pp. 19–56.

The Intergovernmental Conference procedure was used to consider treaty amendments for EMU and EPU, which resulted in the Maastricht Treaty. See below.

[32]There are two principal types of Community legislation: "directives," which set Community policy but must be implemented by national legislation, and "regulations," which are directly binding on European citizens and entities.

[33]See SEA, Articles 17 and 18. Qualified majority is a weighted voting system: There are 76 votes in the Community (10 each for France, Germany, Italy and the United Kingdom; Spain has 8; Belgium, Greece, the Netherlands and Portugal 5; Ireland and Denmark 3; and Luxembourg 2). A qualified majority is 54 votes.

The movement toward qualified majority voting was helped by the accession of Spain and Portugal to the Community; the growing size convinced many member-states that decision by consensus was increasingly impracticable.

through the use of the "cooperation procedure," while establishing tight time deadlines to keep the process on track.[34]

On the political level, the changes were more modest and, in many cases, simply represented treaty codification of existing political practices. The Treaty established a formal, legal basis for European Political Cooperation, although under an intergovernmental institutional framework separate from the Community's core economic activities (Title III of the SEA). Similarly, the European Council achieved Treaty status (Article 2), but rather than reiterating the detailed description in the 1983 Stuttgart Declaration on European Union, the SEA left the Council's responsibilities largely undefined. The SEA also expanded the Community's competence to include research and technology development, environmental regulation, and workplace health and safety; and it expanded the scope of "regional policy."[35]

THE ROLE OF THE UNITED STATES IN THE EUROPEAN COMMUNITY'S DEVELOPMENT

In the aftermath of World War II, the United States supported moves toward greater European union as a means of reintegrating Germany

[34]Under the cooperation procedure, the Parliament has two opportunities to review a proposed Community directive. After the Commission drafts a proposal (under its exclusive right of initiative) it goes to the Council, which asks the Parliament for its opinion. On this "first reading" the Parliament may accept, reject, or amend a directive. It then reports to the Commission and Council. While in principle the Commission may ignore the Parliament's amendments, in practice the Commission (which sees the Parliament as an ally against the intergovernmental Council) typically accepts the amendments. This revised proposal becomes the basis for the Council's consideration.

After the Council reaches a decision by qualified majority vote (called the "common position"), the Parliament conducts a "second reading" under strict time limits where it may reject, accept, or amend, then report back to Council and Commission. If Parliament accepts the common position, the directive is returned to Council for action by qualified majority. If Parliament rejects it outright, it also returns to the Council, where it can be adopted only by unanimous vote. If Parliament adopts amendments, the amendments go back to the Commission. If the Commission accepts Parliament's amendments, the Council may pass the amended directive by qualified majority or return to the original proposal (but only by unanimous vote). If, however, the Commission does not accept the Parliament's amendment, the Council must act unanimously. In practice, Parliament rarely amends at the second reading. See John Fitzmaurice, "An Analysis of the EC's Cooperation Procedure," *Journal of Common Market Studies,* June 1988, pp. 389–400.

The European Parliament also has a right of co-decision (in effect, a veto) over the Community's budget. But this power is less than it might appear because it cannot alter "compulsory" spending, which includes most major expenditures, such as the CAP. It has a veto over adding new members to the Community and concluding agreements with non-member states.

[35]Title II, Subsections III–VI, of the SEA.

with its former West European adversaries, facilitating post-war economic recovery and ending the antagonisms that had twice drawn the United States into Europe's quarrels. With the growing East-West conflict, the United States saw a more united Europe as essential (both politically and militarily) to maintain the Cold War balance in Europe and as a means to achieve European acceptance of Germany's rearmament.

In the late 1950s, the United States, for the most part, saw no conflict between European integration and the transatlantic security community. Secretary of State John Foster Dulles observed in 1956 that "European integration and the development of NATO are complementary and not mutually exclusive processes."[36] U.S. support for European integration reached a rhetorical zenith during the Kennedy administration, reflected in President Kennedy's 1962 Independence Day address[37] and in calls for a European pillar in defense. The administration linked support for integration to a transatlantic partnership in both economics and defense.[38] On that basis, the United States supported Britain's entry into the Community in the early 1960s.

But new tensions developed in the mid-1960s over issues such as de Gaulle's veto of Britain's EC application, balance of payments and burdensharing controversies, and France's withdrawal from NATO's unified command. European integration, and especially the prospect of an evolving French-German axis, appeared to some Americans as a rival to transatlantic political, economic, and security structures.

U.S.-European conflict came to a head in the controversy surrounding Secretary of State Kissinger's April 1973 speech launching the "Year of Europe." Kissinger's initiative sought to provide a strategic

---

[36]Quoted in Oliver Debouzy, *The Debate on the American Presence and Role in Europe* (European Strategy Group, January 1991), p. 35.

[37]"We believe that a united Europe will be capable of playing a greater role in the common defense, of responding more generously to the needs of poorer nations, of joining with the United States and others in lowering trade barriers, resolving problems of commerce and commodities and currency, and developing coordinated policies in all economic, political and diplomatic areas. We see in such a Europe a partner with whom we can deal on a basis of full equality in all the great and burdensome tasks of building and defending a community of free nations. . . . The first order of business is for our European friends to go forward in forming the more perfect union which will some day make this partnership possible." *New York Times*, July 5, 1962, p. 2.

[38]Thus while supporting European integration, President Kennedy called for Europe to lower its external as well as internal trade barriers (including tariffs and the CAP). See Gary C. Hufbauer, "An Overview," in G. C. Hufbauer, ed., *Europe 1992* (Washington, D.C.: The Brookings Institution, 1990), p. 4 [hereinafter, *Europe 1992*].

blueprint for transatlantic relations, linking political, economic, and security objectives through a new transatlantic charter. But the proposal met a chilly reception in Europe, reflecting concerns that it was designed to extend U.S. influence over all aspects of European policy. In response, the nine members of the EC adopted the "Declaration of European Identity," stating their intention to "strengthen their own cohesion and contribute to the framing of a genuinely European foreign policy."[39]

The United States responded with concern that the European proposal would lead to more confrontational U.S.-European relations on important foreign policy issues. Kissinger stated that "To present the decisions of a unifying Europe to us as *faits accomplis* not subject to effective discussion, is alien to the tradition of U.S.-European relations. The attitude of the unifying Europe . . . seems to attempt to elevate refusal to consult into a principle defining European identity."[40] The conflict was defused when the EC Foreign Ministers adopted in May 1974 the "Gymnich formula" (calling for consultations with the United States prior to discussion in EPC).[41]

Although the United States and the EC continued to conduct a number of meetings at senior official levels, high-level interchange was limited; EC President Delors went only once to Washington in his first four years in office.[42] Economic policy remained a source of contention, from the balance of payments crises of the early 1970s to the international economic instability created by growing U.S. budget deficits and the soaring dollar in the early 1980s. As the Single Market Program gathered steam, some in the United States began to fear the construction of a "Fortress Europe" in trade.

With a new administration in Washington in 1989 and the pressure of events in Europe, the U.S. approach to the EC evolved quickly. In a May 1989 speech at Boston University, President Bush set forth his administration's approach to U.S.-European relations:

---

[39]The Copenhagen Declaration, December 14, 1973.

[40]Quoted in Debouzy, *Debate on the American Presence,* p. 45.

[41]"[B]efore a member of the EPC could inititate consultations on a certain issue, provided the others agreed, the state in the chair would begin consultations with the United States. If there was no unanimity on such consultations, then they could take place bilaterally with the United States." Ibid. A revised approach to transatlantic consultation was agreed to in NATO's Ottawa Declaration of June 1974 See A. Menon, A. Forster, and W. Wallace, "A Common European Defence?" *Survival,* Autumn 1992, pp. 101–102.

[42]Henri Froment-Maurice and Peter Ludlow, "Towards a European Foreign Policy," in *Governing Europe,* Center for European Policy Studies Paper No. 45, 1990, p. 11. Delors did participate in several summit meetings of the G-7.

> The United States welcomes the emergence of Europe as a partner in world leadership. We are ready to develop—with the EC and its member states—new mechanisms of consultation and cooperation on political and global issues, from strengthening the forces of democracy in the Third World, to managing regional tensions, to putting an end to the division of Europe.

These ideas were fleshed out by Secretary Baker in his December 12, 1989, speech in Berlin.

> As Europe moves toward its goal of a common internal market, and as its institutions for political and security cooperation evolve, the link between the United States and the European Community will become even more important. We want our trans-Atlantic cooperation to keep pace with European integration and institutional reform. To this end, we propose that the United States and the European Community work together to achieve, whether in treaty or some other form, a significantly strengthened set of institutional and consultative links.[43]

Some Europeans viewed Secretary Baker's proposal with suspicion. France, in particular, doubted U.S. motives, fearing that the United States sought to extend the leverage it exercises in the security field (through NATO) to the EC's broader economic and political realm. In Europe there was talk of the United States wanting a "seat at the table."[44] After extended negotiations (during which both sides abandoned key short-term political objectives),[45] the United States and the EC reached agreement on a "Transatlantic Declaration," signed in Paris on November 20, 1990. The Declaration stated:

> To achieve their common goals, the European Community and its member states and the United States of America will inform and consult each other on important matters of common interest, both political and economic, with a view to bringing their positions as close as possible without prejudice to their respective independence.

---

[43]*New York Times,* December 13, 1989.

[44]See, e.g., *Guardian,* November 11, 1990.

[45]The United States sought a commitment from the EC to reduce agricultural subsidies; the EC wanted a U.S. pledge on stabilizing the dollar's exchange rate. They also disputed the site of the various consultations. The Transatlantic Declaration provides that the Foreign Ministers/Secretary of State meetings will take place "alternately on either side of the Atlantic" but is more ambiguous on the location of the other meetings (the consultations between Presidents will take place "in the United States and Europe"). More generally, the dispute centered around the U.S. attempt to focus on consultations among the Thirteen, while Europeans (especially France) preferred to see the agreement as bilateral between the United States and the Twelve. *Guardian,* November 21, 1990.

The Declaration also agreed that "a framework is required for regular and intensive consultation," including:

- Biannual consultations between:

  –the Presidents of the European Council and Commission, and the U.S. President

  –EC Foreign Ministers and the Commission and the U.S. Secretary of State

  –EC Commission and the U.S. Cabinet;

- Ad hoc consultations between the Foreign Minister of the country holding the EC Presidency and the U.S. Treasury Secretary;
- Briefings ("as currently exist") by the EC Presidency to U.S. representatives at the ministerial level of EPC.[46]

CONTINUITY AMIDST CHANGE

This history of Europe's efforts to achieve greater political and economic integration since the Second World War reveals a number of recurring issues that continue to shape the debate over Europe's future in the 1990s. Several stand out:

- *The goal of integration:* a "political union," including foreign policy and defense versus a free trade association;
- *The process of collective decisionmaking:* supranational institutions versus intergovernmental arrangements;[47]
- *Economic philosophy:* deregulation and neoliberalism versus interventionist economic policy; and
- *Geographic scope:* a small, homogeneous community versus a broad association of European nations.

Positions on these issues are interrelated. For example, "Eurofederalists" who favor the broader goal of political integration tend to see a small Community as the most fruitful route toward political integration, while those who focus on the purely economic benefits of integration tend to support enlargement.

Although debates within the Community have led to shifting alliances, Western Europe's post-war history shows that most of the major nations have adopted relatively consistent approaches over

---

[46]Transatlantic Declaration, November 20, 1990. The United States and the President of the EC Council (at that time, Ireland) had agreed on most of these new procedures on February 27, 1990.

[47]This choice is sometimes characterized as one between a Community uniting "peoples" and one uniting "nations."

time. France, although a leading advocate of a close political union (including security issues), has favored intergovernmental strategies, an activist industrial policy, and a smaller, tightly knit membership. The United Kingdom (and, to a considerable extent, Denmark) has shared France's preference for an intergovernmental approach but with different objectives: greater focus on the common market and free trade, support for a broader Community with greater national diversity, and a transatlantic rather than European approach to security. Germany shares France's interest in a political/security union but is more inclined to a free trade approach and prefers strong supranational institutions. Germany's growing concern with instability in Eastern Europe and its historical political and economic ties with several "neutral" nations increasingly leads it to favor relatively rapid EC expansion. Italy agrees with Germany on supranationalism, but its own powerful state economic sector leads Italy to favor greater economic intervention at the Community level. As for including defense in the "union," Italy, once thought of as strongly "European," is increasingly siding with the United Kingdom against the Paris-Bonn axis.

Many of the smaller EC nations share the supranational preference; they see the "communitarian" institutions, especially the EC Commission, as a way to protect their interests against domination by the larger states.[48] But there are differences among the small states as well: the Netherlands favors a transatlantic approach to security and free market economics, while Belgium is a leading voice for strengthening the Community's role in security and defense and a more activist industrial policy. Ireland's neutrality leads it to oppose EC involvement in defense (although it has not sought to impose this view on the Community).

Integration poses a particular dilemma for the Community's newer, less affluent members. On the one hand, membership in the Community has played a critical role in the democratic transformation of Greece, Spain, and Portugal. In addition, the Community has brought considerable economic benefits for all three countries (for Spain and Portugal, in the form of enhanced investment and growth; for Greece, primarily in substantial economic aid). To a large degree, their future economic success depends on a vibrant economic Community. Yet there is a risk that the larger, more developed countries will dominate a more powerful Community and will pursue in-

[48]Dutch Foreign Minister Hans Van den Broek has called the Commission a "factor of objectivity" in contrast to "the more subjective point of view of the individual countries." *NRC Handelsblad*, June 29, 1991 (FBIS-WEU-91-138, July 18, 1991, p. 18).

terests that differ from the priorities of the Community's weaker nations. For the EC's most developed countries, economic stability and low inflation are a priority: as net payers to the Community budget, they tend to resist expanding Community outlays. The poorer nations focus on economic development and improving economic parity; they are more prone to running large budget deficits and inflationary macroeconomic policy and want to expend Community resources to defray the costs of development. As a result, these countries are enthusiastic about the principle of a deeper Community but anxious on specific measures. They are also reluctant to support expanding the EC, especially to include former communist countries, fearing both economic competition and a diversion of the Community's economic development funds.

Table 2.1

European Attitudes on Political and Economic Integration Prior to the Maastricht Treaty

	Security Included	Supranational	Economic Activism	Broadened Membership
Belgium	Yes	Yes	Yes	No
Denmark	No	No	No	Yes
France	Yes	No	Yes	No
Germany	Yes	Yes	No	Yes
Greece	Yes	Yes	Yes	No
Ireland	No	Yes	Yes	No
Italy	Yes	Yes	Yes	Yes
Luxembourg	Yes	Yes	No	No
Netherlands	No	Yes	No	Yes
Portugal	No	Yes	Yes	No
Spain	Yes	Yes	Yes	No
United Kingdom	No	No	No	Yes

In the end, the future of European integration will turn to a large degree on the resilience of the nation-state as the organizing political principle in modern Europe. The intense public debate over ratifying the Maastricht Treaty has demonstrated the extent of European discomfort over transferring sovereignty to a "technocratic" government in Brussels. Although most of the analysis in this Report concerns top-down policy decisions (substantive and institutional), perhaps the most critical questions concern attitudes of the peoples of Europe themselves. Is a European identity emerging? Are citizens prepared to look to Brussels rather than their own capitals for the expression of their political, economic, and social aspirations and for the protection of their interests? Will the decisions at Maastricht boost public support for the integration process or trigger a backlash against new encroachments on traditional national sovereignty?

On the whole, EC member-states with the longest tradition of nationhood and more homogeneous populations have tended to favor intergovernmental solutions that preserve a strong sense of national identity. Countries for which nationhood is a relatively new development—notably Germany, Italy, and Belgium as well as the Netherlands—seem less wedded to preserving national prerogatives.[49] This division also reflects differences between states with highly centralized governments (France, the United Kingdom) and those that share power with local or regional entities (Germany, Belgium, Spain). Although some Eurovisionaries speak of a United States of Europe, their vision is competing with an alternative, less centralized image of Europe's future, as expressed by Danish Foreign Minister Uffe Ellemann-Jensen:

> In the United States you had a land area almost empty of people to which different cultures, races and peoples came pell-mell. And from this melting pot a nation grew. The peoples and cultures of Europe are fixed. We are not a melting pot and hopefully we never will be. In Europe we can reach agreement on more and more and break down ever more barriers between us. But you cannot compare the two situations.[50]

---

[49]The frequently scathing Dutch criticism of the French approach vividly illustrates this dichotomy. For example, Dutch Foreign Minister Van den Broek recently observed that he had "gotten the feeling on several occasions that certain larger member countries, in spite of the interests they themselves have in the Community . . . are still being influenced in their actual behavior by a certain inclination towards the past, when every state was 100 percent sovereign and when there was still no question of any supranational discipline." *NRC Handelsblad,* June 12, 1990 (FBIS-WEU-90-140, July 20, 1990, p. 2).

[50]*Berlingske Tidende,* July 8, 1990 (FBIS-WEU-90-134, July 12, 1990, p. 28).

3. TO MAASTRICHT AND BEYOND: THE ELEMENTS OF EUROPEAN INTEGRATION

As 1990 dawned in Europe, two important trends were, in parallel, pushing the European Community's members to take major new steps to reshape the Community's role and its institutions. In the economic sphere, the success of the 1992 program and the growing macroeconomic interdependence of European economies through the European Monetary System (EMS) led Community leaders to consider once again establishing a European Economic and Monetary Union (EMU).[1] On the political front, the transformation of the European political landscape, beginning in 1989 with the democratic revolutions in Eastern Europe and the accelerating movement toward German unification, coupled with the Iraqi invasion of Kuwait in August 1990, generated new interest in enhancing EC foreign and security policy cooperation and in improving the functioning of Community institutions. To deal with these two challenges, the Community launched two Intergovernmental Conferences (IGCs), one on EMU and another on European Political Union (EPU), that were to culminate in the December 1991 Maastricht Treaty.[2]

THE FRANCO-GERMAN BARGAIN

At its core, the dynamic leading to Maastricht stemmed from a broad Franco-German bargain on both economic and political issues. On the economic side, France had a strong interest in EMU. Ever since President Mitterrand abandoned his reflationary economic strategy in 1983, France had come to realize that the Bundesbank constrained macroeconomic policy for all EC countries participating in the European Exchange Rate Mechanism (ERM), and France wanted a greater say over those policies that affected its national economic well-being. The answer was EMU—collectively decided monetary policy. Conversely, Germany had the most to lose from EMU—giving

[1]The original effort at EMU failed in 1971. See Section 2, n. 21, supra. It was relaunched in 1988, when the EC leaders commissioned the EC President to prepare a report on EMU. At Strasbourg in December 1989, the EC decided in principle to move forward on EMU, but it was not until the political dimension ripened in 1990 that actual treaty negotiations began.

[2]The European Council meeting that produced the agreement was held on December 9–10, 1991. EC heads of state and government signed the treaty at Maastricht on February 7, 1992.

up national control over monetary policy and subordinating the Bundesbank and the deutschemark, symbols of Germany's economic miracle, to Community control. For German leaders, EMU was acceptable only if it brought corresponding benefits to Germany—closer European political integration, a key part of Germany's overall strategy for gaining approval of German unification, and a more democratically accountable Community.

France, historically intergovernmental in its approach to constructing the Community, had serious reservations about Germany's goals for institutional reform. But the changing political landscape in Europe enhanced France's willingness to accept a more supranational structure as a means to assure continuing French influence in European political affairs.

France's willingness to agree to an IGC on EPU was driven largely by security issues; once France accepted the reality of a unified Germany and its continued membership in NATO, the need to bind Germany to "Europe" became a major French objective.[3] France's concerns stemmed in part from its fear that Germany's enhanced economic and political strength might lead it to act more independently, to the detriment of its European partners, especially France. In addition, France, which had long sought to develop a European security and defense identity independent from NATO, hoped to use the period of European restructuring to tie Germany to this project. For France, both issues grew in importance with the prospect that the United States might withdraw from Europe as the Cold War drew to a close.[4]

In the immediate aftermath of German unification, following on the heels of the political revolutions in Central and Eastern Europe,[5] Germany was particularly open to France's entreaties. Germany was

---

[3]Other EC states have shared France's concern. In Denmark both the governing coalition and the Social Democrats became more enthusiastic about European integration in the wake of German unification. Denmark's Foreign Minister Uffe Ellemann-Jensen observed: "Now we will suddenly have in the middle of Europe a large German state which will change such an incredibly large number of the balances that we have in the economy, at the political level, and in security policy. That is why we all are forced to re-evaluate our own positions on what the Europe of the future will look like." *Berlingske Tidende,* July 8, 1990 (FBIS-WEU-90-134, July 12, 1990, p. 27).

[4]French Prime Minister Cresson observed: "It is evident that the United States is disengaging from Europe. But it can't leave and ask us Europeans not to have a defense of our own." *Wall Street Journal,* July 15, 1991, p. 1. Some U.S. critics of France's policy have argued that France's policy was to deliberately provoke U.S. withdrawal as a means to foster European independence.

[5]The creation of democratic and capitalist governments in Central and Eastern Europe and the end of the Cold War also placed an important additional issue on the Community's agenda: the prospect of further Community enlargement. See Section 7, below.

eager to reassure its neighbors (not least France) that unification posed no risk of a more independent, potentially threatening Germany in the economic or political dimensions.[6] Moreover, as the Soviet military risk receded, NATO's long-term viability seemed increasingly uncertain, and Germany, too, saw European security integration as a prudent hedge against the prospect of partial or total U.S. disengagement from Europe and as a useful framework for a more activist German foreign policy as well.

The result was a grand, if implicit, Franco-German bargain: Germany would support the move toward EMU and an expanded security role for the Community as part of an IGC that would also address EC institutional reform; France would accept strengthening the supranational character of the Community in order to get EMU and European defense.[7] In the run-up to the special Dublin EC summit in April 1990, President Mitterrand and Chancellor Kohl joined in calling for an IGC on European Political Union to run in parallel with the EMU IGC. Their language was general, but included in it was a specific commitment to give the Community a foreign and security policy dimension.[8] The European Council formally endorsed the decision to hold an IGC on EPU at the June 1990 summit in Dublin, with Mrs. Thatcher's reluctant assent.[9]

The Gulf War both stimulated and complicated the move toward EPU. Europe's relatively ineffective military response to Iraq's invasion of Kuwait convinced many that European security cooperation, including defense matters, needed dramatic improvement.[10] At the same time, the Gulf crisis underscored the importance of U.S. leader-

---

[6]One commentator analogized Germany's enthusiasm for European integration during the debate over German unification with its earlier willingness to support the ECSC in the early 1950s, calling German policy during both periods a "sovereignty for integration bargain." David Buchan, "A Strong Centre, A Worried Periphery," *Financial Times,* August 6, 1990.

[7]As Chancellor Kohl stated at the start of a meeting with President Mitterrand just weeks before Maastricht: "There is not only a political, but also a practical link between the two intergovernmental conferences. They form an indivisible whole. The treaty on political union is the vital counterpart to the treaty on economic and monetary union." *Le Figaro,* November 14, 1991, p. 4.

[8]The letter called for measures "to reinforce the union's democratic legitimacy, to make its institutions more efficient, to ensure economic, monetary and political cohesion and to define and set in motion a common foreign and security policy." *Economist,* July 7, 1990, p. 29.

[9]A negative vote would not have changed the outcome since the Council can convene an IGC by majority vote, as happened in 1985 with the IGC that led to the SEA.

[10]See Trevor C. Salmon, "Testing Time for European Political Cooperation: The Gulf and Yugoslavia 1990–1992," *International Affairs,* Vol. 68, No. 2, 1992, pp. 236–247.

ship and the need to maintain the transatlantic tie, particularly for Germany. Thus, while Germany was willing to include defense explicitly on the EPU agenda (in a joint Kohl-Mitterrand letter on the eve of convening the EPU IGC in December 1990), German policy also became increasingly sensitive to not alienating the United States in the process of developing a European security identity.[11]

The road to Maastricht triggered a comprehensive and often heated debate over Europe's future, sweeping across a broad range of often interrelated substantive and procedural issues. In the negotiations, the EC leaders revisited the four key issues identified in Section 2 of this Report that had characterized the Community's internal debate since its inception. Part 2 of this Report will analyze these debates in detail, but it is useful to begin with a broad overview of the decisions made at Maastricht to understand the interlocking dynamic of the discussions.

THE PARAMETERS OF THE DEBATE LEADING TO MAASTRICHT

The Goal of Integration

The debate leading up to Maastricht featured fundamental conflicts in three key areas over the goal of integration: economics, internal security (immigration and crime), and foreign policy. With the Single European Act, the Community had accepted a genuinely "communitarian"[12] approach to many aspects of the internal market. But to some, led by Germany and France, the task of completing the "economic" Community remained unfinished. They argued that the logic of economic integration required a communitarian approach to macroeconomic policy (including coordination or even Community-supervised national fiscal policies, a common interest and exchange rate policy, and a single currency). In addition, some nations (especially Germany) contended that a truly "barrier-free" Community required common action on problems of immigration and crime, areas left un-

---

[11]For example, Secretary Baker and Foreign Minister Genscher in a joint statement issued May 10, 1991, stated that "NATO should be the principal venue for consultation and the forum for agreement on all policies bearing on the security and defense commitment of its members under the North Atlantic Treaty."

[12]In the parlance of EC debates, this is often termed a "federal approach." But Community members differ over the meaning and implications of "federal" in the Community context, so for purposes of clarity, communitarian is used here to mean a collective, supranational mechanism, typically supported by the use of qualified majority voting in the Council of Ministers and a significant role for the European Parliament.

touched by the Single Act. Their opponents, led by the United Kingdom (and to a lesser extent, Denmark), argued that the SEA went far enough; the Single Market did not require a single currency and further integration in economic or internal security policy would impermissibly trammel national prerogatives.

In the sphere of international relations, France and Germany (supported to greater or lesser extent by Belgium, Spain, Italy, Greece, and Luxembourg) argued that, since its inception, the Community's goal was "political union," which necessarily included a common foreign and security policy as well as a common defense. Their approach was strenuously resisted by the United Kingdom, the Netherlands, Denmark, and Portugal, which preferred to confine the Community to economic affairs, leaving foreign, security, and defense policy to NATO.

The Community's decisions at Maastricht represented a clear further step toward "deepening the Community," although in many areas the European leaders did not go as far as some hoped. The Community adopted a timetable and a procedure for implementing EMU.[13] The EC leaders agreed to closer coordination on immigration and crime, although these policies will mostly remain outside the communitarian procedures. They reached agreement on the idea of EC citizenship, extending some voting rights to all EC citizens in their country of residence. On security policy, the leaders adopted a framework for a Common Foreign and Security Policy (CFSP). But the future of a common defense remained murky: the Council agreed that the CFSP would "eventually [result in] the framing of a common defence policy, which might in time lead to a common defence."[14]

Economic Philosophy

Maastricht saw a sharp debate over the degree to which the Community should adopt a laissez-faire approach to the Single Market, focusing on two dimensions—"social policy" (primarily workers' rights) and industrial policy. On social policy, the United Kingdom found itself virtually isolated from other Community nations, which argued that the "business-oriented" communitarian approach of the 1992 program required a parallel communitarian approach to such issues as workers' pay, employment rights, and occupational safety. The United Kingdom remained adamant in its opposition, leading the Community leaders to adopt a solution that may

---

[13]The EMU Agreement is discussed in detail in Section 6, below.

[14]The agreements on CFSP and defense are discussed in Section 5.

have broad implications for the future: an agreement by the Eleven to go forward without the United Kingdom to establish a regime for EC social policy based on qualified majority voting.

On industrial policy, the United Kingdom was more successful in attracting allies for its non-interventionist approach. Backed by Germany and the Netherlands, the EC leaders declined to adopt qualified majority voting for granting firms subsidies or anti-trust exemptions, thus sharply reducing the likelihood that the Community would become involved directly in shaping Europe's industrial and technological landscape.

The Process of Collective Decisionmaking

The debate over the Community's goals largely (but not entirely) mirrored the cleavages over intergovernmental versus supranational decisionmaking. Those who favored a broader vision of the Community's goals (led by Germany) tended to push for greater authority for the communitarian institutions (European Parliament and Commission) and expanded majority voting across the range of Community activities, from economic issues to immigration to the Common Foreign and Security Policy. Those with a narrower vision attempted to preserve the intergovernmental character of decisionmaking in new areas of Community activities and to separate clearly those new activities from the communitarian institutions involved in the Single Market. France represented a rather unique case: favoring a broad vision of the Community's goals but an intergovernmental approach. In some areas, such as strengthening the European Parliament, however, France was forced to subordinate its intergovernmental preference to gain Germany's support for deepening the Community.

To a large extent, Maastricht represented a victory for the intergovernmentalists. The Treaty slightly expands the scope of communitarian activities to include consumer protection, health, education, and "trans-European networks" (telecommunications, transport, and energy) as well as some aspects of environmental policy. The Treaty also brings industrial policy and culture within the Community framework but requires unanimous action by the Council. The Community adopted the "pillar approach," establishing separate, predominantly intergovernmental procedures outside the communitarian framework for crime/immigration[15] and security policy (allowing only limited qualified majority voting under the CFSP). The Parliament's role was strengthened slightly, but the Parliament is still denied a significant role in non-communitarian activities.[16] Despite the limited strengthening of the Community's supranational character, however, some of Maastricht's critics attacked the Treaty for concentrating too much power in Brussels.

Geographic Scope

Although the issue of enlargement fell outside the scope of the two IGCs, the Maastricht summit represented something of a psychological watershed in this dimension, as the Council agreed to open discussions with new applicants to the Community beginning in 1992. But the leaders deferred most of the difficult questions, including the criteria for admission, timing, and any necessary institutional modification necessary to accommodate an enlarged Community.[17]

THE CONTROVERSY OVER RATIFICATION

Each of the 12 EC leaders left Maastricht claiming victory for his objectives, with a shared belief that only technical work was needed to convert the Maastricht agreement into the new constitutional framework for Europe. But storm clouds were gathering even before the ink was dry: German public opinion, whipped up by colorful and sometimes provocative journalism, began to question the wisdom of abandoning the sacred deutschemark. In Denmark, despite the support of virtually all the major political parties, polls showed an even division between support and opposition to the Treaty—an ominous sign in view of Denmark's constitutional requirement requiring treaty ratification by referendum. The Treaty was attacked by both left and right in the United Kingdom; and in France, some expressed disappointment in Maastricht's limited achievements, while others criticized the ceding of French sovereignty in areas such as voting rights for non-French citizens.

The growing opposition to Maastricht was fueled by President Delors's comments on the need for substantial institutional reform before undertaking enlargement and a draft Commission proposal on

---

[15]Under Maastricht, the Community would gain jurisdiction over nations' policies on short-term visas, with unanimity required in the Council until 1996 (except in an emergency, when the Council is authorized to act by majority vote).

[16]Institutional reform is discussed in Section 4.

[17]On enlargement, see Section 7.

that subject for the Lisbon summit scheduled for June 1992. The perception that Maastricht was only a first step toward further centralization—summed up in a *Financial Times* headline, "Delors Signals More Powers for Brussels"—stoked the opposition in Denmark and throughout the Community.[18]

The Danish "no" vote on June 2, 1992, by the smallest of margins (50.7 percent to 49.3 percent, less than 50,000 voters), created an atmosphere of crisis among EC leaders. Although all vowed to press ahead with ratification and rejected the idea of modifying the Treaty, the path toward implementing Maastricht suddenly seemed strewn with obstacles. President Mitterrand reversed his previous opposition to holding a referendum on the Treaty. Prime Minister Major withdrew the Treaty from parliamentary consideration, hoping that the political atmosphere might improve in the fall. Commission President Delors, who, for many in Denmark and elsewhere in the Community, symbolized the distant, unaccountable technocracy of Brussels, vowed to reduce the Commission's policy ambitions and to reinforce the concept of subsidiarity.[19] The British government, assuming the Presidency in an atmosphere of near crisis, sought to seize the opportunity to push for its preferred vision of a broader, more loosely knit Community. Compounding the crisis atmosphere was the Community's continued failure to broker a political solution to the conflict in Yugoslavia.

Ireland's overwhelming vote (by a margin of 2 to 1) on June 18, 1992 in favor of ratification calmed the sense of panic, but opinion polls showed support for Maastricht plummeting throughout the Community, and France's narrow "yes" on September 20 raised at least as many questions on Europe's future as it answered.

Although there were common threads running through the ratification debate throughout the Community, in each of the major countries the issues were filtered through unique national prisms.

France

The French debate over Maastricht quickly became intertwined with the fading political fortunes of the governing Socialist party and its leader, President Mitterrand. Although the government hailed the

---

[18]*Financial Times*, April 8, 1992, p. 2.

[19]In the run-up to the Lisbon summit in June 1992, Delors said that the EC should avoid involvement in internal security, justice, urban policy, social security, health, culture, and education and play a lower profile role on the environment and adjudicating trade disputes. *Economist,* June 27, 1992, p. 56.

Treaty as a triumph for France and its objectives at Maastricht, the agreement failed to save the Socialists from a disastrous showing in the regional elections in March 1992. Although Mitterrand initially insisted that France could ratify the Treaty and adopt the necessary modifications to the French Constitution without resorting to a referendum, he quickly switched course after the Danish vote and set a referendum for September 20, with the hope that the apparently broad popular support for the Treaty (upwards of 70 percent approval) might lift his own political fortunes. Instead, the opposite happened: many in France decided to take the referendum as a plebiscite on Mitterrand, and his own unpopularity, combined with an effective "no" campaign, drove down public approval for the Treaty.

Most of the Socialist leadership rallied around the Treaty, except the "Gaullist" Socialist faction led by former Defense Minister Jean Pierre Chevènement. Both the far left (Communists) and far right (National Front) opposed the Treaty, while the traditional opposition was in disarray: Valery Giscard D'Estaing's Union pour la Democratie Française (UDF) strongly supported the Treaty; and while his rival, former Prime Minister Jacques Chirac, equivocated, the majority of his party, the Rassemblement pour la République (RPR), joined the opposition.[20] Nonetheless, the French Assembly and Senate both adopted the necessary constitutional changes by a wide margin, and they were approved overwhelmingly in a special Congress (a procedure established by the French Constitution for adopting amendments).[21]

Most of the opponents based their opposition on the specifics of the Treaty itself rather than on the idea of deeper integration—for Europe but against Maastricht. Nonetheless the bill of particulars remained for the most part rather vague. The provision allowing non-French EC nationals to vote in French municipal elections was frequently singled out for criticism as an unacceptable intrusion on sovereignty, an issue that touched deep roots of growing French popular anxiety over immigration.

The outcome of the referendum remained uncertain right up to the balloting, with confusion heightened by frantic currency markets in the week before the vote, stretching the European Exchange Rate Mechanism (ERM) to the breaking point. The narrow margin of vic-

---

[20]The anti-Maastricht element of the RPR was led by Philippe Séguin and Marie France Garaud, who authored an anti-Maastricht tract entitled *De L'Europe en Géneral et de la France en Particulier*. Chirac himself said he would vote for the Treaty but declined to support it actively.

[21]*Financial Times*, June 20–21, 1992, p. 2.

tory (51.05 percent to 48.95 percent) staved off a humiliating defeat for the government and the governing class, but it deeply divided the French public. Young city residents and those who lived near borders with other EC countries on the whole favored the Treaty; the middle-aged, rural, and smaller town populations tended to oppose.

Germany

The extent of opposition to Maastricht in Germany caught most observers by surprise, coming so soon as it did after German unification. There had been warning signs in the fall of 1991 that the Sozialdemokratische Partei Deutschlands (SPD) would criticize Chancellor Kohl's failure to win a substantially strengthened Parliament. But opinion polls showed broad support for European integration, and most assumed that Germany would not risk alienating its fellow EC members by actually opposing the Treaty.

Public discontent over the Treaty crystallized around the decision to adopt a plan for EMU—notwithstanding that Germany gained many of its key objectives in devising the plan's specifics. The power of the deutschemark as an acceptable and cherished symbol of Germany's reborn nationhood after the Nazi era was an important factor, but even the intellectual community raised doubts about the wisdom of a single currency, at least without substantially greater convergence of the European economies. In the end Chancellor Kohl was obliged to promise that he would consult with the Bundestag before entering into EMU, even though the Maastricht Treaty, by its terms, gave the right of parliamentary approval only to the United Kingdom. And German economic officials began to suggest that they would insist that the new currency be called a Euromark, rather than ecu, and that the European Central Bank (ECB) be located in Germany.

The third area of controversy concerned the rights of Germany's 16 Länder to participate in formulating German negotiating positions in the context of modifying the Rome Treaty. The Länder's leaders complained that Kohl had compromised rights and responsibilities granted to them by the German Basic Law, without adequate consultation or participation. Here, too, Chancellor Kohl had to promise to do better in the future to gain the Länder's support, which was critical since they make up the upper house (the Bundesrat) of Germany's Parliament, and to adopt the constitutional changes necessary to implement Maastricht requires two-thirds approval of both chambers. In light of these compromises, the German Parliament approved the Treaty overwhelmingly in December.

The German public discontent over Maastricht was colored by a wide range of domestic controversies surrounding the governing coalition, including the enormous financial cost of unification, mounting discontent over immigration exacerbated by new emigrants from the East and refugees from the conflict in the former Yugoslavia, and a heated debate over Germany's role in international relations, including deploying the Bundeswehr outside Germany and NATO for missions with the United Nations or the WEU. In some ways, the debate over Maastricht is symptomatic of a wider German struggle to define what is acceptable in the pursuit of national self-interest now that the Cold War has ended and Germany is no longer divided. The debate raises fundamental questions of whether the next generation of German leaders will be as faithful to the grail of integration as their predecessors.[22]

United Kingdom

The Danish vote put U.K. Prime Minister John Major in the unlikely position of a principal champion of the Maastricht Treaty. Having hailed his success in the Maastricht negotiations and responsible as the leader of the country holding the EC Presidency for guiding the EC through the crucial months of the second half of 1992, Major adamantly insisted that the Treaty was a good one, that no re-negotiation was possible, and that Britain would ratify. The Eurocritics in his own party, temporarily silenced by Major's skilled maneuvering before Maastricht and his surprisingly large victory at the polls in April, got a second wind and intensified their efforts to defeat the Treaty. Labour, which had sought to position itself as more European than the Tories prior to the British election, showed signs of reverting to past Euroscepticism, and it was possible to imagine, at least theoretically, a lineup consisting of right-wing Conservatives and left-wing Labour that could block ratification. Major's European policy problem was compounded by the United Kingdom's continued economic difficulties, blamed by most, including Chancellor Lamont, on German economic policy, which forced the United Kingdom to suspend its participation in the ERM the week of the French referendum.

Major hoped to use the U.K. EC Presidency to demonstrate that the United Kingdom was "at the heart of Europe" and to use the discomfort over the Danish vote to push U.K. objectives, especially rapid enlargement and a more stringent approach to subsidiarity. But the

[22]For a discussion of the German debate, see Ronald D. Asmus, "Germany and America: Partners in Leadership?" *Survival*, November/December 1991, pp. 546–566.

U.K. leadership was partially undermined by continued conflicts over Yugoslavia, which led many to question the Community's efficacy, at least in its current procedures, and by loss of credibility when Major had to abandon his determined defense of the pound in the ERM. In the end, Major beat a tactical retreat, deferring final parliamentary action until after the Danish question is resolved, most likely in the spring of 1993.

On a technical level, the French referendum left the Maastricht Treaty barely alive (a "no" would have brought an end to the ratification process), but the tiny margin, coupled with growing doubts throughout the Community, meant that leaders would need to agree on clear steps to improve the Treaty. At the Edinburgh summit, the Twelve EC leaders managed to cobble together a series of compromises that seem likely to permit ratification by Denmark and the United Kingdom by mid-1993.[23] The contentious post-signing debate has raised an important question. Is Maastricht yet another step on the road to "ever closer union"? Or will it in fact represent the last, rather limited achievement of the Eurofederalists in the face of pressures to retain the nation-state as the dominant actor in a loosely confederal Europe from Brest to Brest (or beyond)?

Part 2 of this Report explores in detail key elements in the process of greater European integration: institutional reform (Section 4); foreign and defense policy (Section 5); economic integration (Section 6); and enlargement of the Community (Section 7).

---

[23]At the EC's Edinburgh summit on December 11–12, 1992, the EC leaders adopted a procedure that would allow Denmark to "opt out" of the Maastricht Treaty's provisions on EMU and defense. This agreement, "legally binding, but only for the Danes," is designed to facilitate a second Danish vote without requiring re-negotiation of the Treaty or re-ratification by the ten EC members who had completed ratification by January 1, 1993. *Wall Street Journal,* December 14, 1992, p. A6; *Financial Times,* December 14, 1992, p.2.

PART 2

THE MAASTRICHT TREATY: SECURITY, ECONOMIC, AND INSTITUTIONAL DIMENSIONS

4. REFORMING THE COMMUNITY'S INSTITUTIONS: LEGITIMACY AND EFFICACY

The Single Market Program expanded the scope of the EC's activities, leading many governments and political leaders to question the adequacy of the decisionmaking structure created in 1957. They identified two central problems: efficacy and political legitimacy. As the Community's tasks became more complex and numerous, the intergovernmental bias of the Rome Treaty, which lodged most authority in the Council, seemed a barrier to quick and decisive action. Imaginative leadership at the Commission succeeded in enhancing the Commission's power, but the dominant role of the Council continued to limit the Community's ability to adopt needed but controversial legislation. The problem became more acute with the Community's expansion to 12 members and the consequent difficulty of achieving unanimity. Moreover, the Commission itself, enlarged to 17 members, was also in some cases a barrier to timely and effective action.

The SEA took a first step toward improving the Community decisionmaking process by expanding majority voting in the Council. While the Rome Treaty explicitly contemplated majority voting, French objections, culminating in the de facto national veto enshrined in the Luxembourg Compromise of 1966, meant in practice that the Council adopted all important decisions by consensus. The SEA opened up majority voting for implementing the Single Market Program but left large areas of the EC's jursdiction unaffected.

The increasing size and scope of Community activities also enhanced concerns about the political legitimacy and accountability of the EC decisionmaking process. There was a growing belief that the Community suffered a "democratic deficit," a problem that grew more pressing as the EC's role expanded. The "deficit" had three elements: a weak Parliament, a bureaucratic Commission, and a secretive Council.

For a Community comprised of states committed to parliamentary democracy, the weakness of the European Parliament (EP) seemed especially serious. Even under the special cooperation procedure for Single Market rules, the Parliament has a limited voice in legislation. In most areas, except aspects of the EC budget, the European Parliament's role is little more than advisory.

Even with enhanced power, the European Parliament's ability to act as a democratic check on Community decisions is limited; as a practical matter, there was little connection between the electorates' views on European issues and its members. Members of the European Parliament (MEPs) are, for the most part, elected on the basis of their national political affiliations, and so MEP campaigns tend to be conducted on the basis of national rather than "European" issues.[1] Although the national parties are affiliated in EC-wide groupings,[2] these groupings include widely divergent national parties that have no common platform on which to conduct MEP campaigns.[3] Purely "national" concerns sometimes lead to splits within groups or to unholy alliances across them.

Since the first MEP election by direct vote, two groupings, the Socialists and the European People's Party (EPP), primarily Christian Democrats, have shared what power the Parliament possesses, alternately holding the Presidency. Since neither comes

---

[1]The significance of MEP elections is further diluted by the low voter turnout, which was only about 41 percent in the June 1989 election.

[2]There are 518 members of the European Parliament, 81 from each of the "Big 4" (France, Germany, Italy, the United Kingdom); 60 from Spain; 25 from the Netherlands; 24 each from Belgium, Greece, and Portugal; 16 from Denmark; 15 from Ireland; and 6 from Luxembourg. After the 1989 EP elections, there were 10 groupings (including the U.K. Conservatives as a separate group): Socialist Group (180); European People's Party (EPP) (122); Liberal and Democratic Reformist Group (49); European Democrats (34); Greens (28); United European Left (28); European Democratic Alliance, primarily the U.K. Conservative party (22); Group of the European Right (17); Unity Group (14); and Rainbow Group (14). Nine are independent.

[3]For the first decade after direct MEP elections, the U.K. Conservative party stood outside the principal center-right grouping, the European People's Party. In 1989, the Conservatives applied to join, but were rejected because some, especially the Dutch and Italians, were concerned about policy divergences on a broad range of issues, including EMU, social policy, and a strengthened European Parliament. In 1991, the EPP voted to admit the Tories, in part due to a change in Conservative party tone with the ascension of John Major and in part under the influence of German Christliche Demokratische Union (CDU) leaders, who wished to expand the EPP's influence in the Parliament. The British Conservatives finally joined the EPP group in April 1992. *The Times,* May 9, 1992, p. 15. Nevertheless, major policy differences persist. For example, British Conservatives vocally oppose referring to the Community's "federal" future, yet the EPP platform states that "only institutions of a federal nature can satisfy the aspirations of Europeans who wish to share common destiny." *Financial Times,* June 19, 1991, p. 16. By contrast, France's center-right party, the RPR, has remained outside the EPP. The RPR, with its Gaullist roots, is deeply suspicious of supranational integration, which sets it apart from most European Christian Democrats. *Liberation,* May 3, 1991, p. 6.

The British Labour party, while a member of the Socialist Group in the European Parliament, has opposed creating a supranational Socialist party that would bind national parties to policy decisions taken by majority vote. *Guardian,* June 4, 1991, p. 8.

close to a majority, however, any important decision must be taken by a broad coalition, further limiting the Parliament's clout.

The Commission, with considerable power as a result of its sole right of initiative and its advantages in technical expertise, seemed even further removed from political accountability. While the Commission President is chosen by consensus by the member governments, individual Commissioners are chosen by their national governments with little or no influence from the Community at large, and once chosen, the Commission is highly insulated from political checks of any kind during the life of its term.[4]

Under the present system, the principal "democratic" element is the Council, which derives its legitimacy from the fact that its constituent members (national governments) are themselves democratically elected. But this legitimacy is attenuated because national governments are chosen only in part by their views on Community issues; domestic policy considerations are far more important. Moreover, the Council's accountability is further limited because its deliberations are secret.

In the view of some, the advent of increased majority voting in the Council threatened to further weaken democratic control. They argued that, where majority voting prevails, the Council can make decisions over the dissent of one or more countries, arguably "disenfranchising" the voters of that country. This seems a curious argument in a democracy, since by the nature of parliamentary democracy, minorities on any given issue are disenfranchised. The argument is doubly weak in the Community context, where considerations of comity loom much larger than in national parliaments, and decisions are rarely taken by majority except with the implicit acquiescence of the outvoted states.[5] Nonetheless, the growth of majority voting crystallized concerns about the European Parliament's weakness and the Commission's lack of direct political accountability—the "democratic deficit."

The Maastricht debate on institutional reform turned on three issues:

---

[4]As noted above, the Commission can be sacked by the Parliament on a vote of no confidence, but this remedy is drastic. Commissioners also appear before parliamentary committees for questioning, but the limited size and expertise of the Parliament's staff constrain the utility of this method of oversight. Perhaps the most important oversight of the Commission is the Council of Auditors, created in 1977, which scrutinizes Community expenditures.

[5]Some of the confusion stems from the Council's dual personality as both a legislature and an executive. It is true, as some have argued, that the Council is not "collectively" accountable to anyone, but neither are legislatures.

- How much streamlining to improve the efficacy of the Community, particularly through majority voting?
- How important a role for the Parliament? and
- How to draw the line between the Community's jurisdiction and matters reserved for national or local governments?[6]

The intergovernmentalists on the whole opposed increased majority voting and a bigger role for Parliament. This led them to favor what became known as the "pillar approach" to constructing the Community: while the economic component of the Community would be governed by majority voting and a stronger role for Parliament, other Community activities, such as CFSP and internal security would retain their own structures, with little majority voting and a nominal role for Parliament. Thus the Community would consist of separate pillars for each of its major activities. For the intergovernmentalists, the national veto in a strong Council that has power of appointment over Commission members was the ultimate and sufficient guarantee of democratic accountability. France, Denmark, Ireland, Luxembourg, and the United Kingdom advocated the pillars approach, which was reflected in the Luxembourg Presidency's draft treaty in the spring of 1991.[7] But France faced a dilemma: intergovernmental in orientation,[8] France nonetheless saw that political reform toward a more supranational approach was necessary for Germany's support on EMU.

Germany, along with other supranationalists, favored the "tree approach": a single institutional structure to cover all Community

---

[6]For an account of the IGC on EPU, see Richard Corbett, "The Intergovernmental Conference on Political Union," *Journal of Common Market Studies,* September 1992, pp. 271–298.

[7]The Luxembourg Presidency presented its initial views in the so-called "non-paper" of April 1991. The paper proposed a treaty structure for the European Union with three distinct chapters: an expanded Rome Treaty, CFSP, and Trevi (Interior Ministers). Commission President Delors called the non-paper "a violation of the basic principles that inspired the founding fathers of the Treaty of Rome." *Independent,* April 18, 1991, p. 12. The pillars concept was continued in Luxembourg's draft treaty presented at the June 1991 European Council meeting, modified to include an eventual goal of unifying the three.

[8]The French commitment to intergovernmentalism crosses party lines. At the extraordinary European "Assizes," in which both MEP and national parliamentarians met in Rome from November 27–30, 1990, to adopt recommendations on political union, virtually all the French Socialists and members of the RPR abstained on the final document (approved by a vote of 150 to 13, with 26 abstentions) on the grounds that the Assizes' proposal took too much power from the Council. Only the UDF representatives voted solidly for the group's recommendations. In contrast, all representatives from Germany, Italy, and Belgium, as well as most of Britain's Labour party representatives voted in favor. *Le Monde*, December 2–3, 1990.

activities, with enhanced majority voting in the Council and increased parliamentary responsibility, including a stronger parliamentary role in approving members of the Commission. They preferred to build democracy directly into the Community institutions to assure accountability. Belgium, Germany, Greece, Italy, the Netherlands, Portugal, and Spain generally favored this approach.[9] Germany in particular insisted on the need to accompany expanded Community powers in EMU with a parallel strengthening of the Parliament. In Germany's view, an Intergovernmental Conference on EMU was acceptable only if accompanied by a conference to amend the Rome Treaty's institutional structure to improve its democratic accountability.

Not surprisingly, the European Parliament's proposal for institutional reform was the most supranational and went furthest in strengthening Parliament's powers: it called for co-decision by the Council and Parliament (each must affirmatively approve legislation),[10] sharing the right to initiate legislation with the Commission, greater involvement in security policy, and the right to elect the Commission President.[11]

The Commission supported Germany's call for a stronger Parliament. Although an enhanced parliamentary role would arguably come at

---

[9]The Netherlands' Presidency adopted the tree approach in its initial draft. But virtually all EC members harshly criticized the Dutch proposal, particularly those provisions that brought foreign policy and immigration into the communitarian framework and strengthened the Parliament's powers. Only Belgium broadly supported the initial Dutch draft. As a result, the Netherlands quickly retreated to the three pillars framework proposed by the Luxembourg Presidency. See *Financial Times,* September 25, 1991, p. 2, and October 2, 1991, p. 14; *Guardian,* September 28, 1991, p. 24; *Wall Street Journal,* September 25, 1991, p. A9; *Economist,* September 21, 1991, p. 64, and September 28, 1991, p. 59. Some commentators attributed the Dutch "fiasco" to the fact that the Foreign Ministry was overburdened by trying simultaneously to manage both the Intergovernmental Conferences and the Yugoslavia crisis. See *De Volksrant,* October 5, 1991, p. 3 (FBIS-WEU-901-204, October 22, 1991, p. 17).

[10]The Parliament itself had proposed that it have the right of "co-decision"—a requirement that Parliament affirmatively pass all legislation. Only Germany, Italy, and Belgium supported this substantial increase in the Parliament's role. *Financial Times,* August 13, 1991, p. 2, and November 29, 1991, p. 2.

[11]The proposal, adopted by the Parliament in October 1990, was based on a report by U.K. Labour party MEP David Martin. The Parliament's proposal also called for opening Council meetings to the public to increase accountability.

Another proposal (supported by many in France) that fell out of favor called for creating a second chamber of the Parliament to represent national parliaments (along the lines of the original U.S. Senate). Some called for representing the regions in the second chamber.

For the most part, national parliaments share the view of the European Parliament, with the exception of the two most intergovernmental countries, the United Kingdom and France.

the partial expense of the Commission as well as the Council, the Commission tends to see the Parliament (the other primarily communitarian institution) as its ally in the larger struggle for control between the supranationalist institutions and the intergovernmental Council. But while the Commission supported enhancing some of Parliament's powers, it oppposed sharing the right to initiate legislation with Parliament. It advocated extending the cooperation procedure, but not co-decision, and also sought a greater role for itself in foreign and security policy.

The Kohl-Mitterrand letter in December 1990 sought to strike a balance between the Council and the Euro-institutions (Commission and Parliament) by giving the Parliament co-decision for "truly legislative acts" (undefined).[12] The Parliament would gain the right to confirm the EC Commission President and later the Commission as a whole. Parliament and the Council could jointly agree to confer new areas of jurisdiction on the Community.

The letter proposed that the European Council assume the role of "arbitrator, guarantor, and impulse-giver for coherent integration on the path toward a European union," acting as a rule by majority voting, with limited exceptions specifically set forth in the revised Treaty. The Council would decide broad policy questions on foreign and security policy by consensus but could implement decisions by qualified majority vote. On domestic policy the Kohl-Mitterrand letter proposed to expand the EC's authority in the areas of environment, health care, social policy, energy, research and technology, and consumer protection. The Council would decide questions in those areas by qualified majority voting, and the cooperation procedure would apply. It also proposed to bring the Trevi process under the Community's umbrella by creating a Council of Justice and Interior Ministers to address immigration, visa policy, right of asylum, drug trafficking and use, and organized international crime. The Rome summit in December 1990 followed the general lines of the Kohl-Mitterrand proposal, adding the issue of trans-

---

[12]In its submission to the IGC, the Commission adopted this concept of an EC "law" as setting forth basic elements of a subject matter, as opposed to detailed implementation, which would be left to the member-states. It would replace the current "directives." See *Europa Institute,* pp. 52–53. If the Council and Parliament disagreed on provisions of a proposed law, they would meet in a "conciliation committee" (similar to a conference committee in the U.S. Congress) to work out their differences. A version of the conciliation process made its way into the Maastricht Treaty.

European transportation (a high priority for less developed countries such as Portugal).[13]

One of the hottest disputes in the EPU IGC was the debate over whether to refer explicitly to a "federal" future for the EC. For the intergovernmentalists, especially the United Kingdom, federal connoted supranational, and Prime Minister Major threatened to veto any treaty text that contained the term. Ironically, for Germany and other supranationalists, federal implied a more decentralized Community.

For foreign and security policy, the dividing line between intergovernmentalists and supranationalists was in some respects less important than the conflict between a transatlantic and a European approach to defense. Thus, the Netherlands and Portugal normally supported supranationalist solutions, but they nonetheless opposed a defense role for the Community, while intergovernmentally oriented France led the charge for giving the European Union a defense identity. Still, the distinction between supranationalism and intergovernmentalism retained some relevance: although the Netherlands preferred NATO for defense, it advocated bringing foreign policy within the Rome Treaty structure, with an enhanced role for Parliament and the Commission.

In the end, Maastricht produced a broad, although not complete, victory for the intergovernmentalists. Although there were modest additions to the Community's competence under the Rome Treaty framework, the Common Foreign and Security Policy and the Trevi process (internal security and immigration)[14] retained separate procedures, brought together only under the hortatory "chapeau" of an ill-defined European Union.[15] The United Kingdom succeeded in

---

[13]At the European Council meeting on December 14 and 15, 1991, the member-states adopted a communiqué directing the IGC to consider the Kohl-Mitterrand proposals, though it did not specifically endorse them. The British Prime Minister, John Major, considered this a kind of victory. "We have a menu for the intergovernmental conferences. Our favorite dishes are on that menu, so are the favorite dishes of others and the Community has not yet determined what orders to place." London Press Association, December 15, 1990.

[14]The one exception is in the area of visas, where the Community procedures will apply. Until 1996, the Council must act unanimously in developing a list of countries whose nationals will require visas (except in the case of an emergency caused by the threat of a sudden influx of immigrants, a qualified majority may establish a visa requirement for up to six months); thereafter, decisions will be by qualified majority vote. Article 100c, Maastricht Treaty.

[15] Thus Title I of the Maastricht Treaty establishes the "European Union" (Article A) and states that the "Union shall be secured by a single institutional framework." But the Treaty has a separate Title V, establishing "A Common Foreign and Security

excising references to the Union's "federal goal," both in the preamble and the language calling for a new Treaty revision in 1996. It also eliminated wording that called, in the long run, for integrating the two intergovernmental pillars into the communitarian framework and succeeded in including general language defining the principle of subsidiarity.

The European Parliament gained some new powers, although they fell far short of what advocates for a more active parliamentary role had hoped. The Maastricht Treaty creates a new "conciliation" procedure,[16] which will give the Parliament an enhanced voice on Single Market legislation, consumer protection, worker training, health care, trans-European networks, and aspects of environmental and research policy.[17] The result is to create a complex patchwork of procedures: affirmative parliamentary assent,[18] the conciliation

---

Policy," and Title VI, "Provisions on Cooperation in the Fields of Justice and Home Affairs."

[16]Article 189b. The procedure is sometimes called a "negative assent" procedure. It is a modification of the cooperation procedure described in Section 2, n. 34. As with the cooperation procedure, the Commission initiates a proposal and the Council, acting by qualified majority, adopts a common position. The Parliament then has three months within which to act. If it does nothing, the Council can adopt its common position. If it amends the common position, the Council can adopt the amendments (by qualified majority, if the Commission agrees with the amendments; unanimously, if the Commission disagrees). If the Council rejects the amendments, the matter is referred to a "Conciliation Committee" composed of the members of the Council (or their representatives) and an equal number of MEPs. If the Conciliation Committee reaches a compromise, under a six-week time limit, the compromise can be approved by a qualified majority of the Council and a majority of the Parliament. If they do not reach agreement, the Council can adopt the proposal by qualified majority, unless the Parliament vetoes the proposal by an absolute majority of its members within six weeks of the Council's action. If the Parliament rejects the Council's common position outright, the matter is also referred to a Conciliation Committee, but in this case, the initiative belongs to the Parliament: it can either confirm its earlier rejection and thus kill the proposal, or after taking into account the discussions in the Conciliation Committee, vote to adopt amendments (triggering the normal procedure for handling parliamentary amendments).

[17]The conciliation procedure applies to legislation on free movement of workers (Article 49); freedom to establish businesses (Article 54/2); self-employed persons (with some limitations) (Article 57); the internal market (Article 100a); incentive programs in the fields of education, vocational training, culture, and public health (but not mandatory requirements) (Articles 126, 127, 128, and 129); consumer protection (Article 129q); guidelines and priorities for trans-European network programs (but not financial support) (Article 129d); the overall level of funding for research and development (but not specific program funding) (Article 130i); general action programs for the environment (but not actual directives) (Article 130s).

[18]This applies to action on the discretionary portion of the EC budget (Article 206), international agreements that create reciprocal rights and obligations or which have important budgetary implications (Article 238), and adding new members to the Community (Article O).

procedure, the cooperation procedure,[19] parliamentary consultation, and no parliamentary involvement.[20]

If adopted, the Maastricht Treaty will give the Parliament the right to approve the nomination of the members of the EC Commission as a body (Article 158). The Parliament also gained the right to set up committees of inquiry (Article 138c), to appoint an ombudsman (Article 138e), and to review Community finances.[21]

In addition to sorting out the roles of Council, Commission, and Parliament, the IGC sought to address the division of responsibilities between Brussels and national governments. There was broad agreement that strengthening the Union should not usurp functions that properly belong to nations but considerable division on how and where to set the line. Some favored specifically delineating powers and substantive jurisdiction to be reserved to national governments; others preferred to enumerate specifically the Union's authority.[22] Most preferred a generic approach, which became known as "subsidiarity," a concept already used informally at the EC, though without an agreed definition.

According to one definition of subsidiarity, adopted by the European Parliament in its 1984 proposals for strengthening the Union, "the union shall act to carry out those tasks *which may be taken more effectively in common than by member states*" (emphasis added). This formulation would grant broad scope to the Community's jurisdiction. Jacques Delors offered a narrower formulation: "it means that a problem is handled at a higher level *only when it cannot be handled at a lower level.*"[23] Former EC President Roy Jenkins offered yet a third definition between the two: the Community should concentrate on "those functions which will, beyond reasonable doubt,

---

[19]The current cooperation procedure will apply to intra-EC transport (Article 75); working environment, including health and safety (Article 118a); financial support for trans-European networks (Article 129d) and the regional funds (Article 130d); limited aspects of the research and development program (Articles 130j, k, l); environmental legislation (Article 130s); and development cooperation with non-Lomé Convention countries (Article 130w).

[20]Even in the area of Common Foreign and Security Policy, the Parliament is given modest rights, including consultation "on the main aspects and basic choices" of CFSP and the right to ask the Council questions and make recommendations. Article J.7, Maastricht Treaty, p. 127. The Treaty grants the Parliament similar rights in the field of Justice and Home Affairs. Article K.6, Maastricht Treaty, p. 134.

[21]*Financial Times,* December 12, 1991, p. 6.

[22]This approach would mirror the U.S. Constitution, which enumerates powers for the federal government, and reserves all other powers to the states (10th Amendment).

[23]*El Pais* (special supplement), July 19, 1990, p. 4 (emphasis added).

deliver significantly better results because they are performed at the Community level."[24]

The Maastricht agreement adopted an explicit definition of subsidiarity, but its ambiguity raised doubts over its practical utility as well as its enforceability: "In areas which do not fall within its exclusive competence, the Community shall take action, in accordance with the principle of subsidiarity, only if and in so far as the objectives of the proposed action cannot be sufficiently achieved by the Member States and therefore, by reason of the scale or effects of the action, be better achieved by the Community."[25]

A final element related to institutional reform was the adoption of Spain's proposal for creating "European citizenship." While current EC law allows citizens of an EC state to work in any other, more restrictive provisions govern the right to take up residence, vote, etc.[26] The Treaty establishes a new definition of European citizenship, and grants EC nationals the right to vote in local and European Parliament elections in their place of residence.[27]

The patchwork of institutional compromises in the Maastricht Treaty jeopardized its public acceptability and, in the end, threatened its ratification. The subsidiarity clause's ambiguous wording failed to convince skeptics that there was an effective check on expanding Brussels's powers and contributed to the Danish "no" vote on ratification. Large sections of the German public, led by the SPD, criticized Chancellor Kohl for his failure to achieve the promised strengthening of the European Parliament as a necessary quid pro quo for EMU.[28] In France, nationalists from both the left and right

---

[24]*Financial Times,* August 28, 1990. Jenkins's formulation is from a speech given in 1977.

[25]Article 3(b). This basic approach was further elaborated at the December 1992 Edinburgh summit. See *Conclusions of the Presidency,* European Council in Edinburgh, 11–12 December, 1992 [hereinafter *Edinburgh Conclusions*] Part A, Annex 1, "Overall Approach to the Application of the Subsidiarity Principle," SN 456/92 (mimeo).

[26]For example, under current Community law, right of residence is guaranteed for only three months while seeking work in another EC country. If work is obtained, there is a five-year right of residence, extendable for five additional years. *European Unification* (EC Commission, 1989), pp. 40–41.

[27]Article G(9) of the Maastricht Treaty, adding a new Article 8, 8b, 8c to the Rome Treaty.

[28]One German paper called it the "disequilibrium between economic and political integration." *Hannoverische Allgemeine,* December 12, 1991, reprinted in the *German Tribune,* December 22, 1991, p. 1.

challenged the European citizenship provisions as an impermissible interference with France's sovereignty.

Commission President Delors and the leaders of the Twelve sought to calm public doubts at the Lisbon summit, particularly on the issue of subsidiarity, with assurances that they would hold the Brussels bureaucracy to a tight standard. The Community leaders took further steps to reinforce their commitment to subsidiarity in the Birmingham summit in October 1992, but their actions failed to stem public concern. The Edinburgh agreement reiterated the EC's commitment to subsidiarity and called for more open Council deliberations.[29] Whether or not Maastricht is ultimately ratified, the broad-based public outcry over the nature of EC governance has demonstrated that the issue of democratic accountability is not simply academic and could prove a major brake on the process of ever closer union.

---

[29]See *Edinburgh Conclusions,* "Transparency–Implementation of the Birmingham Declaration," Part A, Annex 3.

5. THE EC'S ROLE IN FOREIGN AND DEFENSE POLICY

The debate over the Community's role in foreign and security policy lay at the heart of the Maastricht deliberations because it crystallized many of the key disagreements over the EC's destiny. It was a contest between two visions: a loose, large free trade confederation that left security either to national policy or to other institutions (primarily NATO, and to a lesser extent, the Conference on Security and Cooperation in Europe [CSCE]) versus a tightly knit, smaller Europe with highly integrated foreign policies, military forces, and greater independence (especially from the United States). The United Kingdom and France represented the two poles of this debate, although France, because of its much cherished independence in the field of security, was in some respects an odd champion for a supranational approach to foreign and security policy.

But the alternative designs were not drawn on a blank slate; over the preceding two decades, the Community had involved itself increasingly in foreign policy issues beyond those economic considerations, such as trade, explicitly committed to the EC by the Rome Treaty. A coordinating mechanism, European Political Cooperation (EPC), had become an integral part of European foreign policymaking. The evolution of EPC formed the backdrop to the debate over a Common Foreign and Security Policy leading up to Maastricht.

EPC: THE ROAD TOWARD A COMMON FOREIGN AND SECURITY POLICY

EPC began at the Luxembourg summit of 1970, where the Community's heads of state and government agreed "to cooperate in the sphere of foreign policy."[1] In the initial years, EPC's most notable successes were associated with the negotiations leading to the

---

[1]On the history of EPC, see Alfred Pijpers et al., eds., *European Political Cooperation in the 1980s* (Martinus Nijhoff, 1988); Henri Froment-Meurice and Peter Ludlow, "Toward a European Foreign Policy," in *Governing Europe* (Center for European Policy Studies, 1990), pp. 14–22; Note, "A Community Within the Community: Prospects for Foreign Policy Integration in the European Community," *Harvard Law Review*, Vol. 103, No. 5, March 1990, pp. 1072–74; Roy Ginsberg, *Foreign Policy Actions of the European Community.*

Helsinki Final Act of 1975.[2] Although the member-states endeavored to coordinate positions at the UN General Assembly, both France and the United Kingdom resisted efforts to extend that coordination to the Security Council. During the early years, the Middle East was a major preoccupation of EPC, particularly in the wake of the 1973 Arab-Israeli war. However, EC members found it hard to reach common ground and the process led to conflict with the United States, particularly when the Community seemed not to support the Camp David process.[3] Relations between the United States and EPC remained haphazard throughout much of the 1980s.[4] Policy toward South Africa also generated sharp divisions, and Community disarray in response to the Soviet invasion of Afghanistan marked a low water mark in the evolution of common foreign policy.[5]

The EPC's shortcomings were evident in the EC's effort to achieve consensus on imposing sanctions in response to international crises: South Africa, Iran after the hostage taking, the Soviet Union after the 1981 Polish crisis, and the Falklands. Sanctions also illustrate the complex interplay between EPC and the common external policies of the EC. For example, in the case of the Falklands, the European Council initially voted to adopt sanctions against Argentina pursuant to Article 113 of the Rome Treaty, which allowed for common action; but as support for sanctions began to waver (Italy and Ireland backed off from their previous support), the Community was forced to switch the basis of its actions to Article 224, which requires action by individual member-states.[6]

---

[2]The EC played two roles in the Helsinki negotiations. For trade issues in Basket II (economic issues), the Commission itself represented the Community nations, an extension of its Rome Treaty responsibilities in this area. On the broader political issues, the nine member-states established an informal coordinating committee of their CSCE delegation heads. According to John J. Maresca, "the Nine were reasonably successful in their effort to follow joint policies on political issues in the CSCE, although not with the same discipline as resulted from the legal commitment to follow the same line on trade questions." John J. Maresca, *To Helsinki* (Duke University Press, 1985), p. 19.

[3]Since the Venice Declaration of 1980 (suggesting a Palestinian role in the Middle East peace process), EPC involvement with problems of that region has diminished considerably, although the EC has sought to participate in the 1992 Middle East Peace Conference.

[4]The process of consultation between the United States and the EC took place under the Gymnich formula adopted in 1974. See Section 2, n. 41, above.

[5]The Community took 19 days to respond to the Afghan crisis. The need to act more quickly and decisively led the Council (in the 1981 London Report) to agree to crisis response procedures.

[6]See Gianni Bonvicini, "Mechanisms and Procedures of EPC," and Simon Nutall, "Where the Commission Comes In," in *European Political Cooperation in the 1980s*, pp. 65–66; 112–113.

With the SEA, EPC formally became part of the Treaty structure, and the Twelve agreed to "endeavour jointly to formulate and implement a European foreign policy."[7] They also took a cautious step toward Community involvement in security policy, agreeing

> that closer cooperation on questions of European security would contribute in an essential way to the development of a European identity in external policy matters. They are ready to coordinate their positions more closely on the political and economic aspects of security.[8]

But EPC remained outside the Community's normal decisionmaking process: eventually given its own Secretariat by the SEA[9] but kept separate from the Commission's structure.[10] Nonetheless, there has been a growing convergence between the two processes, given that the 12 Foreign Ministers act both as the principal consultative body for EPC and as the General Affairs Council for normal Community business.[11] The result has been what Reinhardt Rummel has called a "composed foreign policy," consisting of the Community's common

---

[7]SEA, Article 30(1).

[8]SEA, Article 30(6a). This provision has its roots in the London Declaration of 1981, where the Foreign Ministers noted that the "flexible and pragmatic" approach of EPC allowed for discussions of "certain important foreign policy questions bearing on the political aspects of security."

An earlier effort to involve the Community more deeply in security policy, the Genscher-Columbo initiative (1981) met considerable resistance from member-states, and even the SEA's general reference to security policy led to a legal challenge in neutral Ireland. The difficulty of including security on the EC agenda contributed to the decision to revitalize the WEU in 1984; it also affected the EC's role in the CSCE, particularly the Stockholm CDE negotiations. See E. Regelsberger, "EPC in the 1980s," in *European Political Cooperation in the 1980s.*

[9]Prior to establishing the Secretariat, the rotating Presidency was solely responsible for administering EPC. This created enormous problems of continuity and burden (especially on the smaller member-states), problems which were partially eased by the institution of the Troika, formalized in the 1981 London Report. The Troika, which consists of the current, immediate past, and next EC Presiding nations, collectively represents the EC in foreign policy matters.

[10]The SEA, Article 3(b), did provide, however, that "The Commission shall be fully associated with the proceedings of Political Cooperation."

The European Parliament has an extremely limited role in EPC, as set forth in Article 30(4) of the SEA, which committed the Twelve to "ensure that the European Parliament is closely associated with European Political Cooperation. To that end, the Presidency shall regularly inform the European Parliament of the foreign policy issues which are being examined within the framework of Political Cooperation and shall ensure that the views of the European Parliament are duly taken into consideration."

[11]The SEA, Article 30 ¶3(a) explicitly authorized the Foreign Ministers to discuss foreign policy issues at the monthly meetings of the Council of the EC, as well as at the SEA-mandated four EPC meetings each year.

external policies, joint policies agreed through EPC, and individual national responses.[12]

Like other activities of the Community, the structure and substance of EPC has been shaped by the member nations' general outlook on European integration. The overall intergovernmental approach is a product of the strong views of France and the United Kingdom, which carry particular weight on matters of foreign policy. But over time there has been some rapprochement between the intergovernmentalists and supranationalists (especially Belgium and Italy), which has permitted the Commission's growing involvement in EPC activities.

The specific foreign policy interests and perspectives of individual states have heavily colored EPC's evolution. Ireland's neutrality initially caused EPC to tread cautiously on matters of security policy, while Denmark has taken pains to ensure that EPC does not disrupt its strong foreign policy ties to the other Nordic nations.[13] Greece has often posed difficult problems in achieving consensus as a result of its distinctive foreign policy (particularly under former Prime Minister Papandreou) and the unique problems caused by the Cyprus conflict. EPC has proved a valuable tool for German foreign policy, allowing it to keep a low profile while playing a larger international role, without reviving fears of a dominant or independent Germany. EPC also aided Germany in developing support for Ostpolitik.

EPC's development highlighted its two principal weaknesses: the commonly leveled charge that EPC is "reactive" (a charge the Community itself applied to EPC in the London Report of 1981) and its dependence on consensus. As one commentator has observed: "in the absence of clearer and more binding procedures for the construction of a consensus, organizational improvements in EPC are possible but are likely to be marginal; it is the essence of the problem that the decisionmaking process is neither binding nor pre-eminent in the national context."[14]

The Gulf War sharpened the debate over the EC's future role in foreign and defense policy. For those who favored a stronger, more ex-

---

[12]See Reinhardt Rummel, "Speaking With One Voice—and Beyond," in *European Political Cooperation in the 1980s.*

[13]Denmark appended a declaration to the SEA stating that the provisions on EPC were not intended "to affect Denmark's participation in Nordic cooperation in the sphere of foreign policy." On the politics of EPC, see Françoise de la Serre, "The Scope of National Adaptation to EPC," in *European Political Cooperation in the 1980s*, Ch. 9.

[14]Gianni Bonvicini, "Mechanisms and Procedures of EPC," in *European Political Cooperation in the 1980s,* p. 66.

plicit EC role in defense, the shortcomings in Europe's response demonstrated the need for more effective mechanisms.[15] The EC's deep involvement in the Yugoslavia crisis is also likely to affect the ultimate shape of the Community's new role in foreign policy and defense. As with the Gulf, some have argued that it demonstrates the need for more streamlined procedures and a standby military intervention capability; others see the crisis as proving that the divisions within the EC are too deep to allow an effective common foreign policy, much less a defense role.[16]

FOREIGN POLICY AND DEFENSE IN THE MAASTRICHT TREATY

Germany and France initially led the effort to include foreign policy on the agenda of Community reform. The Kohl-Mitterrand letter of April 1990 called for "a common foreign and security policy," but it was silent on defense. The two leaders did not make clear what changes to EPC they intended to create a CFSP; given the two countries' divergence on whether to pursue an intergovernmental or supranational approach, the ambiguity may have been intentional.

The Iraqi invasion of Kuwait and the deployment of European ships to enforce the embargo against Iraq brought the defense question to the fore. Although Europe acted quickly to impose sanctions against Iraq, there was more dissension over economic aid to Jordan, Egypt, and Turkey, and the military response was uneven. The debate took on a new, more concrete dimension when Italy's Foreign Minister, Gianni De Michelis, tabled a proposal in September 1990, during the Italian EC Presidency, for merging the WEU and EC.[17] The response

[15]For example, Delors remarked: "According to the experts, the EC did everything within its power. It was the first to condemn the violation of Kuwait's independence and to promote the embargo. 'Yes,' the public says, 'but it was not seen to act consistently with respect to the developments which took place later.' There is a feeling of frustration and questioning among the public which the heads of government have understood very well. As a result, following the cessation of hostilities and the noting of a certain laxity, dynamism and desire to move forward—which will give the EC a political personality and the means to exercise it in foreign and security policy—are apparent." *La Vanguardia,* April 14, 1991 (FBIS-WEU-91-083 April 30, 1991, p. 1).

[16]For a more detailed analysis of the EC's role in Yugoslavia and its likely impact, see James B. Steinberg, *The Role of European Institutions in Security After the Cold War: Some Lessons from Yugoslavia,* RAND, N-3455-FF, 1992.

[17]In 1984, the Foreign and Defense Ministers "revived" the WEU, stating their "determination to make better use of the WEU framework in order to increase cooperation between the member-states in the field of security policy and to encourage consensus."

to his initiative fell into two predictable camps: the Atlanticists—the United Kingdom,[18] Portugal,[19] the Netherlands, and Denmark as well as Ireland (which opposed a defense dimension because of neutrality); and the Europeanists—France, Italy, Spain, Belgium, and Luxembourg. Germany was caught in the middle: committed to working with France to expand the EC's security role, under pressure from the United States to retain NATO's primacy as the forum for West European security policy and the framework for integrating German military forces, and in the middle of a wrenching national debate brought on by the Gulf crisis over whether to permit non-NATO missions for the Bundeswehr.

Although few countries signed up explicitly to De Michelis's proposal,[20] it proved an important impetus to an agreement by France

---

In the 1987 Platform on European Security, the WEU linked its own efforts to the broader question of a security role for the EC. "We recall a commitment to build a European Union in accordance with the Single European Act, which we all signed as members of the European Community. We are convinced that the construction of an integrated Europe will remain incomplete as long as it does not include security and defense."

The WEU had taken on increasing prominence in recent years as a result of its role in two Gulf conflicts: the minesweeping operation in 1987 (on August 20, 1987, the WEU political directors declared in The Hague that the right of free shipping in the Gulf was a "vital European interest") and the European naval response to Iraq's invasion of Kuwait. See Robbin Laird, *The Europeanization of the Alliance* (Boulder, Colo.: Westview Press, 1991), Ch. 2.

[18]The United Kingdom's opposition to an EC defense role spans both major parties. In a speech to the Royal United Services Institute in January 1991, former U.K. Labour party leader Neil Kinnock stated: "The EC should really have no competence in defense matters." He argued that including defense in the EC would pose a barrier to Eastern European states' membership and cause friction with the USSR. *The Times,* January 24, 1991, p. 8.

[19]Portugal's socialist opposition is more sympathetic to the Paris/Bonn position. *Publico,* April 19, 1991 (FBIS-WEU-91-098, May 21, 1991).

[20]*Financial Times,* November, 1990. Spain tabled a more modest version of the De Michelis proposal in December 1990, calling for gradually incorporating the WEU into the EC, beginning with synchronized timetables for EC and WEU ministerials and rotating presidencies. (In April 1991, the EC heads of government met simultaneously with WEU defense and foreign policy ministers for the first time; the non-WEU EC members—Denmark, Ireland, and Greece—as well as the Commission were invited to attend.) Spain also proposed that the Twelve undertake a mutual defense agreement along the lines of the Brussels (WEU) Treaty (a position supported by the Commission) and coordinate their positions in multilateral security and disarmament negotiations.

and Germany on the contours of Community foreign, security, and defense policy. In their December 7, 1990 letter to the Italian EC Presidency, President Mitterrand and Chancellor Kohl proposed that "foreign and security policy . . . should be extended to all spheres. . . . In addition, political union should include a real security policy which would eventually lead to a common defense." They defined five priority areas for CFSP: relations with the USSR, implementing the Paris CSCE Charter and follow-on CSCE activities, disarmament negotiations, development policy, and relations with Mediterranean countries. Following De Michelis's suggestions, they proposed that the IGC on political union "study how the Western European Union and the political union could establish a clear organic relationship and thus how the WEU, made more operational, could ultimately form part of the political union."[21]

As later fleshed out by the German and French Foreign Ministers, the Franco-German approach envisioned that a decision on the future links between the WEU and EC would be made around 1996–97, in anticipation of the Brussels (WEU) Treaty's 1998 expiration. This Franco-German proposal received support from Italy, Spain, Greece, and Belgium. In response, Britain, Denmark, the Netherlands, and Portugal offered their own amendment in the IGC, explicitly reserving defense for NATO. Ireland, too, opposed any link between the WEU and the EC.[22]

Although the Atlanticists fervently opposed incorporating the WEU into the EC, they supported a December 1990 British proposal to enhance the European security identity by creating an out-of-area intervention force under WEU auspices. This proposal thus transformed the debate over an EC role in defense to one over the future of the WEU—would it be a bridge ("passerelle") between NATO and the EC, leaving NATO supreme in matters concerning European security, or the nascent defense arm of the EC?

For Jacques Delors, this transformation of the debate from one of substance (should the EC have a defense role) to one of institutions (what link between the EC and WEU) threatened to mire the IGC in premature conflicts.[23] France's view was similar: it was eager to secure a commitment to giving the EC a defense role in the future but wanted to postpone discussion of the modalities until considerably

[21]*Le Monde,* December 9–10, 1990, p. 1.

[22]*Economist,* April 20, 1991, p. 49.

[23]*Le Monde,* October 12, 1990.

later, when the geostrategic situation in Europe has evolved and the future U.S. role in Europe has become clearer.[24]

Germany's ambivalence over the EC's defense role strained the Franco-German relationship. Although German leaders reiterated their commitment to the principles of the Kohl-Mitterrand letter of December 1990 and the Genscher-Dumas proposal of February 1991, French European Affairs Minister Elisabeth Guigou expressed concern about German "apathy" toward the question of defense in the EC.[25] Chancellor Kohl was caught in an awkward conundrum: how to square a defense role for the EC with the continued viability of NATO, which he believed necessary to maintain the U.S. commitment to Europe. The problem was further compounded by Kohl's effort to improve relations with the United Kingdom and to keep the United Kingdom on board the broader agenda of the two IGCs while remaining faithful to the Franco-German "couple."

Germany's dilemma became sharper when the United States weighed in with its own views about European security integration. In a demarche to the 11 NATO members of the EC in February 1991 (the "Bartholomew telegram"), the United States indicated that it supported strengthening European joint foreign and security policy and a European defense pillar. But the United States insisted that the new arrangements should not lead to a European caucus in NATO, disrupt the NATO-integrated military structure, or undermine NATO's collective security guarantees among all 16 NATO members.[26] The conflict between transatlantic and European defense arrangements came into the open over NATO's proposed multinational rapid reaction force, which France viewed as a deliberate attempt to preempt on-

---

[24]The French opposition party leaders, although in many cases less "pro-Europe" than the government, have also supported a defense role for the EC. See the interviews with former Finance Minister Eduard Balladur and Republican Party leader François Leotard in *Financial Times,* September 21, 1990.

[25]*Le Monde,* June 25, 1991, p. 4.

[26]*Independent,* March 6, 1991, p. 9. See also Menon et al., "A Common European Defence?" p. 105. Later, in a joint communiqué issued on May 10, 1991, Secretary Baker "affirmed that the United States is ready to support arrangements the European Allies decide are needed for the expansion of a common European foreign, security, and defense policy," but Genscher in turn stressed that "A European security and defense identity should be reflected in the development of a European pillar within the Alliance." The statement made no mention of a European security identity's link to the EC. "U.S.-German Views on the New European and Trans-Atlantic Architecture: Secretary Baker and Minister Genscher Joint Statement," U.S. Department of State Dispatch, May 13, 1991, p. 345–346.

going efforts to develop a European defense identity through the EC-WEU.[27]

The debate over the Community's role in security policy intensified in the months leading up to the Maastricht summit. Most of the Community's members rejected the draft Dutch proposal that would put foreign and security policy squarely within the communitarian machinery, yet there was little consensus on an alternative. On October 4, 1991, the United Kingdom and Italy unveiled a proposal to strengthen the role of the WEU both "as the defence component of the [European] Union and as the . . . European pillar of the Alliance."[28] The two countries agreed that members of the WEU should create an autonomous "European reaction force" for contingencies outside the NATO area, with a peacetime planning cell to develop contingency plans and conduct exercises. For security issues that fall under the Washington Treaty, however, NATO would remain "the essential forum for agreement on policies." To facilitate coordination between the WEU and NATO, they called for transferring the WEU Secretariat to Brussels and building new links between the two organizations. The proposal won quick support from the other Atlanticist countries, Denmark, the Netherlands, and Portugal.[29]

Although Italy argued that the proposal represented an important British concession in favor of a European defense identity,[30] it failed to satisfy either France or Germany. The French and German Foreign Ministers invited "like-minded" EC countries to an informal meeting to discuss alternative plans, a move the Netherlands sharply criticized as usurping the role of the Presidency.[31] Instead, the French, German, and Spanish Foreign Ministers met on October 11, and on October 14, Kohl and Mitterrand sent a letter to the Dutch

---

[27]For France, moving to multinational structures that include the United States would create serious obstacles to an all-European or even a "double-hatted" (WEU and NATO) European military capability. President Mitterrand raised his concerns directly with Chancellor Kohl at the Franco-German summit on May 31, 1991. *Frankfurter Allgemeine Zeitung,* June 1, 1991, p. 2.

[28] *Declaration on European Security and Defence* , Policy Statement 62/91, October 4, 1991.

[29]*Economist*, October 12, 1991, p. 56.

[30]Foreign Minister De Michelis stated: "For the first time, the British accepted the prospect of a common defense." *La Stampa,* October 15, 1991, p. 7 (FBIS-WEU-91-216-A, November 7, 1992, p. 6).

[31]*Independent*, October 9, 1991, p. 8.

Foreign Minister outlining their alternative approach to European defense.[32]

The Franco-German initiative stated that the objective of political union is "to assert its identity on the international scene, notably by the implementation of a common foreign and security policy which will eventually include common defense." They called for creating an "organic link" between the Union and the WEU, which would implement the Union's decisions.[33] They proposed creating a WEU planning group and military units relevant to the WEU's mission and made no distinction between military operations within or outside the NATO area. In a postscript, the two leaders noted that "Franco-German military cooperation will be increased beyond the existing brigade. The strengthened Franco-German units could thus become the core of a European corps which could include the forces of the other WEU member states. This new structure could also become the model for closer military cooperation among WEU member states."[34] The letter also specified a number of areas for joint action under the proposed CFSP.[35]

The Franco-German initiative served several purposes: it restored Franco-German leadership on the security policy debate in the wake of the Anglo-Italian proposal; solidified the Franco-German link that was perturbed by the U.S.-German initiative to create a North Atlantic Cooperation Council (NACC) embracing members of NATO

---

[32]"Union Politique Initiative Franco-Allemande" Lettre addressé par M. le President de la République et M. le Chancelier Helmut Kohl à M. Ruud Lubbers, Premier Ministre du Royaume des Pays-Bas, President en exercise du Conseil European, Paris et Bonn, October 14, 1991 (mimeo), reprinted in *Le Monde*, October 17, 1991, p. 4. A translation appears in FBIS-WEU-91-102, October 18, 1991, p. 21. Although the letter is dated October 14, the proposal was publicly unveiled on October 16. See *New York Times*, October 17, 1991, p. 1.

[33]To solve the problem of EC members who were not yet WEU members, the letter proposed inviting all EC members who also belong to NATO (Denmark and Greece) to join the WEU; they offered observer status to non-NATO EC members (i.e., Ireland).

[34]It is unclear who initiated the proposal; officials in both capitals attribute the initiative to the other. *Frankfurter Allgemeine Zeitung*, October 17, 1991, p. 2, attributes the idea of a Franco-German Corps to Chancellor Kohl. In any case, the decision was made by the two leaders personally and held within a very small circle of advisors; senior Foreign and Defense Ministry officials in both countries were taken by surprise at the announcement.

[35]The areas included: political and economic relations with the Soviet Union, Central and East European countries, the Mediterranean area and the Near and Middle East; the CSCE process; relations with the United States under the Transatlantic Declaration of November 1990; the UN and other international organizations and humanitarian measures. For security policy, the letter highlighted: European arms control policy, participation in peacekeeping, nuclear non-proliferation, and the economic aspects of security, including arms export controls.

and the former Warsaw Pact;[36] and provided a new basis for the continued stationing of French troops in Germany.[37] German officials took pains to play down the potential conflict with NATO and the United States, stating that a European defense was "a long term prospect"[38] and "This is nothing outside NATO, but something to strengthen NATO in case of defense."[39] Indeed, many argued that the Franco-German Corps would bring France closer to NATO.[40] But the Kohl-Mitterrand letter and subsequent official statements left many issues unclear, including the Corps size and structure, its mission, and the relation between German forces' NATO obligation and their new role in the Corps.[41]

The British Foreign Minister immediately criticized the proposal,[42] a view echoed by officials in Denmark,[43] while Italy's Foreign Minister downplayed the differences between the two initiatives.[44] Spain, Belgium, Luxembourg, and Greece supported the initiative.[45] The U.S. reaction was muted;[46] U.S. officials focused their attention on

---

[36]U.S. Secretary of State Baker and Foreign Minister Genscher unveiled the NACC proposal on October 3. France objected, on the grounds that it was an inappropriate extension of NATO's sphere of competence. *Washington Post*, October 4, 1991, p. 19; *Financial Times,* October 9, 1991, p. 14.

[37]In September 1990, after the conclusion of the 2 + 4 talks leading to German independence, President Mitterrand announced that France planned to withdraw its troops from Germany because the legal justification for stationing those troops as occupation forces had lapsed. The new Franco-German agreement provided a new rationale, since each country would station forces on the other's territory (German forces would be stationed in Strasbourg as a part of the headquarters for the proposed Franco-German Corps). *Le Figaro*, October 17, 1991, p. 4.

[38]*The Times*, October 17, 1991, p. 10.

[39] *Financial Times*, October 17, 1991, p. 2.

[40]*Die Welt*, October 17, 1991, p. 2; *Süddeutsche Zeitung*, October 17, 1991, p. 4.

[41]Germany's Defense Minister stated that Germany would not create new troops for the Corps but that NATO requirements would have priority. Agence France Presse, October 17, 1991 (FBIS-WEU-91-202, October 18, 1991, p. 1); *Independent*, October 18, 1991, p. 10; *Frankfurter Allgemeine Zeitung,* October 18, 1991, p. 6.

[42]*Financial Times*, October 17, 1991, p. 1.

[43]*Berlingske Tidende*, October 17, 1991, p. 9 (FBIS-WEU-91-204, October 22, 1991, p. 28).

[44]*Le Figaro*, October 17, 1991, p. 5.

[45]*Guardian,* October 17, 1991, p. 10; *Christian Science Monitor*, October 18, 1991, p. 6.

[46]*Wall Street Journal*, October 18, 1991, p. A10. Defense Secretary Cheney said, "I think our concern would be that whatever forces are assigned to the new entity would not be subtracted from those forces assigned to NATO." *Independent*, October 22, 1991, p. 12. U.S. Ambassador to the United Kingdom, Raymond Seitz, warned that U.S. policy was based on the assumption that European security policy would be handled in a transatlantic context; if that assumption changed, it would trigger a U.S.

resolving the potential conflict with NATO at the upcoming November 7–8 NATO summit in Rome.[47]

Although the summit began in an atmosphere of tension,[48] NATO leaders succeeded in reaching a compromise that appeared to satisfy all parties by recognizing both the legitimacy of an independent European defense identity and the primary role of NATO under the Washington Treaty. Building on the Copenhagen statement on "NATO's Core Security Functions in the New Europe," the Rome Declaration "recogni[zes] that it is for the European Allies concerned to decide what arrangements are needed for the expression of a common European foreign and security policy and defence role," while reiterating that the "Alliance is the essential forum for consultation among its members and the venue for agreement on policies bearing on the security and defence commitments of Allies under the Washington Treaty."[49] The accompanying "Strategic Concept" further noted that "integrated and multinational European structures, as they are further developed in the context of an emerging European Defence Identity, will also increasingly have a similarly important role to play in enhancing Allies' ability to work together in the common defence."[50] The primary area of disagreement in Rome was not over the European defense identity, as expected, but rather on whether NATO should expand its political role.[51]

---

withdrawal from Europe. "If there is a separate and competing decision-making body on security issues, then we are in for tough times." *Guardian*, October 31, 1991, p. 14.

[47]The summit was called to complete work on NATO's new strategic concept.

[48]President Bush openly challenged the European NATO members to reaffirm NATO's primacy and their continued intention to support keeping U.S. troops in Europe. "If, my friends, your ultimate aim is to provide independently for your own defense, the time to tell us is today." *Washington Post,* November 8, 1991, p. 1.

[49]¶6, Rome Declaration on Peace and Cooperation, November 7–8, 1991, *NATO Communiqués 1991* (NATO Office of Information and Press, Brussels, n.d.), p. 27.

[50]"The Alliance's New Strategic Concept," ¶52, Press Communiqué S-1 (91) 85, November 7, 1991 (mimeo). It is noteworthy that, after initial hesitation, France not only participated in drafting the NATO Strategic Concept but also endorsed the final document (though France remained careful to distance itself from those portions of the document related to the integrated military command and NATO military doctrine).

[51]France in particular was critical of the effort to give NATO a more political role, especially through expanded contacts with East European nations through the proposed North Atlantic Cooperation Council (NACC). President Mitterrand stated: "The alliance is a good one, but it is not the Holy Alliance" (a reference to the 1815 Alliance of Prussia, Austria, and Russia). Mitterrand also refused to sign the NATO Declaration on the Soviet Union, arguing that it was outside NATO's competence. Agence France Presse, November 8, 1991 (FBIS-WEU-91-217, November 8, 1991, pp. 3, 5).

France and Germany interpreted the NATO summit as implicitly endorsing their effort to build a European defense identity as part of the IGC on EPU. As the negotiations leading to Maastricht approached their final stage, they focused on two key objectives: (1) strengthening the CFSP by including in the Treaty a list of priority areas for common action as well as for qualified majority voting and (2) incorporating an explicit reference to the European Union's role in defense. The United Kingdom, by contrast, vigorously opposed their ideas on CFSP; for defense, Britain was willing to support a stronger WEU and to concede that the Union could have a role in defense "policy" but argued that defense itself should be left to NATO for in-area contingencies and to an autonomous WEU for out-of-area actions.[52]

The result, like so much of the Maastricht agreement, was a compromise that left key issues for the future. The leaders agreed to strengthen the Union's role in foreign and security policy by establishing procedures for "common positions" and "joint action,"[53] outside the communitarian structures of the Rome Treaty,[54] but binding (at least politically) on all members.[55] In a victory for Britain, the Treaty does not define in detail the priority areas for the CFSP and allows qualified majority on joint actions only after a prior unanimous vote authorizing its use.[56]

---

[52]*Guardian*, November 8, 1991, p. 11.

[53]The Treaty distinguishes between "common" policies, designed to improve "systematic cooperation between Member States" (implemented through the procedures set out in Article J.2) and "joint action" (Article J.3).

[54]Thus the Commission and European Parliament have much more limited roles under CFSP. For example, unlike the areas of Community competence under the Rome Treaty, the Commission shares the right of initiative, and Maastricht provides only that "The Commission shall be fully associated with the work carried out in the common foreign and security policy field." Article J.9. The Presidency of the Council is responsible for implementing the CFSP. Article J.5. Similarly, the Parliament's role is limited to consultation "on the main aspects and the basic choices" of CFSP and the right to remain informed and ask questions or make recommendations to the Council. Article J.7.

[55]The Treaty imposes (at least hortatorily) a stronger obligation on members for joint action, as compared with the common policy. In general, the Treaty provides: "The Member States shall support the Union's external and security policy actively and unreservedly in a spirit of loyalty and mutual solidarity. They shall refrain from any action which is contrary to the interests of the Union or likely to impair its effectiveness as a cohesive force in international relations. The Council shall ensure that these principles are complied with." Article J.1(4). However, for joint action, the Treaty explicitly states: "Joint actions shall commit the Member States in the positions they adopt and in the conduct of their activity." Article J.3(4).

[56]Articles J.3(2) and J.8(2). In an annexed Declaration, however, the EC leaders stated: "The Conference agrees that, with regard to Council decisions requiring unanimity, Member States will, to the extent possible, avoid preventing a unanimous

The provisions on defense represent a split decision.[57] The key language provides that "The common foreign and security policy shall include all questions related to the security of the Union, *including the eventual framing of a common defence policy which might in time lead to a common defence*" (emphasis added). Thus the United Kingdom was successful both in slowing the move to a common defense *policy* and in deferring entirely the question of the European Union's responsibility for defense per se. France and Germany, however, succeeded in including a firm commitment to review the defense question in 1996 in conjunction with the need to renew the Brussels Treaty in 1998. They also won inclusion of language stating that the WEU "is an integral part of the development of the Union" and that the Union may request the WEU to "implement decisions and actions of the Union which have defence implications," though not the right to "instruct" the WEU.

The nine EC members that made up the WEU further spelled out the relationship between the European Union and WEU in a declaration adopted at a parallel WEU meeting in Maastricht. The "Declaration on the Role of the Western European Union and Its Relations with the European Union and with the Atlantic Alliance"[58] straddles the divide between Atlanticists and Europeanists, while explicitly acknowledging the organic link between the WEU and the European Union: "The WEU will be developed *as the defence component of the European Union* and as a means to strengthen the European pillar of the Atlantic Alliance" (emphasis added). To underscore the relationship to the European Union, the WEU Maastricht Declaration outlines procedures to link the two institutions and, in a separate declaration, invites all EC states to join the WEU, while limiting non-EC NATO European states to associate membership.[59] The WEU

decision where a qualified majority exists in favor of a decision." Declaration on Voting in the Field of the Common Foreign and Security Policy," Maastricht Treaty, p. 239. For decisions that require expenditures from the EC budget, the Council must act unanimously. Article J.11.

[57]The defense provisions of the Treaty appear in Article J.4.

[58]The WEU declaration is incorporated in the "Declaration on Western European Union" annexed to the Maastricht Treaty, p. 242.

[59]"States which are members of the European Union are invited to accede to WEU. . . or to become observers if they so wish. Simultaneously, other European Member States of NATO are invited to become associate members of WEU in a way which will give them the possibility of participating fully in the activities of the WEU." "Declaration of the Member States of the Western European Union issued on the Occasion of the 46th European Council Meeting on December 9 and 10, 1991, at Maastricht," annexed to the Maastricht Treaty, pp. 245–246. Greece insisted on language assuring the right of all EC members to join the WEU as the price for its agreement to the Maastricht Treaty; the language on associate membership was

states also agreed to set up a "planning cell" to undertake closer cooperation on logistics, transport, training, and strategic surveillance and to examine and define appropriate missions, structures, and means for military units answerable to the WEU.[60]

DEVELOPMENTS AFTER MAASTRICHT

After Maastricht, it became quickly apparent that the agreed Treaty represented only the beginning of the debate on the Community's role in security policy. The first controversies grew out of the Community's continuing effort to respond to the Yugoslavia crisis, fueled by Germany's threat to recognize unilaterally Slovenia and Croatia, which most EC states felt violated the spirit of the CFSP agreement.[61] The Community faced additional embarrassment over Greece's continued veto over recognizing Macedonia.[62]

EC states continued to battle over Maastricht's meaning for creating a European defense identity. Most of the conflict centered over the role of the WEU and the proposed Franco-German Corps. The United Kingdom insisted that Maastricht preserved the WEU's autonomy and assured its tie to NATO. To cement this view, Britain offered a series of proposals to link the WEU to NATO institutions and to focus the WEU's efforts on out-of-area actions. The British Defense Secretary, Malcolm Rifkind, said that Britain did not "rule out a role for the WEU inside the NATO area, in humanitarian operations, for

---

included in turn to reassure Turkey that its interests would not entirely be neglected. *Washington Post*, December 11, 1991, p. 1. Greece was admitted to full WEU membership in autumn 1992. Denmark, the other member of both NATO and the EC, but not the WEU, is divided on whether to join the WEU; Foreign Minister Ellemann-Jensen supports WEU membership, while the Social Democrats are opposed. *Berlingske Tidende*, February 11, 1992, p. 2 (FBIS-WEU-92-030, February 13, 1992, p. 42); *Arbeiderbladet*, March 3, 1992, p. 11 (FBIS-WEU-92-044, March 5, 1992, p. 23).

[60]They also agreed to examine proposals for enhanced armaments cooperation "with the aim of creating a European armaments agency."

[61]In the face of Germany's threat to act alone, the other EC nations agreed to a compromise in which the EC's Yugoslavia arbitration panel, headed by French Judge Robert Badinter, would review all the Yugoslav republics' applications for recognition according to their conformity with guarantees of human rights, democracy, and renouncing the use of force. When the panel recommended recognizing Slovenia but not Croatia, the conflict between Germany and its EC partners flared again, as Germany made clear that it intended to recognize Croatia in any event. Ultimately, the other EC states bowed to Germany's policy preference. See Steinberg, *The Role of European Institutions in Security After the Cold War*.

[62]The Badinter panel concluded that Macedonia met the EC's criteria for recognition, but the eleven other member-states declined to act over Greece's objection. At the June 1992 Lisbon summit the Twelve stated that they were prepared to recognize Macedonia only if it agreed not to use the name "Macedonia"; in effect endorsing Greece's position.

example," but "NATO would have to give its agreement first."[63] Britain also fought hard to maximize the associate members' involvement in WEU deliberations and to preserve the "transparency" of the WEU's activities.[64]

France and Germany focused their efforts on developing the Franco-German Corps. At Germany's invitation, they held a "seminar" in February 1992 to discuss ideas for the Corps with other European states over Britain's objection that the WEU was the proper forum for discussions of defense policy.[65] France and Germany further elaborated their concept at the Franco-German summit in La Rochelle on May 21–22, 1992, when they announced that they would create a planning staff for the Corps on July 1, 1992, in Strasbourg, France, with the aim of creating an operational unit of some 35,000 troops by October 1, 1995. Although the two leaders re-extended their invitation to other EC members to contribute to the Corps, none to date have joined. Kohl and Mitterrand both stressed the compatibility of the Corps with NATO,[66] but several U.S. officials spoke openly about their concerns that the Corps would harm NATO.[67]

---

[63]"A Decade of Change in European Security," Rt. Hon. Malcolm Rifkind, Centre for Defence Studies, Kings College, London, May 14, 1992 (mimeo). The United Kingdom initially proposed co-locating the new WEU planning cell with NATO's planners at Mons, Belgium, or even sharing staff, and suggested that WEU members "dual-hat" their NATO representatives to serve as WEU representatives when the WEU Secretariat moved to Brussels. For military forces, the British rejected the idea of separate peacetime command structures or units, arguing that the WEU could draw on existing forces and headquarters if the need arose for actions out-of-area.

[64]The United Kingdom was concerned that the WEU would make decisions and present them as *faits accomplis* in the context of NATO deliberations, binding on all WEU members even in discussions within NATO's North Atlantic Council (NAC). The United Kingdom sought to ensure that the NAC would be the primary forum for security discussions. According to Britain, the Maastricht language setting forth associate members' roles ("other European Member States of NATO are invited to become associate members of WEU in a way which will give them the possibility of *participating fully* in the activities of the WEU") required at least a majority vote to exclude them from WEU meetings. France and Germany seemed to favor a rule that would allow excluding associate members on the vote of three full members.

[65]Other WEU members, especially Italy, were also concerned at what some viewed as a Franco-German attempt to "hijack" the European defense identity under the guise of the Corps. Former Italian Defense Minister Virginio Rognoni said that the Maastricht agreement "did not ask us to act two by two, but all together in common." *Washington Post,* May 27, 1992, p. A21.

[66]Kohl: The Corps "will contribute to strengthening the Alliance." Mitterrand: "We want the presence of Americans in Europe. We know what we owe to NATO." *New York Times,* August 23, 1992, p. 1.

[67]See, e.g., remarks of William Taft IV, U.S. Ambassador to NATO, *Washington Times,* May 22, 1992, p. 7. By contrast, Secretary Richard Cheney said that the Corps "is probably basically a sound proposal." *New York Times,* May 23, 1992, p. 1.

Despite the continued high-level commitment to the Corps in both France and Germany and the nominal agreement spelled out in the La Rochelle communiqué, there remained unresolved differences between the two on the structure and missions of the Corps and its relation to NATO. Both countries accepted that the Corps could come under NATO's operational control in the event of an in-area contingency. But German leaders took pains to stress that German forces assigned to the Corps would continue to have independent NATO assignments, while under France's approach, both German and French forces would belong to the Corps in peacetime and come under NATO control only after a political decision by each of the two countries (preferably as an intact corps rather than as separate national forces).[68]

Defining its missions proved particularly difficult, given the limitations in Germany's Basic Law on the use of the Bundeswehr. The La Rochelle communiqué defined three tasks for the Eurocorps:

- Joint allied defense under either the Brussels or NATO Treaties;
- "Maintaining or re-establishing peace"; and
- "Humanitarian missions."

As traditionally interpreted by Germany's political leaders, the Basic Law limits the Bundeswehr to national defense and collective responsibilities under NATO, precluding out-of-area actions or in-area use not under NATO command. While leaders of the Christliche Demokratische Union (CDU) saw the Corps (as well as the development of the WEU) as a further argument for amending the Basic

---

[68]The La Rochelle communiqué states that "the formations [of the Eurocorps] are primarily subordinated to the Corps and are intended for joint missions." This could conflict with NATO's assertion that "the primary responsibility of forces answerable to the WEU will remain NATO's collective defence under the Washington Treaty." Final Communiqué, Ministerial Meeting of the North Atlantic Council in Oslo, Norway, June 4, 1992, ¶7.

In the case where the Eurocorps is used as part of a NATO mission, the La Rochelle communiqué states it should be on the basis of a political agreement with NATO,which "presupposes that the troops subordinated to the European Corps . . . are primarily subordinated to the Commanding General of the Corps and are used together with its staff." ¶3.2.2.

The communiqué gives an illustrative list of forces for the Eurocorps but the German ground forces are labeled "to be determined." Germany proposed to resolve the conflict by assigning to the Corps only those forces that did not already have a role in NATO's Rapid Reaction Corps. Nonetheless, there remains a potential conflict, since all German forces have a NATO mission (except those assigned in the eastern part of Germany until the Soviet forces finally depart in 1995). Thus the forces that Germany is likely to associate with the Corps also have an assignment with NATO's main defense forces.

Law, leaders of the Sozialdemokratische Partei Deutschlands (SPD) (with the support of many in the Freie Demokratische Partei [FDP]) criticized attempting to use the Corps as a back door means of expanding the Bundeswehr's role, even for peacekeeping or humanitarian operations.[69] France, by contrast, proposed that the Corps be available for a full range of missions, in and out-of-area.

The Basic Law also proved a stumbling block to Germany's approach to developing the WEU since supporters of the restrictive interpretation refused to acknowledge the WEU's legitimacy to undertake autonomous actions. France implicitly supported Germany's diffident approach, preferring to focus on the Corps rather than on the WEU for developing Europe's independent military capability, as Britain advocated.

Although both France and Germany repeatedly referred to the Corps as a "European" corps, other countries were reluctant to commit forces. Belgium and Spain expressed the greatest interest, but Belgium was limited by the fact that it had already committed its small contingent of ready forces to NATO's Rapid Reaction Corps (RRC), posing a difficult, if not insuperable, potential conflict in responsibilities.

While France and Germany proceeded with planning for the Eurocorps, the United Kingdom and others pressed ahead with redefining the role of the WEU. At a meeting in Bonn, Germany, on June 19, 1992, the leaders of the nine WEU nations took a number of steps to enhance the WEU's role and capabilities.[70] They offered to allow WEU forces to serve as peacekeeping forces under the CSCE or United Nations, created a new liaison relationship with the eight countries of Central Europe, and agreed to semiannual meetings of

---

[69]These criticisms predated the Maastricht agreement. See *Frankfurter Allgemeine Zeitung,* November 7, 1991, p. 2 (FBIS-WEU-91-225, November 21, p. 8); Berlin ADN, November 6, 1991 (FBIS-WEU-91-126, November 7, 1991, p. 9). For the CDU view, see the interview with Karl Lamers, CDU/CSU Bundestag group spokesman on foreign policy, in *Frankfurter Allgemeine Zeitung*, March 23, 1992, p. 6. On the same issue, former Foreign Minister Genscher, a leader of the FDP, outlined his view that military actions out-of-area should only take place under UN auspices (including the CSCE to the extent that it becomes a regional organization under Chapter 8 of the UN Charter), an approach which implicitly rules out military activities solely under WEU sponsorship. As a result of the German government's decision to send a destroyer and airborne surveillance aircraft to the NATO/WEU forces monitoring the embargo against Serbia in July 1992, the SPD brought the issue of the constitutional limits on deploying the Bundeswehr to the German constitutional court, but the court has not yet ruled.

[70]Western European Council of Ministers, "Petersberg Declaration," Bonn, June 19, 1992 (mimeo).

Chiefs of Defense Staffs. They agreed to a definition of missions, including common defense under Article 5 of the NATO and Brussels Treaties; and humanitarian, peacekeeping, and crisis management tasks (including "peacemaking"). Each WEU member agreed to designate which military units and headquarters it would make available for WEU missions. The members accepted that some of the forces would have NATO missions, but these would be made available "after consultation with NATO."

The WEU nations finally resolved the problem of the relationship between WEU members and NATO countries not part of the WEU (associate members). The Council agreed to permit associate members to participate fully in WEU meetings except where a majority of the member-states vote to restrict the sessions. Similarly, associates can participate in WEU actions unless a majority of WEU members vote no. Associates can send liaison staff to the WEU planning cell and speak but not vote in the WEU Council. Anticipating the problem of a potential conflict between a full member (Greece) and an associate (Turkey), the WEU stated that no WEU member could invoke the mutual assistance article of the Brussels Treaty against a NATO member.

On November 20, 1992, Greece signed a protocol admitting it as the 10th member of the WEU, while Turkey, Norway, and Iceland became associate members. Denmark and Ireland plan to limit their involvement to observer status.

THE FUTURE OF SECURITY COOPERATION IN THE EUROPEAN COMMUNITY

Developments since Maastricht suggest that the idea of a European defense identity has some momentum. But there are large obstacles in the path of a truly effective, autonomous European military capability. At present, there is no obvious consensus on when Europeans might use these forces. Humanitarian, peacekeeping, and rescue operations seem the most likely, but this would represent a very limited expression of a European defense identity. As the Yugoslavia crisis shows, there is considerable European reluctance to commit forces to combat situations, even in nearby areas of instability that have the greatest impact on European security.[71] Moreover,

[71]Some, especially French officials, have argued that the EC's reluctance to become engaged militarily in Yugoslavia is attributable to the lack of existing capability and that the plans for creating the Corps and other European structures will enhance Europe's willingness to take action in the future. It seems more probable that the

European forces have significant capability shortfalls for large-scale military operations, particularly for deployment and operation out of Europe. Analysts and European military leaders cite military lift, surveillance, intelligence, and communications as the most pressing shortcomings. Although individual nations have proposed beefing up Europe's capability and the WEU is specifically charged with coordinating West European efforts in these areas, budget limitations suggest that they will make modest improvements at best and that Europe will continue to need U.S. assistance in major contingencies. This is not to say that a more focused effort will not improve European capabilities for future contingencies such as the Gulf War, but rather that Western Europe will still require close transatlantic cooperation in security.

The future for the European defense identity will turn on many developments, only some of which are directly under European control. The extent of future U.S. involvement in Europe is a key factor. A sharply reduced U.S. commitment, not only in the number of U.S. military forces stationed in Europe but in the level of political involvement, could, but need not necessarily, lead to more intensive European efforts; the alternative, less likely but not inconceivable, is a renationalization of European defense. The nature and level of instability on Western Europe's periphery—Eastern Europe and the former Soviet republics, the Mahgreb, and the Middle East—will dictate to some degree the need for a greater, more coordinated effort.

The evolution of the Community itself, especially the degree to which the Community expands, is an important consideration. If the bonds among member-states continue to deepen, they are likely to see eye-to-eye more frequently on questions of security, enhancing the prospect for a common response. However, a larger Community, particularly one that embraces the Cold War neutrals, could make achieving consensus more difficult. The current members have stressed to new applicants that they must agree to all the Community's *acquis*, including the willingness to participate in the Common Foreign and Security Policy, but whether that will extend to defense is a separate question, particularly since the Community was forced to let Denmark "opt out" of common defense as a price for its ratifying the Maastricht Treaty. Even France, which is the most fervent advocate of a common defense, seems prepared to concede that a

---

Community's failure to act in Yugoslavia is attributable to a lack of political consensus rather than inadequate means.

subset of the full Community membership should reserve the right to act in the military field.[72] On the other hand, including the Central European countries in the Community could bring security problems closer to home, increasing the need—and willingness—to act jointly.[73]

Finally, the evolution of EC members' national outlook, especially Germany, will be critical. An effective European capability is unimaginable without German participation, yet it is unclear whether the German public, and hence its political leaders, will agree to a broader role for the Bundeswehr. Under Chancellor Kohl, Germany has continued to expand the list of permissible missions, but it is uncertain how far the public will continue to support him if Germany begins to suffer casualties in foreign military operations.[74] There is also a risk that Germany will conclude that a European defense structure is inadequate to replace diminishing U.S. involvement, and will feel the need to take measures to assure its own security interests, particularly as Germany becomes more involved in Central and Eastern Europe. At the extreme, this could lead to German interest in developing its own nuclear deterrent.

Whether Germany feels compelled to nationalize its defense will depend in part on France's willingness to commit to an integrated European defense. Changes in the European security environment and domestic budget constraints have eroded de Gaulle's legacy of France's strategic independence, most clearly evident in the proposals for the Franco-German Corps. But a key question is whether France is prepared to commit its nuclear deterrent to the service of the European Union. President Mitterrand has hinted that in the future France may be prepared to move in that direction, but that outcome is by no means certain.[75] In addition, key Community members, in-

---

[72]Former Italian Foreign Minister De Michelis has also spoken of the possibility of a "variable geometry" for defense as the Community enlarges. *Die Presse,* March 23, 1992, p. 3 (FBIS-WEU-92-058, March 25, 1992, p. 3).

[73]The issues associated with enlargement are discussed in greater detail in Section 7.

[74]German Defense Minister Volcker Rühe has spoken of a "culture of restraint" that would constrain German actions in the future (*Handelsblatt,* August 14–15, 1992, p. 3) and suggested that barriers related both to psychology and capability would limit German out-of-area operations for a decade. *Süddeutsche Zeitung,* July 17, 1992, p. 4.

[75]In a speech on January 10, 1992, President Mitterrand stated: "is it possible to draw up a European [nuclear] doctrine? That question will quickly become one of the major questions raised by the building of a common European defense." *Le Monde,* January 12–13, 1992, p. 1. But Admiral Lanxade, French Chief of Staff, indicated that such a change was not imminent. *Le Monde,* January 14, 1992, p. 8. Defense Minister Pierre Joxe recently stated that France "could already envision multilateral [European] consultation on the use of nuclear weapons and the enlargement of the nuclear

cluding the United Kingdom, the Netherlands, and Denmark, still retain a strong Atlanticist orientation. This is likely to change as the United States draws down its European forces and refocuses its security policy away from Europe, but whether this will lead those countries to accept a European defense is unclear.[76]

In short, it is simply too soon to say where the process of European defense is headed. The EC conference called for 1996 may mark the next crucial watershed.[77]

---

guarantee," Pierre Joxe, speech at the opening of a Colloquium on "The New Strategic Debate," September 29, 1992 (mimeo). Jacques Delors had earlier observed: "I cannot help thinking that if, one day, the EC has a very strong political union, nuclear arms could be transferred to that political authority." *Le Monde,* January 14, 1992, p. 8. See also *The Times*, January 6, 1992, p. 1. French public opinion shows strong support for a common European defense, but the reaction to giving up the independent deterrent is more mixed. *Economist*, January 18, 1992, p. 48.

Former German Foreign Minister Genscher hinted that he agreed with the need to address the role of French nuclear forces in implementing European security policies. *Die Welt,* January 8, 1992, p. 8 (FBIS-WEU-92-005, January 8, 1992, p. 10).

[76]In the United Kingdom, for example, both the Conservatives and Labour opposed the Franco-German Corps. *Financial Times*, February 10, 1992, p. 5. In Denmark, a pre-Maastricht poll found that 56 percent of Danes preferred maintaining the NATO-centered security system, while only 23 percent favored more European military cooperation. *Berlingske Sondag*, December 8, 1991, p. 8 (FBIS-WEU-92-014, January 22, 1992, p. 20).

[77]A related element of European defense integration concerns weapon system development and procurement. European governments and defense firms are already involved in extensive intra-European collaborative projects. Through the Independent European Program Group (IEPG), the European members of NATO (minus Iceland) are developing a common approach to European procurement policy and, through the EC, armaments coordination is shaped by aspects of economic policy (competition, research and development, and procurement) that affect "dual use" equipment and technologies. The EC's potential role was further enhanced by Article 30(b) of the SEA, which provided that "The High Contracting Parties are determined to maintain the technological and industrial conditions necessary for their security. They shall work at the national level, and, where appropriate, within the framework of the competent institutions and bodies."

But direct EC involvement has been limited by Article 223 of the Rome Treaty, which reserves the right of individual nations to decide on defense procurement. There was considerable discussion of repealing or modifying Article 223 as part of the EPU IGC, but no action was taken and European Defense Ministers strongly prefer to leave defense collaboration to the IEPG. In the meantime, the expanding role of the WEU, and the agreement to allow broad participation by NATO members who are not members of the WEU, has led to new interest in bringing the IEPG efforts within the purview of a proposed WEU European Armaments Agency. See "Petersberg Declaration," ¶I(13), and the IEPG Oslo declaration, March 6, 1992. For an analysis of the process of defense industry integration and the role of the EC and IEPG, see James B. Steinberg, *The Transformation of the European Defense Industry,* RAND, R-4141-ACQ, 1992.

6. ECONOMIC INTEGRATION: MOVING TOWARD ECONOMIC AND MONETARY UNION

From the European Coal and Steel Community through the Rome Treaty and the Single European Act, the effort to deepen European economic integration has played a major role in the European Community's construction. The Maastricht Treaty represents a further step down this path. The Community's decision to adopt a timetable and procedures for EMU; the agreement of all but the United Kingdom to institutionalize the "social dimension" of Community economic policy; and a modest broadening of the Community's role in areas such as consumer protection, health, education, and trans-European networks represents the principal economic developments of the new Treaty. At the same time, the prospect of EMU triggered some of the most heated debates over Maastricht's ratification, calling into question whether Maastricht's centerpiece, EMU, is any closer to realization. This section reviews the broad trends in Community economic policy, beginning with an assessment of the effort to complete the Single Market, then turns to the debate over EMU and social policy. It concludes by examining the continuing debate over the Community's budget, including recent proposals for reforming the Common Agricultural Program (CAP), and "regional" policy, the key element of the Community's effort to enhance "cohesion" by reducing imbalances between the more and less developed countries and regions.

ECONOMIC INTEGRATION AMONG THE TWELVE

Even before the Community launched its ambitious 1992 program, the economies of the Western European nations had achieved considerable interdependence. Both intra-EC and intra-Western European[1] trade had grown dramatically in importance and helped fuel European economic growth.[2]

---

[1]Western Europe for the purposes of this discussion includes the 12 members of the European Community (Belgium, Denmark, France, Germany, Greece, Ireland, Italy, Luxembourg, the Netherlands, Portugal, Spain, and the United Kingdom) and the seven members of the European Free Trade Association (Austria, Finland, Iceland, Norway, Sweden, Switzerland, and Lichtenstein).

[2]For a more detailed discussion of the extent of European economic integration, see C. Cooper, J. Steinberg, and M. Shires, *The Evolution of the European Economy: Implications for Transatlantic Relations*, RAND, N-3432-FF, 1992.

Several indicators demonstrate the growing integration of European markets. Intra-regional trade increasingly dominates the European economy. Overall, intra-EC trade grew from 32.9 percent to 59.6 percent of all trade by EC countries from 1950 to 1991, and intra-regional trade (Western Europe) rose from 44.4 percent of all trade (exports plus imports) to 67.4 percent (Table 6.1).

Table 6.1

European Intra-Trade as Percentage of Total Trade (in thousands of U.S. dollars)

	1950	1960	1970	1980	1990	1991
Total EC trade	38,184	90,034	241,611	1,463,881	2,787,272	2,825,522
Total EC intra-trade	12,556	35,532	124,777	766,513	1,633,277	1,683,744
Intra-trade as percentage of all EC trade	**32.9**	**39.5**	**51.6**	**52.4**	**58.6**	**59.6**
Total WE trade	45,069	106,693	284,657	1,703,365	3,240,883	3,257,864
Total WE intra-trade	19,995	56,520	178,630	1,055,721	2,174,261	2,195,485
Intra-trade as percentage of all WE trade	**44.4**	**53.0**	**62.8**	**62.0**	**67.1**	**67.4**

SOURCE: International Monetary Fund, *Directory of Trade Statistics,* Washington, D.C., various years.

Converging price levels[3] and wages[4] within the Community show the

[3]A price study by Eurostat shows that the variation in tax-inclusive prices of "Equipment Goods" (machinery, instruments, vehicles, and ships) within the EC-9 (excluding Greece, Portugal, and Spain) decreased by 9.3 percent in the period from 1975 to 1985. While not as impressive as "Equipment Goods," the variation in tax-included prices on consumer goods such as food, textiles, clothing, household appliances, energy, and services decreased by 2.4 percent during the same period. "The Economics of 1992," *European Economy,* No. 35 (Commission of the European Communities, March 1988), pp. 119–121. Some of the impact of converging inflation rates may be attributable to the European Monetary System. See Kenneth A. Froot and Kenneth Rogoff, "The EMS, the EMU and the Transition to a Common Currency," NBER Working Paper No. 3684, April 1991, summarized in *The Effects of Greater Economic Integration Within the European Community on the United States: Fourth Follow-Up Report,* USITC Publication 2501, April 1992, pp. 4-6, 4-7. [Hereinafter *U.S.I.T.C. Fourth Follow-Up Report.*]

[4]*Economist,* January 25, 1992, p. 66.

effects of increased trade interdependence. There are also indications of an increasingly integrated European financial market.[5]

But in the mid-1980s many barriers to open trade within the Community remained, and the EC had not yet achieved two of its principal long-standing goals—completing the Single Market and Economic and Monetary Union. With the adoption of the SEA, the Community turned its attention to achieving the first of these two goals.

EC 1992

The White Paper on Completing the Market and the SEA's ratification provided both the substantive road map and the procedural tools for moving the Community toward free movement of peoples, goods, services, and capital. The Commission identified some 280 directives[6] needed to overcome key remaining barriers to an open market. Although the challenge appeared daunting, the business and financial communities' broad enthusiasm, spurred on by the Commission's own

---

[5]Corner and Tonks reviewed individually the correlation coefficients of the five major European stock markets with those of Europe, the United States, and Japan. The study found that for three of the stock markets reviewed, Germany, the Netherlands, and Italy, the markets became more closely correlated with the other European markets than with the other world markets, reflecting a level of increased integration between the markets. The remaining two markets, France and the United Kingdom, showed the opposite, although for France the increase in the correlation coefficients was almost equal between the two markets. While these results are affected by a wide variety of world-wide effects, including timing aspects of deregulation, improved information technologies, and the integration of international financial service firms, they do provide some indication of the convergence of EC capital markets.

Their study also found that stock market performance between EC countries was much more strongly correlated in the post-EMS period (1980 to 1986) than during the pre-EMS period (1973 to 1979), indicating further interdependence. D.C. Corner and I. Tonks, "The Impact of the Internationalisation of World Stock Markets on the Integration of EC Securities Markets," in M. Macmillan, D. G. Mayer, and P. van Veen, eds., *European Integration and Industry* (Tilburg: Tilburg University Press, 1987), pp. 229–246.

[6]The precise number of directives in the Single Market Program has varied over time as the Commission adjusts to ongoing developments but has never strayed far from 280.

[7]The Cecchini Report found that completing the internal market would lead to a one-time increase of 5 percent in the Community's GDP (above any growth that might be experienced in the absence of completing the market). The studies concluded that consumer prices would be deflated by an average 6 percent and produce economies in the public sector of around 2.2 percent of GDP. Paolo Cecchini (English edition, J. Robinson, ed.), *The European Challenge, 1992: The Benefits of a Single Market* (EC

analysis of integration's economic benefits (the Cecchini Report),[7] proved an important motor to the process.[8]

Some aspects of the 1992 project proceeded with relatively little difficulty. In the area of technical barriers (differing national standards for products, business and professional licensing, etc.), the Community achieved rapid progress by leaving much of the detail work to industry and by adopting in most cases a rule of reciprocal or mutual recognition (a product or a service that was permitted under one member country's laws would be permitted throughout the Community).[9] The Community has also made substantial strides toward the free movement of capital—nine countries have completely removed their exchange controls (Ireland can continue until 1992, Portugal and Greece until 1995).[10] Financial services raised many difficult questions. About 30 directives deal with banking, securities, and insurance. Substantial progress has been made on banking and more recently in insurance, based on the use of mutual recognition supported by a core of "essential standards" applied community-wide. Some outstanding issues remain in investment services. For public procurement, the EC adopted a directive, effective January 1, 1993, that will open bidding on a non-discriminatory basis to all qualified firms throughout the Community for previously "excepted" sectors (water, energy, transport, and telecommunications), which together account for some 7–8 percent of the EC's GDP,[11] but the directive

Commission, 1988). Other analysts have reached different results, although all show a real gain. See sources cited in *Europe 1992*, p. 8.

[8]One study distinguishes between "market-led" forces (primarily global competition and technology) that contributed to achieving the 1992 goals and policy-led factors (such as mutual recognition). See Steven Woolcock et al., *Britain, Germany and 1992: The Limits of Deregulation* (New York: Council on Foreign Relations Press, 1991).

[9]As early as 1979, the EC Court had ruled (in the *Cassis de Dijon* case) that products made and marketed under the laws of one member-state could be marketed throughout the Community (allowing exceptions on the grounds of health, safety, or tax policing). But until the Community began to implement the 1992 program, the Commission focused its efforts on developing common standards ("harmonization") that would apply throughout the Community. This approach proved cumbersome and time-consuming (the directive that allowed architects to practice throughout the Community took 17 years to develop), and the Commission largely jettisoned it in the interest of completing the internal market by the January 1, 1993, deadline. In its place, the Commission adopted relatively brief "essential requirements" (such as solvency and capital ratios for banking investment and insurance services) to supplement mutual recognition.

[10]Nicholas Colchester and David Buchan, *Europower* (Economist Books, 1990), p. 93. The elimination of capital controls is now threatened by the currency upheaval caused in part by the controversy over EMU. See below.

[11]Colchester and Buchan, *Europower,* p. 87. The Council has also adopted a directive opening up intra-EC competition for public services contracts. *Financial Times,* December 20, 1991, p. 2.

continues to allow EC countries to discriminate against non-EC bidders.[12]

Other issues proved more troublesome. Only in July 1992 did the EC countries reach a compromise on harmonizing their value-added taxes (VAT), an important step toward removing frontier controls within the Community.[13] The goal of free movement of people has proved difficult to achieve because of differing national perspectives on how to deal with terrorism, drugs, and the prospect of large-scale immigration from Eastern Europe, the Soviet Union, and North Africa.[14] As a precursor to EC-wide free movement of peoples, five nations (France, Germany, and the Benelux countries) signed the Schengen Agreement on June 19, 1990, providing for passport-free travel between their countries, harmonizing visa requirements for third countries, exchanging information on criminals, and establishing common criteria for asylum and the right of hot pursuit. Italy joined Schengen

---

[12]EC bidders are given a 3 percent price advantage over non-EC competitors, who must also assure that half of all contracts go to EC nationals. *The Times,* September 7, 1990.

[13]The EC agreed on a 15 percent minimum standard VAT rate for four years, with a reduced rate of 5 percent for some items and a number of exceptions. This will require Germany and Spain to raise their standard rates slightly. The Finance Ministers also set minimum excise taxes on cigarettes, alcohol, and gasoline, with 0 percent rate on wine. This legally binding agreement followed an earlier political commitment to the 15 percent minimum. *Financial Times,* June 26, 1991, p. 2, and July 29, 1992, p. 2.

[14]The Twelve appended a declaration to the SEA preserving the right of individual governments to develop their own policies in these areas. Most of these problems are now handled on an intergovernmental basis. There is a working group of the Twelve on immigration; and the "Trevi" group of Interior Ministers was created in 1975 for cooperation on crime, drug trafficking, and terrorism. The Maastricht Treaty further institutionalizes cooperation in this area, primarily on an intergovernmental basis.

The problem of immigration has a differential impact on the Community's member nations. The largest non-EC immigrant populations are in France (6.5 percent of France's population) and Germany (5.2 percent). *Financial Times,* March 12, 1990. Increasingly, the Mediterranean states (especially France, Italy, and Spain) worry about migration from North Africa. Nations closest to Eastern Europe and the former Soviet Union express growing concern at the prospect of massive immigration, particularly from the former Soviet republics. Prior to the USSR's dissolution, Soviet authorities suggested that as many as three million Soviet citizens per year might immigrate, mainly to Western Europe. *Independent,* September 25, 1990. More recently, the refugee crisis brought on by the fighting in the former Yugoslavia has focused attention on immigration and asylum policy.

To date, most of the Community's effort has centered around developing a common "negative list" of countries whose citizens must obtain visas before entering any EC country. This task has proved difficult, given the divergent approaches taken by different EC states: France is most restrictive, while southern EC nations and Denmark require few nationals to obtain visas.

in the late fall of 1990, followed by Spain and Portugal, and most recently Greece.[15]

The effort to implement the Schengen Agreement demonstrates the problems of building a border-free Europe in the face of individual national concerns.[16] Agreement was stalled at one time or another as a result of German insistence on including East Germans in the barrier-free travel zone (a problem mostly solved by unification), French worries about Arab terrorism, Dutch sensitivity on the privacy aspect of Schengen and its impact on national asylum policies, and the potential consequences for Luxembourg's banking laws on the Schengen Information System (designed to help in cross-border policing).

Extending the Schengen approach to the Twelve is even more complex and controversial. The European Council, at the Rome summit in December 1990, "noted with regret that a delay has occurred in relation to the programme [of free movement of persons]. It wants the necessary decisions, in particular on the crossing of external borders, to be taken at an early date to ensure that the 1 January 1993 deadline is met."[17] The Commission also expressed its sense of frustration over progress in free movement of peoples in its Work Programme for 1991, observing that substantive results were "awaited with impatience."[18] In order to overcome the resistance of the United Kingdom, Ireland, and Denmark, the EC is considering a "two-speed" approach, in which all 12 members would agree to the substantive proposals, but individual countries could opt out of specific provisions.[19] To date, the United Kingdom and Ireland resist passport-free borders for all entrants who come from another EC destination.

The political impetus to completing the market received a considerable boost from the generally enthusiastic reaction of the European business community.[20] Even before the legal framework was imple-

---

[15]The Schengen Agreement will take effect following ratification by all signatories; only France and Belgium have ratified thus far.

[16]The five countries signed an initial agreement at Schengen in 1985 on barrier-free travel but took five years to resolve the many complex issues. See *Economist,* November 23, 1991, p. 58.

[17]As stated in the Rome Communiqué.

[18]*The Times,* January 21, 1991.

[19]*Daily Telegraph,* June 14, 1991, p. 1.

[20]Prior to 1985, industry-sponsored initiatives such as Per Gyllenhammer's European Round Table helped move the idea for the Single Market Program to the top of the Community's agenda. See Ludlow, *Beyond 1992,* pp. 27–30. Moravscik, in

mented, European entrepreneurs began to adapt their strategies to the prospect of a Europe-wide market. Takeovers, mergers, and joint ventures in Community states increased by 45 percent in 1987.[21] The new climate seemed especially propitious for U.S. multinationals operating in Europe, which were uniquely well suited to take advantage of lowered non-tariff barriers within the EC.[22] Unlike "national champion" firms, whose sales were tied primarily to a single European nation (and whose welfare was often zealously protected by its national government through subsidies and protectionism), the multinationals arguably were among the first truly European firms.

While Community institutions have made considerable progress in developing and adopting the required 1992 legislation, national parliaments have lagged in enacting the directives into national law. By early 1992, the Commission had completed all of the roughly 280 proposed directives established by the 1985 White Paper, and the Council and Parliament had passed approximately 230.[23] But far fewer measures have been adopted in all 12 EC countries.[24]

ECONOMIC AND MONETARY UNION[25]

Eliminating the legal and administrative barriers to intra-Community trade will not, in itself, lead to a fully integrated economy

---

"Negotiating the Single European Act," however, argues that the role of business in bringing about agreement on the SEA has been overstated by some.

[21]Colchester and Buchan, *Europower,* p. 34.

[22]In 1988, affiliates of U.S. multinational firms in Europe had sales of approximately $620 billion. *Europe 1992*, p. xix.

[23]*Financial Times,* December 30, 1992, p. 11. *Der Tagesspiegel,* January 5, 1992, reprinted in the *German Tribune,* January 17, 1992, p. 7.

[24]Italy, for example, has passed only about half the directives cleared through the Community's machinery. *Financial Times,* December 30, 1991, p. 11. The U.S. International Trade Commission estimates that, as of December 1991, EC states had fully adopted less than half (56) of the 136 directives for which the deadline had passed. *U.S.I.T.C. Fourth Follow-Up Report*.

[25]"Monetary Union" refers to the complete integration of national monetary policy. This includes intra-EC exchange rates and issuing legal tender. It is often used synonymously with a single European currency, although other schemes (such as permanently fixed exchange rates) are consistent with monetary union. It also implies a common mechanism for setting monetary policy through a common central bank or other joint mechanism. As a practical matter, this also implies the power to set interest rates.

"Economic Union" is a broader concept that includes both macroeconomic elements (coordinating member-states' fiscal policies, such as budget deficits) and microeconomic policy (competition, industrial policy, infrastructure investments). See *Economist,* July 7, 1990, pp. 25–27; "One Market, One Money," *European Economy,* No. 44 (Commission of the European Communities, October 1990), p. 9.

so long as the Twelve pursue independent macroeconomic policies (especially interest and exchange rate policies). For this reason, the Commission, supported by most Community members, set Economic and Monetary Union (EMU) as the next major goal after completing the internal market.[26]

EC nations took a first concrete step toward coordinated exchange rates with the "snake" in 1972, followed by the European Monetary System (EMS) in 1979. The heart of EMS is the Exchange Rate Mechanism (ERM) in which member-states commit to keep the fluctuation in the value of their currency within a narrow band against other participating currencies.[27]

As a practical matter, the ERM has led to a gradual convergence of member-states' macroeconomic policies toward the policies followed by Germany, the country with the strongest currency, the deutschemark. If countries try to run more expansionist or reflationary policies—through lower interest rates, higher budget deficits, or increased money supply—their currencies weaken, forcing them to abandon or moderate their preferred policy to remain within the agreed currency band.[28] The impact of this discipline contributed to France's macroeconomic policy about-face in March 1983, when President Mitterrand abandoned the reflationary path of his first two years in office to follow a policy that tracked the Bundesbank.

---

[26]The EC has a long-standing political commitment to EMU. See, for example, the 1970 Werner Report (commissioned at the EC's Hague summit in 1969), which called for implementing EMU by 1980. But the economic climate in the early 1970s led to growing divergence in European economic and fiscal policies, scuttling the effort in its early going.

The SEA reiterated the Community's commitment to EMU. It led to appointing a committee of experts under EC President Delors, who produced the Delors Committee Report in April 1989, which formed the basis for the current effort toward adopting EMU.

[27]The ERM centers around the ecu, which is a fixed basket of member-state currencies. Each national currency is assigned a "central rate" against the ecu (which can be realigned by agreement of the member-states, as has happened several times during the life of the ERM). These central rates give a matrix of bilateral central rates between each of the member countries. Under the ERM, countries pledge to intervene in the market to assure that their currency does not deviate (up or down) by more than 2.25 percent from the established bilateral rate. Spain, which joined the ERM in June 1989, the United Kingdom (October, 1990), and Portugal (April 1992) have somewhat greater flexibility; they are allowed fluctuations of up to 6 percent. Greece is not a member of the ERM. Italy and the United Kingdom suspended their participation in the ERM during the exchange rate crisis in September 1992, see page 86, below.

[28]Some economists have questioned the empirical support for the conventional wisdom concerning the Bundesbank's influence over long-term EMS interest rates outside Germany. See Heinz-Dieter Smeets, "Does Germany Dominate the EMS?" *Journal of Common Market Studies,* September 1990.

Since most European governments now live within the deutschemark zone and must conform their own policies to the decisions of the Bundesbank, the result is a near de facto single currency over which ERM states, other than Germany, have no say.[29] This led to renewed interest in creating a single European Central Bank to determine monetary policy for the entire Community.[30]

EMU advocates have also pushed a single currency on the grounds of efficiency. A study prepared for the EC estimated that savings of ecu 8 to 13 billion ($11–18 billion at 1990 exchange rates) would flow from the reduced transaction costs associated with a single currency; other savings would lift the total to ecu 13 to 19 billion ($18–26 billion). Further microeconomic savings should flow from reduced exchange rate uncertainty.[31] According to the study, EMU would produce the greatest benefit for smaller EC countries (Belgium, Luxembourg, Ireland, Denmark, and the Netherlands); their GDP would increase by 0.9 percent compared with 0.5 percent for larger countries.[32] Others have argued that the financial benefits are limited, and the cost in reduced monetary policy flexibility severe.[33]

The debate over EMU has revolved around six questions:

1. A fixed timetable and an irrevocable commitment to a single currency versus an evolutionary, open-ended approach;

---

[29]This consequence is reinforced by the Community's decision to end all exchange controls, which means that capital can freely move from weak to strong currencies, further enhancing the need of weaker currencies to shadow the Bundesbank's policies.

[30]The attitude of Denmark's Prime Minister, Poul Schluter, one of the most ardent defenders of national sovereignty prerogatives, illustrates why, for most EC countries, EMU is viewed as a net gain for national control. "[F]or a number of years it has been the West German Bundesbank that has determined the conditions for Danish interest policy. We in Denmark have been merely an echo. In direct and close monetary cooperation, we will no longer be an echo. We will be able to howl before the decisions are made." *Aftenposten,* September 29, 1990 (FBIS-WEU-90-206, p. 34). In 1988, then Italian Finance Minister Giuliano Amato called the proposal for a common central bank "an agreed loss of autonomy" by all EC states instead of the de facto unilateral loss of autonomy to the Bundesbank. Colchester and Buchan, *Europower,* p. 167.

[31]"One Market, One Money," p. 178. See also Michael Emerson and Christopher Huhne, *The ECU Report* (London: Pan Books, 1991), Ch. 2.

[32]"One Market, One Money." The benefits to these states arise primarily from reducing the exchange rate uncertainty and transaction costs associated with currencies not widely used. For small, less developed states, such as Spain, Greece, and Portugal, EMU would impose higher short-term transitional costs but offer larger gains in the future.

[33]See, e.g., the essay by Martin Feldstein, "The Case Against EMU," *Economist,* June 13, 1992, pp. 19–22.

2. An independent European Central Bank versus some degree of political oversight of monetary policy;
3. Commitment to a single policy principle (fighting inflation) versus flexibility (to include employment, growth, etc.);
4. A requirement that member-states' economies "converge" (especially in inflation rates) as a precondition to completing EMU versus using the discipline of EMU to promote convergence;
5. Fixed and enforceable budgetary rules in individual states versus national freedom in fiscal policy;[34] and
6. An automatic financial assistance mechanism to compensate poorer, lower productivity states for the lost power to devalue versus continued reliance on the structural funds.[35]

Disagreements over these issues created a multisided debate within the Community. Most EC countries, led by France (already de facto under the iron rule of the Bundesbank), supported a fixed timetable with a firm goal of a single currency and a European Central Bank. They resisted stringent criteria for economic convergence prior to EMU as a delaying tactic. They also sought some political oversight of the Central Bank's policies.[36] Within this group, states with large

---

[34]See *Financial Times,* February 18, 1991, p. 15. Proponents of enforceable budget rules (especially Germany and the Netherlands) argued that, without firm budgetary rules, individual states could run up large budget deficits, which would be implicitly subsidized by the whole Community in the form of higher Community-wide interest rates and inflation. Conversely, more disciplined countries would not fully reap the benefits of their conservative approach. Others argued that the experience of federal systems (such as the United States, where individual states have their own "fiscal" policies—taxing, spending, and borrowing—but a common currency and monetary policy) shows that a monetary union does not preclude budgetary independence and that markets will differentiate among borrowers (in the form of differential interest rates) based on their creditworthiness.

[35]See "The Rhetoric and Reality Behind European Sovereignty," *Independent,* December 15, 1990. By definition, a single interest rate policy will have a differential impact on regions with different mixes of wage growth, industrial compositions, and the like. The less homogeneous the currency area, the greater the differential impact (particularly where there are constraints on labor mobility). This problem exists for national monetary policy; it could be exacerbated in the more diverse Community-wide area under EMU. In particular, an inflation-fighting strategy will impose a penalty (in the form of lower output) on high inflation regions/countries, leading to the demand for financial compensation mechanisms. See William E. Pettersen, ed., *Beyond the Intergovernmental Conferences* (Europa Institute, 1991), pp. 5–7. On the applicability of the theory of "optimum currency area" to the EC, see *The ECU Report,* pp. 11–15.

[36]Despite some initial reluctance, France accepted that the European Central Bank itself should be independent. Hamburg DPA, April 6, 1990 (FBIS-WEU-90-068, April 9, 1990, p. 1). Rather, the issue of oversight concerned both the relationship between the "economic" and the "monetary" union and the method of selecting the governors of the European Central Bank. In the French view, expressed by French Finance

budget deficits (Italy, Greece, Portugal, Ireland, and Belgium) resisted enforceable budget guidelines that could lead to punitive sanctions.[37] Ireland, Portugal, Spain, and Greece looked for financial assurances to cushion the economic costs of EMU.[38]

Britain, under Prime Minister Thatcher, adamantly opposed EMU. She claimed that EMU would represent "the biggest transfer of sovereignty we've ever had."[39] Germany supported EMU, including a single currency and single Central Bank, but it insisted that the new institution closely mirror the structures and anti-inflationary bias of the Bundesbank and that EMU include a mechanism to force budgetary discipline on the participating states. Some German officials, especially Finance Minister Theo Waigel and Bundesbank President Karl-Otto Pöhl, stressed the need for EC economies to converge before implementing EMU and urged that any EMU agreement avoid fixed timetables. However, German Foreign Minister Genscher supported establishing a timetable to maintain momentum towards

---

Minister Pierre Bérégevoy, "independence is never total." *Guardian,* December 12, 1990.

One particular source of contention was who should have the authority to set external exchange rates. Although exchange rate policy is highly political (it is a frequent source of controversy in the G-7), the principal tool for setting exchange rates is interest rates (the domain of the Central Bank). See *Economist,* July 7, 1990, p. 25. Some EC countries, led by France, worried that the European Central Bank would favor a "strong ecu" to maintain price stability at the expense of EC export competitiveness. *Financial Times,* April 8, 1991, p. 14.

[37]A study in the EC's annual economic report concluded that for these five states, plus the Netherlands, "forecasts based on unchanged policies show that only limited headway will be made in improving budgetary positions in the short run." "Budgetary Policies in Stage I of EMU," *European Economy,* No. 46 (EC Commission, 1990), p. 173.

[38]*Economist,* January 19, 1991, p. 74. Greece's economic performance is so far from the Community average that some economists doubt whether, as a practical matter, Greece could really participate in EMU without special transitional provisions. Spain and Portugal present significant but fewer problems with an appropriate transition period.

[39]Colchester and Buchan, *Europower,* p. 9. As an alternative to a single currency, Britain proposed that the Community create a "hard ecu," a new currency that would circulate in parallel with national currencies. The British proposed to create a European Monetary Fund that would issue ecus in return for national currencies and would administer the Fund's reserves to assure that the "hard ecu" would never be devalued against any national currencies. If successful, nations might choose to adopt the hard ecu as a substitute for national currencies, thus (under the British theory) creating a single currency as a result of competition in the marketplace of currencies. *Financial Times,* June 21, 1990, p. 1.

Germany strongly opposed this idea, fearing the uncertainty that would come from yet another source of monetary policy in the Community. See *Economist,* January 19, 1991, p. 74. France, Italy, and the Netherlands also criticized the proposal. *Financial Times,* July 22, 1990, p. 1.

EMU, a decision that would come back to haunt Chancellor Kohl's government.[40]

At the Strasbourg summit in December 1989, the European Council agreed to convene an Intergovernmental Conference in 1990 on EMU.[41] At the Rome EC summit in October 1990, the European Council (over the objections of Mrs. Thatcher) appeared to reach agreement creating a Central Bank on January 1, 1994 (Stage 2), with full EMU (Stage 3) to begin in 1997.[42] But the language of the communiqué hedged on the question of how much choice governments would have in deciding if and when to move to a single currency.[43] The Rome Communiqué committed the proposed European Central Bank to a policy of inflation fighting: "the monetary institution's prime task will be to maintain price stability; without prejudice to this objective, it will support the general economic policy of the community."[44]

Despite the broad areas of agreement in the Rome Communiqué, the year-long Intergovernmental Conference on EMU (which began in December 1990) showed important divisions among the Twelve. In particular, John Major's arrival as British Prime Minister in November 1990 changed the dynamics of EMU. The Anglo-German relationship warmed considerably, helped by better personal relations

---

[40]*Financial Times,* September 17, 1990, p. 1.

[41]The decision followed the publication of the Delors Committee Report in April 1989, setting forth a three-stage process for EMU. Under the Delors proposal, Stage 1 (from July 1, 1990, until January 1, 1993) would prepare the way for EMU through the accession of all states to the ERM, eliminating all remaining exchange controls and completing the Single Market Program. During Stage 2, a common Central Bank would be created to exist in parallel with national central banks until the beginning of Stage 3 (January 1, 1996), when EC countries would adopt a single currency under the management of the Community's Central Bank.

[42]*Economist,* November 3, 1990, p. 55. Thus the Twelve agreed to delay by one year the start of Stage 2 (compared with the Delors Committee proposal). According to the communiqué: "The second phase will start on January 1, 1994. At the start of the second phase, the new community institution [the European Central Bank] will be established."

[43]The Rome Communiqué stated: "At the latest within three years from the start of the second phase, the Commission and the council of the monetary institution will report to the Ecofin Council and to the General Affairs Council on the function of the second phase and in particular on the progress made in real convergence in order to prepare the decision concerning the passage to the third phase, *which will occur within a reasonable time*" (emphasis added). The text of the communiqué appeared in the *Financial Times,* October 29, 1990.

[44]The broader "economic" union would have, as its goal, "an open market system that combines price stability with growth, employment, and environmental protection and [be] dedicated to sound and sustainable financial and budgetary conditions, and to economic and social cohesion." Rome Communiqué.

between the two leaders, a more conciliatory British tone on European integration, and growing German preoccupation with the need to control its monetary policy through the difficult period of East German reconstruction. The two countries increasingly saw eye-to-eye on the importance of "economic convergence" as a precondition for implementing a single currency (a point stressed by then Bundesbank President Pöhl, following a long line of German economic thinking on EMU).[45]

Germany also seemed to back off its earlier commitment to inaugurate the EC Central Bank during Stage 2. Germany was concerned that potential conflicts between the new European Central Bank and national central banks would produce market uncertainty about monetary policy and argued that there was little point in creating a new institution until it had concrete responsibilities to fulfill.[46] France continued to support a substantial transitional second stage.

The movement away from a firm commitment on a single currency was also fueled by growing doubts among poorer states (notably Spain and Portugal). They worried that the requirement of economic convergence would lead some (the richer) states to go ahead with EMU, leaving others to join later (creating a "two-speed" economic Europe).[47] They also feared that losing the ability to devalue would harm their economies (especially if the new Central Bank followed a rigidly anti-inflationary policy) and that the interests of the larger, more developed EC states would dominate Central Bank policy.[48] Spain in particular sought an agreement that EMU would be accom-

---

[45]*Financial Times,* February 2, 1991, p. 1. The Netherlands, which held the EC Presidency from July 1 to December 31, 1991, supported the idea that convergence should precede a single currency rather than using EMU to facilitate subsequent convergence. Italy and the less developed EC nations opposed the Dutch Presidency's proposal, see *Financial Times,* September 4, 1991, p. 1; September 9, 1991, p. 1; September 13, 1991, p. 14.

[46]*Le Figaro,* February 27, 1991, p. 32; *Financial Times,* March 1, 1991, p. 5; *The Times,* March 5, 1991, p. 22; Hamburg DPA, May 11, 1991 (FBIS-WEU-91-094, May 15, 1991, p. 1).

[47]For this reason, Spain supported France's position on a long transitional Stage 2 as a "break in" phase. See interview with Carlos Westendorp, Spanish Secretary of State for the EC, *ABC,* April 14, 1991 (FBIS-WEU-91-083, April 30, 1991, p. 30); and the remarks of Spanish Finance Minister Carlos Solchaga, *Diario 16,* September 11, 1991, p. 49 (FBIS-WEU-91-189, September 30, 1991, p. 28).

[48]*Economist,* September 15, 1990, p. 61.

[49]Spanish Prime Minister Gonzalez stated, "Spain is committed to the concept of economic and monetary union but expects or hopes for a significant increase in

panied by an "interstate compensation fund" to cushion the impact of EMU,[49] a proposal vigorously resisted by the Commission.[50]

EC Finance Ministers reached consensus on most key issues surrounding EMU at a meeting in Appledoorn, Netherlands, on September 21, 1991,[51] but last minute disagreements continued until the Maastricht summit actually convened.[52] At the EC summit on December 9–10, 1991, the European Council finally agreed on a plan for adopting EMU.[53] Prior to January 1, 1994, all EC states must

---

Community resources to be transferred to the less wealthy members." *Financial Times,* May 9, 1991, p. 15.

Spain has also linked the need for a compensation fund to extending majority voting for non-1992 measures. Costly environmental regulations, for example, "would be fine if the country in question has voted yes, but if it has voted no and has no funds, it makes no sense to implement it. If we want a majority vote, let the Community provide the funds to implement the decisions. . . . Right now, most of the policies in the Community are designed to benefit the richest countries." Carlos Westendorp, Spanish Secretary of State for the EC, *ABC,* April 14, 1991 (FBIS-WEU-91-083, April 30, 1991, p. 30).

[50]Delors observed: "Insofar as we are not in a federal state, it is impossible to promote an interstate compensation fund, such as exists in the FRG [Federal Republic of Germany]. In the EC, the setting up of such a fund would cause a political battle each year which would nullify all the efforts hitherto made in the EC." Delors prefers continued reliance on the EC's structural funds. *La Vanguardia,* April 14, 1991 (FBIS-WEU-91-083, April 30, 1991, p. 1).

[51]*Financial Times,* September 23, 1991, p. 4; *Economist,* September 28, 1991, p. 84. The key breakthrough at Appledoorn was the decision that the third phase of EMU would begin only after a "critical mass" (seven or eight) of EC countries meet previously established criteria for convergence (for inflation and interest rates, budget deficits, and currency stability) but that all countries would participate in the vote to determine which countries qualified under the convergence criteria. This procedure was adopted at Maastricht with one significant amendment: the decision to allow EMU to go forward with as few as two qualifying countries beginning in 1999.

[52]Going into the Maastricht summit, there were two principal areas of disagreement. The first was the extent to which the Treaty should make an "irreversible" commitment to a single currency. France in particular wanted to assure that EMU would go forward by qualified majority vote of the European Council without the need for subsequent national political decisions, even if only a small number of countries meet the convergence criteria. Agence France Presse, December 2, 1991 (FBIS-WEU-91-231, December 2, 1991, p. 7). The United Kingdom sought an "escape clause" (allowing a subsequent parliament to decide whether a country should enter EMU), not only for itself, but for all EC countries. Denmark originally supported the British position, but eventually fell into line with the other 10 EC countries. The second large controversy concerned Spain's insistence that the EC agree to an automatic financial compensation mechanism for less developed countries to facilitate their convergence with the EMU criteria (as well as to offset costs associated with new EC requirements in areas such as transportation and environment). Other unsettled questions included whether to give the Council authority to impose financial sanctions on member-states that run persistent budget deficits, which institution (European Central Bank or the European Council) should have responsibility for external exchange rate policy, and whether countries that failed to qualify for EMU should have voting rights in setting macroeconomic policy.

[53]Maastricht Treaty, Article 109e(2).

abolish all capital controls and, if necessary, adopt a program to assure economic convergence with other EC members.[54] On January 1, 1994, the European Monetary Institute (EMI) will come into being, charged with strengthening the coordination of member-states' monetary policies and preparing the procedures for implementing a single currency.[55] By December 31, 1996 (at the latest), the European Council will review the extent of economic convergence, and if the Council finds (on the basis of a qualified majority vote) that a majority of the member-states meet the criteria,[56] it will set a date for beginning the single currency and creating a European System of Central Banks (ESCB) and a European Central Bank (ECB), which will manage the single currency.[57] Even if a majority of states do not

[54]Under the agreement, convergence will be measured by four principal criteria: price stability (whether the inflation rate is close to the three best performing members of the Community); sustainability of the government's financial position (whether the annual budget deficit is 3 percent or less of GDP and whether the total government debt is 60 percent or less of GDP); exchange rate stability in the EMS (whether the country has stayed within the permitted 2.25 percent band of fluctuation for at least two years); and durability of convergence (convergence of the government's long-term interest rates with other EC states). The Council will also consider other criteria, such as current account balance of payments and unit labor costs. Despite the high degree of specificity in some of the established criteria, the Council retains flexibility in deciding whether a country on the whole has achieved the necessary degree of convergence to participate in the single currency. Article 109j(1), Maastricht Treaty. A "Protocol on the Convergence Criteria" amplifies these requirements further: inflation must be within 1.5 percent of the three best performing countries and average nominal long-term interest rates must not be more than 2 percent above the best performing members. Maastricht Treaty, pp. 185–186.

[55]Articles 109e(1), 109f.

[56]To meet British political concerns, a protocol to the agreement provides that the United Kingdom is not obliged to participate in the final stage of creating a single currency without a separate decision by the British Parliament. The United Kingdom therefore does not count toward determining whether a majority of countries meet the criteria for moving to a single currency. Protocol on Certain Provisions Relating to the United Kingdom of Great Britain and Ireland, Maastricht Treaty, pp. 191–193. Similarly, the Danish Constitution requires a referendum to enter into the single currency: if Denmark has not passed such a referendum by the appropriate time, it too will not count toward the necessary majority. Protocol on Certain Provisions Relating to Denmark, Maastricht Treaty, p. 194.

States that do not meet the criteria receive a "derogation" and do not participate in the ECB; their status will be reviewed every two years or at the request of a country with a derogation. Article 109k.

[57]Article 109j, 109l. The Council agreed that the ESCB will make "price stability" its primary objective. Article 105(1), Maastricht Treaty. External exchange rate policy will also be conducted by the ECB, but the Treaty provides that the European Council may conclude formal agreements with other countries on exchange rates or "formulate general orientations for exchange rate policy," so long as they are consistent with the commitment to price stability. To assure the ECB's independence, members of the Board of Directors will serve eight-year non-renewable terms, removable from office only by the European Court for violating legal obligations. The larger European

meet the criteria by the end of 1997, a single currency will be adopted, beginning on January 1, 1999, for all states that fulfill the conditions.[58] If a nation (other than the United Kingdom) satisfies the convergence criteria, entry into EMU is automatic; that is, there is no opportunity for a prior national political decision on whether to join the single currency.[59] To underscore their determination to move to the third stage by the end of the decade, the EC leaders attached a protocol to the Treaty, declaring "the irreversible character of the Community's movement to the third stage" and directing the Community institutions to take the steps necessary "to enter the third stage irrevocably on 1 January 1999" if it has not occurred earlier.[60]

EMU would also mean increased Community control over member governments' fiscal policies. The Maastricht agreement prohibits European Central Bank financing of EC governments' debts and authorizes the European Council to apply sanctions (including restrictions on borrowing from the European Investment Bank, requiring non-interest-bearing deposits to be placed with the Community, or fines) in the event a nation runs persistently high budget deficits.[61]

Germany and France each won substantial victories in the final outcome. Germany achieved its goal of an independent European Central Bank with a strong commitment to fighting inflation as well as the requirement of economic convergence as a precondition to entering the third stage of EMU (thus virtually assuring a two-speed EMU). France succeeded in enhancing the irreversibility of EMU through two key devices: a provision that would allow EMU to begin in 1997, based on qualified majority voting (rather than unanimity), and the requirement that the third stage will go forward with as few as two qualifying countries in 1999. Chancellor Kohl supported

---

Central Bank Council will consist of the six directors plus the Central Bank presidents from each of the participating member countries.

[58]Article 109j(4).

[59]Of course, any nation could, as a member of the Council, vote "against itself"—that is, vote against finding that it satisfies the convergence criteria. But the qualified majority voting approach permits (at least in principle) fellow EC members to "force" a country to join EMU against its will. The "Protocol on the Transition to the Third Stage of EMU" also provides that all members, whether or not they meet the criteria for convergence, shall "respect the will for the Community to enter swiftly into the third stage," Maastricht Treaty, p. 190. Only the United Kingdom and Denmark are exempt from this element of "irreversibility."

[60]Ibid.

[61]Article 104c(11).

France's efforts, despite reservations by German Treasury and Bundesbank officials.[62]

The United Kingdom and Spain were the principal losers. Although the United Kingdom reserved the right for a future British Parliament to make the final decision on Britain's joining the single currency, it failed in its efforts to extend the "escape clause" to all EC members.[63] The United Kingdom also failed to block the use of sanctions against countries with high budget deficits. Spain was unsuccessful in its effort to include an automatic compensation mechanism for the less developed nations.

Although Maastricht established the framework and timing of EMU, serious economic and political obstacles stand in the way of its eventual implementation. If the EC criteria on convergence were applied to member countries' economic performance at the end of 1991, only France, Luxembourg, and the United Kingdom would have qualified (Germany's 3.6 percent of GDP budget deficit exceeded the 3 percent benchmark). Spain, Italy, and Portugal face significant challenges in meeting the criteria by 1997, while Greece (not yet even a member of the EMS) faces daunting hurdles.[64]

Perhaps even more important, public opinion, which was generally favorable toward EMU at the outset of the Intergovernmental Conference, began to swing against the single currency as the reality came closer. This was most apparent in Germany, where, even before the Maastricht summit itself, public opinion turned sharply against replacing the deutschemark with a single European currency.[65] In

---

[62]*Süddeutsche Zeitung,* December 10, 1991, p. 1.

[63]Denmark originally supported the British position on the escape clause but abandoned that view during the summit in the face of the strong consensus among the other 10 countries.

[64]Some have argued that, with the exception of the fiscal targets (ratio of GDP to public debt and annual deficits), Italy and Spain have a reasonable chance of meeting the convergence criteria in the first round. For example, if German inflation remains at or near its current rate, Italy and Spain would need to reduce their inflation by only 1.5 percent and their interest rates by 2 percent to qualify. See Anatole Kaletsky, "German Weakness Could Open the EMU Door for Southern Partners," *The Times,* December 12, 1991, p. 31.

[65]In a survey released one week before the Maastricht summit, 71 percent of Germans surveyed supported postponing the decision on a single currency, and a similar majority believed that a new currency could endanger German prosperity. Only 3 percent felt that a single European currency would benefit Germany. *New York Times,* December 7, 1991. By contrast, in October 1990, 51 percent of Germans polled favored exchanging the deutschemark for a single currency. *The Times,* November 12, 1990. German industry, too, was skeptical: in a poll conducted for *Wirtschaftwoche* (December 13, 1991, pp. 16–17, FBIS-WEU-92-003, January 6, 1992, p. 11), 55 percent expected disadvantages from a single currency, compared with 39 percent who

the immediate aftermath of the Maastricht agreement, a heated debate broke out among German political leaders, press commentators, and economists over the wisdom of EMU, capped by a letter signed by 62 leading German economists criticizing the agreement on EMU.[66] Although the Bundesbank's leadership supported the agreement, there was evidence of dissension among the full membership.[67] German criticism was fueled by the belief that Chancellor Kohl had failed to gain important institutional reforms (including a strengthened role for the European Parliament) as the needed quid pro quo for Germany "sacrificing" the deutschemark.[68] The SPD agreed to support ratifying the agreement only if the Chancellor promised to consult the Bundestag before entering into a single currency pursuant to the Maastricht Treaty. The German Länder pushed for a commit-

---

anticipated advantages. A later poll found a similar negative view among German (as well as British) business leaders, but a slight overall majority EC-wide believed that a single currency was necessary and in the interest of monetary stability. *Handelsblatt,* February 28–29, 1992, p. 1 (FBIS-WEU-92-040, February 28, 1992, p. 8).

[66]*Frankfurter Allgemeine Zeitung,* June 11, 1992, p. 1; see also the *German Tribune,* June 26, 1992, p. 6. The economists' "eleven theses" focused on the inadequacies of Maastricht's provisions on convergence, the risks of a weakened commitment to price stability, and the dangers for the Community's weaker economies. A rebuttal by three other leading bank economists, Norbert Walter (Deutsche Bank), Ernst Moritz Lipp (Dresdner Bank) and Ulrich Romm (Commerz Bank), appeared in *Frankfurter Allgemeine Zeitung,* June 16, 1991.

Political criticism of the accords ran the spectrum from the SPD (see comments of SPD Bundestag monetary policy spokesman Norbert Wieczorek, *Handelsblatt,* February 19, 1992, p. 14, FBIS-WEU-92-055, March 20, 1992, p. 5) to outspoken conservative CSU member Peter Gauweiler, Bavarian Environment Minister. See *Wirtschaftwoche,* February 14, 1992, pp. 18–19 (FBIS-WEU-92-038, February 26, 1992, p. 6). FDP chairman Otto Graf Lambsdorff, while critical of the overall results of the summit, expressed only mild reservations about EMU. *Handelsblatt,* December 12, 1991, p. 5 (FBIS-WEU-92-007, January 10, 1992, p. 9). The EMU agreement set off a fierce battle in the German press, kicked off by the headline in *Bild Zeitung* (a popular tabloid) proclaiming "The End of the D-Mark" (December 11, 1991, p. 1). Other editorialists who criticized the agreement included Rudolf Augstein of *Der Spiegel* (see, e.g., February 17, 1992, p. 20) and the influential business journal *Handelsblatt* (which ran a series of editorials criticizing the agreement's "loopholes" and the degree of political control over European Central Bank operations). See *Handelsblatt,* December 20–21, 1991, p. 2, December 24, 1991, p. 2, and January 2, 1992, p. 2. *Die Zeit* generally supported the agreement.

[67]See interview with Hans Tietmayer, Bundesbank Vice President. "If the Contracting Parties Follow Rationale of the Agreement, the Union Will Work," *Handelsblatt,* December 17, 1991, p. 6 (FBIS-WEU-91-243, December 18, 1991, p. 11). Bundesbank President Helmut Schlesinger also supported the agreement (see *Handelsblatt,* December 31, 1991, p. 9 [FBIS-WEU-92-002, January 3, 1992, p. 5]), although he criticized the timetable for introducing a single currency. *Die Zeit,* December 20, 1991, p. 21. Representatives from Germany's Landbanks (who sit on the Bundesbank Council) led the criticism. See *Wirtschaftwoche,* January 17, 1992, pp. 21–22, and *Handelsblatt,* February 11, 1992, p. 2 (FBIS-WEU-92-029, February 12, 1992, pp. 16–17).

[68]For a discussion of the debate over institutional reform, see Section 4, above.

ment to greater future involvement in EC treaty negotiations as the price for their support. In order to secure the German Parliament's approval of the Maastricht Treaty, Chancellor Kohl acceded in large measure to these demands, while insisting that they did not amount to amending the Treaty. Similar though less intense concerns have emerged in other EC countries, which stand to benefit from a more Community-wide approach to monetary policy, even if tied to price stability; a European Central Bank presumably would be less constrained by the unique fiscal consequences of German unification in setting EC interest rates.

The future of EMU became even more uncertain in the days preceding the French vote on ratification. The ERM, already under strain from continued high German interest rates, which drove up the deutschemark and made it difficult for weak currencies to maintain their required value, broke under speculative pressure fueled by fears that France would vote no on ratification and reports that the Bundesbank considered the Italian lira and British pound overvalued. Doubts about Europe's future drove investors to the safe haven deutschemark, and the Bundesbank was unwilling to cut German interest rates enough to lessen presssure on the ERM's weaker currencies. After several days of large-scale interventions to maintain the value of the pound and the lira, Italy and the United Kingdom finally decided to suspend temporarily their membership in the ERM.[69] Both John Major and Chancellor Lamont singled out Germany for blame, but this finger pointing provoked a stern response from Chancellor Kohl.[70]

The success of the ERM—five years without a revaluation—had given credibility to the idea of fixed exchange rates and a single currency. The crisis of September 1992 undid in a few short days much of that confidence and seemed to vindicate the single currency skeptics who had argued for a greater degree of economic convergence before moving to EMU.

---

[69]Italy initially devalued the lira by 7 percent in connection with the Bundesbank's September 14 rate cut. But that move did not stop the assault on the lira, and two days later, on September 16, both Italy and the United Kingdom cut their currencies free from the ERM. Spain also devalued on September 14 (by 5 percent) but stayed in the ERM.

[70]*Los Angeles Times,* September 19, 1992, p. A1. Lamont said that the United Kingdom would not return to the ERM until German policy, "which has produced many of the tensions, . . . is actually going to have some changes." He added, "I want to ask some questions about the way in which cooperation between governments works." Kohl replied that "Such a remark is inappropriate for a minister." *New York Times,* September 20, 1992, p. E5.

Despite these political uncertainties, the Maastricht agreement provides new impetus to creating a single EC currency for some, if not all, members, if only to avoid the kind of turmoil experienced in September 1992. Completing EMU would have profound consequences for the Community's future and its relations with the rest of the world. At a minimum, it would transfer all aspects of monetary policy to the Community level and many aspects of fiscal policy: directly, if binding budgetary rules are adopted; indirectly because Community-decided monetary policy will constrain national fiscal policy. It could cause serious political friction among Community members if national political imperatives, such as reducing unemployment in the run-up to an election, came in conflict with the dominant Community economic objective of fighting inflation. As the authors of the EC's own study understood, EMU will prove most effective and least politically problematic where the Community is responding to common external shocks (higher global oil prices, worldwide recession) and most troublesome in the case of asymmetrical shocks that affect only one or a few Community members (accommodating German unification is a dramatic case in point). The implications of EMU for U.S.-EC relations are discussed in Section 9 of this Report.

THE COMMUNITY'S "SOCIAL DIMENSION"

For the most part, the Community's Single Market initiatives focused on the "business" side of the Community equation, with relatively little activity on workers' rights and the labor market.[71] As the 1992 program gained momentum, many inside the Community, especially Socialist governments and Members of the European Parliament (MEPs), began to press for a corresponding initiative in the so-called "social dimension" to accompany the Single Market Program.[72] This effort led to the Social Charter of December 1989, adopted by the European Council over the vigorous dissent of Prime Minister Thatcher.[73]

---

[71]The SEA explicitly expanded the EC's role in areas such as workers' health and safety. SEA Article 21.

[72]At one point, the Socialists in the European Parliament threatened to suspend work on parts of the Single Market Program until the Commission moved more aggressively to develop labor protection legislation. *Guardian,* March 14, 1990.

[73]The impetus for the Charter came from EC President Delors, who proposed it in 1988. The Charter sets forth 12 categories of fundamental rights, including freedom of movement; employment and pay; working conditions; social protection; labor union rights; training; sex discrimination; worker participation and information; health and

The Charter was a political undertaking, not binding on its members. The Commission began to develop a legislative agenda, "the Social Action Program," to translate these principles into Community law, focusing on issues such as minimum wage, working hours, protection for pregnant women and part-time or temporary workers, and extending national benefits when a company subcontracts with an employer from another EC state. Broad British opposition to the Social Action Program led the Commission to try to invoke the streamlined Single Market process, especially qualified majority voting, to advance aspects of the Charter's goals. For example, the Commission contended that its proposal on benefits for part-time workers was appropriate for qualified majority voting because it was designed to eliminate unfair competitive advantage in countries that lack adequate protections.[74]

The limitations of the Social Charter led advocates of a more vigorous EC worker protection policy to try to bring social policy fully into the communitarian procedures, especially the Commission's right to initiate proposals and the provisions allowing qualified majority voting in the Council. Following a meeting of the EC General Affairs Council (in preparation for the first Rome summit preceding the start of the IGC on political union), Italy, holding the Presidency of the Council, noted that, "in most Member States' views, the setting up of the Single Market and of Economic and Monetary Union make it essential to broaden and strengthen the powers of the Community in the realm of social policy, by introducing majority voting in this sphere."[75]

In the initial stages of the IGC, social policy received relatively little attention compared with the dominant controversies over EMU, foreign and security policy, and institutional reform.[76] The Luxembourg Presidency's draft treaty ("non-paper") included a provision extending the Community machinery (including the use of qualified majority voting in the Council) to "the working environment, and, in particular, health and safety protection;—living and working conditions to

---

safety; working minors; pensions; and disabled workers. Colchester and Buchan, *Europower,* pp. 186–187.

[74]See *Economist*, June 29, 1991, p. 64; *Financial Times,* November 27, 1990.

[75]Letter from Gianni de Michelis, President of the General Affairs Council, to Giulio Andreotti, President of the Council of Ministers, SN 4315/1/90 (24.10), Rome, October 23, 1990, ¶3.

[76]Social policy was lumped in with a long list of proposals for expanding the Community's authority in the Kohl-Mitterrand letter on the eve of the IGC (see *Le Monde,* December 9–10, 1990, p. 4) and similarly received only passing mention in the Presidency Conclusions of the second Rome summit of December 14–15, 1990. See Presidency Conclusions, Part 1, ¶4, December 16, 1990 (mimeo).

ensure that workers' basic rights are protected;—the information and consultation of workers."[77] The United Kingdom reiterated its opposition to including workers' issues in the Rome Treaty framework, but opposition to social policy did not come to the forefront of Britain's position until the parliamentary debates preceding the Maastricht summit, in the face of strong Conservative party resistance.[78]

Rather than accept a British veto on social policy, the leaders of the remaining eleven EC nations adopted the groundbreaking approach of going forward with social policy on their own.[79] The Netherlands Presidency conclusions, issued at the end of the Maastricht summit, stated: "The European Council notes that eleven Member States desire to continue on the path laid down by the Social Charter of 1989. To this end it has been agreed to annex to the Treaty a Protocol concerning social policy which will commit the institutions of the Community to take and implement the necessary decisions while adapting the decisionmaking procedures for application by eleven Member States."[80] Although a number of European activities are undertaken by a subset of Community members (nine participate in the Schengen Agreement, and ten EC members belong to the WEU), the social policy agreement represents the first time that the EC machinery itself will be used by a subset of the full Community membership.

The agreement among the Eleven provides for common action, with qualified majority voting, in the areas of workers' health and safety, working conditions, information, and consultation and gender equality.[81] For the areas of social security, job termination rights, collective bargaining and co-determination, employment rights of third

[77]Europe Documents N. 1709/1710, May 3, 1991, Article 118a.

[78]The British government's parliamentary motion on the Maastricht summit, designed to give the Prime Minister a mandate for the final negotiations at Maastricht, stated, inter alia, that the government would work for an agreement that "avoids intrusive Community measures in social areas which are matters for national decision." The opposition Labour party harshly criticized the government's position.

[79]One press report highlighted the conflict between the United Kingdom and its eleven partners: "John Major's determined lone refusal to accept EC plans handing over social policy powers to Brussels threw the Europe summit into turmoil tonight.... The fury of the French and German delegations at what they considered British intransigence at one stage seemed to threaten the collapse of the entire summit." Press Association, December 10, 1991 (FBIS-WEU-91-238, December 11, 1991, p. 2).

[80]European Council, "Presidency Conclusions—Maastricht 9 and 10 December 1991," SN 271/1/91 (Maastricht, December 11, 1991, p. 2).

[81]Agreement on Social Policy Concluded Between the Member States of the European Community with the Exception of the United Kingdom of Great Britain and Northern Ireland, Article 2(1), Maastricht Treaty, pp. 197–201.

country nationals, and Community support for employment and job creation, the agreement requires a unanimous Council vote.[82] The agreement also provides that the Community may delegate responsibility for implementing directives in these areas to management and labor.[83]

Creating a single labor market is critical to enhancing European growth and productivity, yet the task is daunting. The rate of internal migration is much lower in the EC than in the United States.[84] Labor policies differ dramatically among Community members, dividing not only along north/south lines but also between relatively free market countries like the United Kingdom, highly regulated states such as Germany, and Denmark (where labor regulation is primarily a function of government—supervised labor/management negotiation). On the whole, the more developed EC states have supported an expanded role in this area to protect their workers from being undercut by low-wage, low-benefit, limited worker protection policies in the poorer countries. The Social Action Program arguably imposes economic costs on the poorer countries, but because many have Socialist governments, they have supported the social dimension in principle, while opposing specific measures, such as minimum wage regulations, which have a particularly adverse economic impact.[85]

BUDGET POLICY

Conflicts over the EC's budget and regional policy have created two fault lines within the Community: dividing net payer from net receiver states and the poorer from the richer nations. The second divide is primarily north versus south (Ireland also belongs to the "south").

The EC derives its income from four main sources: customs duties, agricultural levies, value-added taxes (VAT), and GDP-related payments by member-states. Customs duties from tariffs levied on goods coming from outside the EC represent about 21–23 percent of the Community's income.[86] Agricultural levies and contributions repre-

---

[82]Article 2(3), Maastricht Treaty.

[83]Article 4, Maastricht Treaty.

[84]Regional net migration in the EC was only 25 percent of the U.S. rate during 1980–85. "One Market, One Money," p. 150.

[85]*NRC Handelsblad*, June 29, 1991 (special supplement), p. 19 (FBIS-WEU-91-158, August 15, 1991, p. 2).

[86]22.7 percent (12.8 billion ecu) in 1991, 20.5 percent (12.9 billion ecu) under the 1992 estimates. *25th General Report of the European Community*, p. 405.

sent the income component of the CAP and come from the duties levied on external agricultural products to maintain the internal guaranteed market prices. There is also some income from the sale of surplus goods on the world markets and on internal duties to control production. All these account for about 4–5 percent of the EC budget.[87] The value-added tax represents the bulk of EC revenues, accounting for some 55 percent. A fixed proportion of the VAT from each country is passed on directly to the Community.[88] The final category of revenues, introduced in 1988 and now accounting for some 22 percent of the total income, is GDP-related contributions, based on a fixed percentage of each country's GDP.[89] This allows the wealth of each member country to partially determine its EC budget contribution.

Throughout the 1980s, the Community budget was a major source of conflict among the EC states, driven by Mrs. Thatcher's determination to alter arrangements that made Britain a substantial net payer to the Community. A series of budget agreements kept political calm.[90] In 1988, the Community made an important breakthrough with a five-year budget agreement. The new accord hinged on three elements: a slight softening of the British attempt to rein in spending on the CAP,[91] a 50 percent increase in EC aid to poorer regions by 1993 (for a total of approximately $68 billion over 1989–93), and Germany's willingness to shoulder a considerable part of the cost. The 1988 budget agreement, which capped EC spending at 1.15 percent of Community GDP for 1988, rising to 1.2 percent by 1992, temporarily freed the EC from the continuous budget wrangling of the

[87]Ibid.

[88]The VAT contribution replaced fixed national contributions in 1960. Under the 1988 agreement, the VAT base for each country is capped at 55 percent of GDP, with a maximum call-in rate of 1.4 percent.

[89]The GDP "resource" is the residual category, so the percentage is fixed to cover the difference between revenues from the other three resources and EC total expenditures. In 1991, the GDP resource amounted to 15 percent (7.4 billion ecu); in 1992, it is estimated to be 22 percent of the total.

[90]Under the first agreement, in 1980, the EC agreed to cut Britain's net payments by two-thirds. At Fountainbleau in 1984, the United Kingdom received a permanent rebate equal to 66 percent of the difference between its VAT payments to the EC and EC funds received back. This arrangement proved particularly advantageous for the United Kingdom during the growth period at the end of the 1980s when VAT receipts grew substantially. According to the *Economist* (November 17, 1990, p. 76), the EC budget rose an average annual 4.3 percent from 1979–90, while the U.K contribution grew only 0.5 percent during that same period.

[91]Under the agreement, the growth in agriculture expenses was limited to 4 percent of the growth in Community GDP.

previous decade and allowed the states to concentrate on the 1992 program (Figure 6.1).

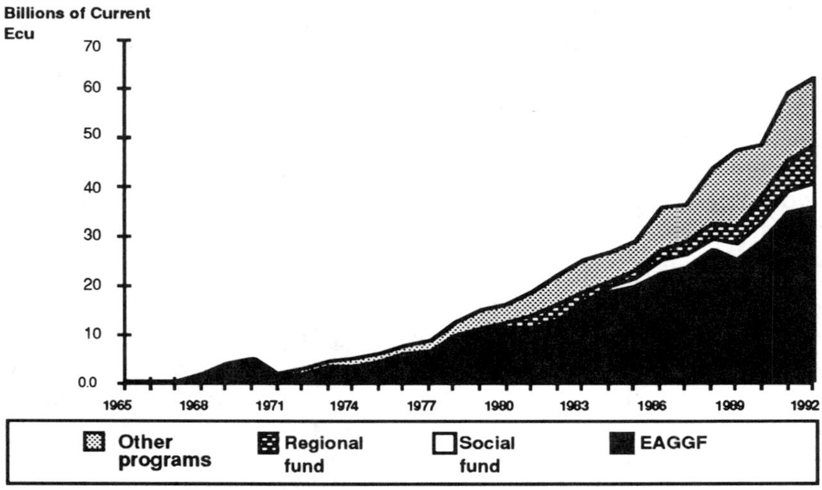

Figure 6.1—EC Budget Expenditures

Under the 1992 budget, the EC will spend about ecu 66 billion ($85 billion): ecu 35 billion (53 percent) on agriculture, ecu 18 billion (27 percent) on regional assistance, and ecu 3 billion (5 percent) on foreign aid. For 1992, Germany is the largest contributor (nearly ecu 18 billion), followed by France (ecu 12 billion), Italy (ecu 9 billion), and the United Kingdom (ecu 8 billion). In 1990, the latest year with complete figures from the EC, the big "losers" (net contributors) were Luxembourg (19 percent of contributions returned in the form of EC spending), Germany (46 percent), the United Kingdom (48 percent), Belgium (56 percent), and France (78 percent). Gainers were Ireland (614 percent), Greece (538 percent), Portugal (219 percent), Denmark (155 percent), Spain (147 percent), and the Netherlands (114 percent). Italy, a net gainer in the early 1980s, is now a net contributor (93 percent of contributions returned).[92]

---

[92]EC Court of Auditors, as reported in *Financial Times*, June 18, 1991, p. 16. Ten billion ecu in EC spending is not attributable to individual countries (including overseas aid). Agricultural spending has a profound impact on the distribution of resources within the Community; thus Denmark and the Netherlands, net gainers counting agricultural spending, are near to the bottom in terms of the percent of revenues returned in non-agricultural spending. The three principal beneficiaries of

The division between net payer and net beneficiary states can further be seen in Table 6.2. In 1989, Germany, the United Kingdom, France, Italy, Belgium, Luxembourg, and Spain (the net payers) contributed ecu 39.4 billion, or 89 percent of the Community budget, while receiving only ecu 23.9 billion, or 54 percent of the Community's disbursements. Greece, Ireland, the Netherlands, Portugal, and Denmark contributed only ecu 5.0 billion, or 11 percent of the budget and received payments totaling ecu 10.1 billion, or 23 percent of EC expenditures. The Netherlands and Denmark are net recipients primarily as a result of agricultural payments, which accounted for over 55 percent of the total EC expenditures in 1989.[93]

The need to reach a new budget agreement for the years beginning with 1993 complicated the negotiations over political union, with Spain in particular pushing for a policy of interstate "compensation" to ensure that poorer states do not become net payers or shoulder additional financial burdens, due to expanding the EC's competence (for example, from complying with new EC environmental regulations), as well as to cushion the expected impact of EMU.[94]

At Maastricht, EC leaders rejected Spain's proposal, adopting instead a commitment to a new "Cohesion Fund," worth up to ecu 2.5 billion, to provide assistance to member-states with less than 90 percent of Community-average GDP for projects relating to the environment and trans-European networks. They also agreed to review the Community's sources of income to consider ways of reducing the regressive elements of the system.[95]

---

non-agricultural spending were Ireland, Portugal, and Greece; followed at some distance by Spain, the United Kingdom, and Italy.

[93]Unofficial data suggest that the group of net payers has remained unchanged since 1989. See *The Times,* November 10, 1992, p. 12.

[94]Spain also proposed that Community revenues come from a more progressive taxation scheme. The current structure poses particularly difficult problems for Spain. Its VAT receipts are relatively high in proportion to GDP, leading to increased Community payments, but it receives relatively less back in CAP and research expenditures (though it does benefit from the regional fund; see below). *Financial Times,* March 12, 1991, p. 4.

[95]Protocol on Economic and Social Cohesion, Maastricht Treaty, pp. 202–203.

Table 6.2

EC Budget for 1989
(in millions of current ecu)

Net Payer States	Payments	Percent	Receipts	Percent	Balance
Germany	11,110	25.1	4,580	10.3	6,530
United Kingdom	6,568	14.8	3,214	7.3	3,354
France	8,623	19.5	5,677	12.8	2,946
Italy	6,606	17.2	6,177	13.9	1,429
Belgium	1,807	4.1	683	1.5	1,124
Luxembourg	73	0.2	8	0.0	65
Spain	3,575	8.1	3,544	8.0	31
Total:	39,363	88.8	23,883	53.9	15,480

Net Receiver States	Payments	Percent	Receipts	Percent	Balance
Greece	566	1.3	2,565	5.8	-1,999
Ireland	371	0.8	1,712	3.9	-1,341
Netherlands	2,700	6.1	3,830	8.6	-1,130
Portugal	458	1.0	946	2.1	-488
Denmark	871	2.0	1,045	2.4	-174
	4,966	11.2	10,098	22.8	-5,132
Unattributable*	0	0.0	10,348	23.3	-10,348
Total:	44,329	100.0	44,329	100.0	0

*Includes overseas aid.

SOURCE: EC Court of Auditors, *Financial Times,* June 18, 1991, p. 16.

On February 11, 1992, the Commission unveiled its proposed budget for 1993–97.[96] It called for raising the ceiling on EC spending from 1.2 percent to 1.37 percent of Community GDP by 1997, 5 percent annual real growth (based on a forecast of an average annual 2.5 percent growth in GDP). This would bring the EC's budget to ecu 88 billion (1992 prices) in 1997 ($112 billion in 1992 dollars). The increase is due primarily to increases in the existing regional funds and the new Cohesion Fund (ecu 11 billion, or $14 billion); additional resources for carrying out Community foreign policy (ecu 3.5 billion, or $4.5 billion); and "competitiveness"—research and development, worker training, and infrastructure investments in transport, telecommunications, and energy (ecu 3.5 billion). The budget projected spending on CAP to rise only modestly—from ecu 35 billion in 1992 to ecu 39.6 billion in 1997, based on adopting the Commission's

[96]"From the Single Act to Maastricht and Beyond: The Means to Match our Ambitions," EC 92/2, February 11, 1992, reprinted in full in FBIS-WEU-92-043-A, March 4, 1992, pp. 1–18.

July 1991 reform proposal.[97] It also offered two suggestions for increasing the "progressiveness" of EC income: capping the VAT base at 50 percent (instead of the current 55 percent) and limiting the maximum call-in to 1 percent. These changes would reduce the VAT-based share of revenues from 55 percent to 35 percent and thus lead to increased reliance on the GDP-based revenues. The Commission deferred proposing changes to the United Kingdom's rebate.[98]

The Commission proposal set off a storm of protest, especially in Germany, which objected to the size of the increase and called for re-examining Britain's rebate, and the United Kingdom, which vowed to retain the rebate and expressed particular objection to the increase in Community research and development efforts. They were joined by other EC members who stood to lose from the reform of the sources of Community revenue—Italy, Belgium, and the Netherlands.[99] Portugal, which held the EC Presidency for the first half of 1992, conceded that it would not complete work on the budget package during its term, foreshadowing a difficult showdown during the United Kingdom's Presidency as the 1993 deadline approached. In the meantime, the Commission scaled down its budget proposal for 1993 to ecu 62.9 billion ($85 billion) a slight drop from 1992 and only 1.09 percent of Community GDP.[100]

At the Edinburgh summit the EC leaders reached a compromise seven-year budget agreement. They decided that the budget ceiling would remain frozen at 1.2 percent of Community GDP for two years (1993–1994) then rise gradually to 1.27 percent (ecu 84.1 billion, or $105 billion in current dollars) by 1999. Spending for regional assistance would grow from ecu 18.6 billion to ecu 30 billion in 1999, including an increase in the Social and Regional Funds (from ecu 18.6 billion to ecu 27.4 billion) as well as the new ecu 2.6 billion Cohesion Fund. The leaders left the U.K. rebate untouched.

In the future, the budgetary conflict could ease somewhat if the Community expands to include the relatively wealthy EFTA nations. But Germany's reduced willingness to bear a substantial share of the

---

[97]That proposal was subsequently superceded by the May 1992 Ministers' agreement, which could further raise the CAP's cost. See below.

[98]See also "The System of Own Resources," Commission of the European Communities COM (92) 81 final, Brussels, March 10, 1992. Ultimately, the Commission would prefer a dedicated revenue source paid directly by taxpayers to the EC, but this is strenuously resisted by most governments.

[99]*Financial Times,* February 12, 1992, p. 1; March 17, 1992, p. 2; March 18, 1992, p. 2; March 24, 1992, p. 1.

[100]*Financial Times,* July 24, 1992, p. 2.

financial burden of "cohesion," coupled with budgetary difficulties in countries such as Italy and Belgium, which must reduce their substantial deficits in order to meet the EMU criteria for convergence, presage continued controversy among the Twelve.

REGIONAL POLICY

The EC's regional policy derives from the preamble of the Rome Treaty, which committed the Community to "reducing the differences existing between the various regions and mitigating the backwardness of the less-favored."[101] Regional policy's importance to the EC grew as the Community took in the "southern" states (Greece, Spain, and Portugal) as well as Ireland. The differential impact of the Single Market Program on poorer states, many of which were highly protectionist and thus vulnerable to reduced trade barriers, further increased the political and economic importance of regional policy.[102]

The Community's "Structural Funds" focus on three areas: agriculture, social policy, and regional development. The largest of these, agriculture, now accounts for about two-thirds of the European Community's budget and is described in greater detail below. Social policy programs are implemented through the European Social Fund (ESF), which is targeted at retraining dislocated workers for new jobs. The Community plans to spend ecu 4 billion on ESF in 1991, about 8 percent of the EC budget.

---

[101]The SEA reiterates this commitment (Article 23), which is known as "economic and social cohesion."

[102]A 1990 EC study assessed the variable impact of the 1992 program on member-states. The study (the "Forty Sector Study") focused on 40 industries that are heavily affected by economic integration. In discussing the impact on southern states, the study recognized that 1992 will cause the diversion of large amounts of production in protected industries, especially capital-intensive machines and industrial goods, to other member-states and an increase in production of labor-intensive goods such as clothing and textiles. As a result of this redistribution of production, the study predicts a significant increase in capital investment in the region (attracted by low wages). The effectiveness of this capital investment will be limited, however, by inadequate infrastructure and a less skilled labor force. Furthermore, the long-term growth prospects of the region's low-tech industries are not optimistic.

Ireland, and to a lesser extent Spain, have the brightest prospects of the group. Ireland has been successful, through very aggressive efforts, in attracting investment in many high-tech areas such as pharmaceuticals, chemicals, machinery, and telecommunications. Similarly, Spain has been able to attract higher-tech investment in office and data processing equipment, chemicals, and electronic equipment. "Medium-term Adjustments in the Southern Member States," *European Economy*, Special Edition 1990, pp. 70–89.

In 1975, the EC established the European Regional Development Fund (ERDF)[103] to address the regional effects of integration, and it substantially revised the program in 1989.[104] Regional support, together with the ESF, will double from ecu 7.8 billion in 1988 to 14.1 billion in 1993, focusing assistance more directly on growth and job-producing investment. ERDF now accounts for about 12 percent of the EC budget. ERDF is structured to favor the poorer "southern" countries. In 1988, for example, 66 percent of the fund was reserved for Greece, Italy, Portugal, and Spain, which when combined only accounted for 36 percent of the Community's population and only 22 percent of the GDP. Although the four poorest EC countries have grown by an average 1.2 percent per year faster than the other states from 1986–90, they have succeeded in narrowing the GDP per capita gap by only 3 percent (from 66 percent to 69 percent) of the Community average.[105] At Maastricht, the EC leaders agreed to create a new Cohesion Fund (discussed above) designed to help the poorer EC countries defray the costs associated with projects on the environment and trans-European networks.

COMMON AGRICULTURAL POLICY

The Common Agricultural Policy[106] is a key element of the Community's economic regime not only because it consumes more

---

[103]The EC will spend ecu 6.3 billion on ERDF in 1991.

[104]Regional effects include such factors as increased unemployment in specific industries due to relocation of production, changing price structures through the opening of the market, and the social effects of monetary union on high-inflation countries.

[105]*Financial Times,* June 18, 1991, p. 16.

[106]"Common" policies concern areas where member-states have ceded to the Community the right to adopt legislation applying throughout the Twelve without further action by national Parliaments. Other areas of common policy include competition, transport, and commercial policy. See Rome Treaty, Article 3.

A complete description of the complex structure of the CAP is beyond the scope of this Report. In simple terms, the Community sets a single common target price for agricultural commodities throughout the Community (the EC has devised an elaborate system to insulate the mechanism against currency fluctuations in the Community, called monetary compensation amounts). A second "intervention price" is established at which price member governments are obliged to buy the commodity from farmers, thus establishing a de facto minimum price (leading to the notorious wine lakes and butter mountains of the late 1980s). To protect the system from agricultural imports (for many agricultural commodities, the world price is considerably lower than in Europe), the Community sets a "threshold" price for imports, and imposes a levy on all imports to bring them up to the threshold price. The Community also pays a subsidy to exporters—the difference between the world price and the Community price. This feature of CAP is at the core of the current dispute in GATT.

than half the Community's budget but also because it is a source of serious political controversy among the member-states and between the EC and its trading partners, especially the United States.

Within the Community itself, the CAP has long been a major source of contention. Disputes over the CAP contributed to the French boycott in 1965–66 and the long-running row between Britain and the principal continental agricultural nations. Because Britain's agricultural sector is a relatively small part of its economy and the United Kingdom had a relatively high proportion of non-EC (thus dutied) trade, British financial contributions, based on a percentage of its customs revenues, substantially exceeded the funds it received back from the Community. The problem was partially solved by capping overall EC farm spending under CAP (in 1989, farm spending declined to less than 60 percent of the EC total)[107] and adjusting the British contribution to the EC. But in the past two years, CAP costs have grown by 33 percent (compared with an 8 percent growth rate 1987–89), and CAP is once again expected to consume 65 percent of the EC's budget.

For a number of years, the Community has been considering reforms to the CAP, impelled by cost of continuing the CAP guarantees, massive overproduction of agricultural products by EC farmers, and considerable pressure from the United States and the Cairns Group of agricultural producer nations, both bilaterally and in the current Uruguay round of GATT negotiations.

The costs of the price and quantity guarantees afforded by the CAP to farmers have represented the bulk of EC spending and have risen continually since the formal implementation of the European Agricultural Guidance and Guarantee Fund (EAGGF) in 1968 (see Figure 6.1). These rising costs[108] are, in part, a function of the growing divergence between official fixed CAP prices and world prices, which are considerably lower. As an example, in 1991, a ton of European wheat produced for $210 cost only $80 on world markets.[109] This difference costs CAP through the subsidies to European farmers when they sell their goods abroad or through the loss incurred when surplus goods purchased from farmers at high prices are sold at lower

For further discussion of the CAP, see Colchester and Buchan, *Europower,* Ch. 9; *European Unification,* pp. 45–49.

[107]*Financial Times,* February 15, 1991, p. 8. "Annual Economic Report," Table 57, p. 274.

[108]In 1968, the EAGGF cost ecu 2 billion; in 1991, it will cost ecu 34 billion.

[109]*Financial Times,* July 10, 1991, p. 6.

world market prices. These guaranteed high prices have also priced the Europeans out of their own markets. Using loopholes in CAP, EC livestock farmers import feed-grains from outside the EC to avoid high domestic cereal grain prices.[110] The CAP price support programs and quantity guarantees have also caused the accumulation of large surpluses of agricultural products in EC storehouses.[111]

The ongoing Uruguay round of the GATT has intensified both intra-EC and external controversy over the CAP program. For the United States and the Cairns Group, reducing trade-distorting agricultural subsidies is the sine qua non for completing the Uruguay round. Their proposals focus on converting non-tariff barriers, such as price and export subsidies and import quotas, to tariffs, with the goal of then reducing the tariffs to zero or near zero over 10 years.[112] The United States would permit some direct payments to farmers, so long as they do not distort trade ("green box"). The United States stresses reducing export subsidies, which the United States claims have the greatest trade-distorting impact.[113]

In July 1990, the EC Agricultural Commissioner Ray MacSharry offered a compromise CAP reform proposal that would cut total agricultural support by 30 percent by 1996 compared with 1986[114] and shift the focus of agricultural payments to direct support, but would retain the Community preference. The Commissioner's plan declined to single out export subsidies for reduction, preferring to base reductions on the overall level of aid to the sector ("aggregate measure of support"). As refined through negotiations within the Community over

---

[110]*Economist,* July 6, 1991, p. 49.

[111]*Le Figaro*, July 10, 1991, p. 26. *Economist,* January 26, 1991, p. 45. In 1991, the EC held more than 500,000 tons of surplus dairy and 700,000 tons of surplus beef; 13 percent of all EC grain is surplus, and EC holdings now amount to some 20 million tons. *Economist,* July 16, 1991, p. 46.

[112]*Financial Times*, April 26, 1990.

[113]Europeans claim that the U.S. position is a self-serving proposal designed primarily to help U.S. grain producers regain their lost world market share; in the 1980s, the EC share of the world wheat market climbed from 13 percent to 20 percent. *Le Point,* September 28, 1991, pp. 19–20. Overall, the U.S. share of world agricultural exports fell from 28 percent in the early 1980s to 21 percent in 1990, while the EC share, under 15 percent in the 1970s, now approaches 20 percent. *Wall Street Journal,* December 3, 1992, p. 1.

[114]In 1986, EC subsidies were approximately ecu 105 billion, compared with ecu 94 billion in 1991 (counting both direct payments and subsidies in the form of higher prices), so the EC proposal represented only about a 15 percent reduction from then current levels of support. The fall in the CAP's cost to ecu 88.5 billion in 1989 was attributable in part to the EC's 1988 reforms and in part to the rising price of U.S. exports due to the late 1980s drought. See *Financial Times,* August 31, 1991, p. 1, and September 26, 1990; *Economist,* November 3, 1990, p. 76, and January 26, 1991, p. 45.

1990–91, the plan also sought to shift the focus of the program away from price supports that favor large, efficient producers (in 1990, some 20 percent of EC farmers received 80 percent of farm payments) toward income support, which would favor smaller producers.[115]

The MacSharry proposal was not only rejected by the United States (which did modify its proposal to allow for a 75 percent reduction in overall farm subsidies over 10 years and a 90 percent reduction in export subsidies),[116] but it was also rejected by many of the EC nations' Agriculture Ministers.

EC countries with larger, more efficient farms, especially the United Kingdom, Denmark, and the Netherlands, objected to giving preference to smaller producers. France feared the impact on its important farm export sector. Farmers in Belgium and Italy joined in sometimes violent protests, while Ireland, Spain, Greece, and Portugal generally supported the MacSharry approach. There was considerable resistance to reform in Germany as well, on the grounds that it would not reduce the overall cost of the program and would harm politically influential farmers. Chancellor Kohl seemed reluctant to press France too hard on agriculture for fear of further politically weakening President Mitterrand, Kohl's key partner in the broader process of European construction.[117] The inability to reach an agreement contributed significantly to the continued Uruguay round deadlock.[118]

---

[115]*Financial Times,* January 24, 1991, p. 14. The EC proposal would also permit "rebalancing"—increasing protection for some threatened sectors, such as oilseeds—while reducing the overall level of support. *Financial Times,* September 26, 1990, and October 5, 1990.

[116]*Wall Street Journal,* October 16, 1990, p. A26.

[117]It is often suggested that, since the late 1950s, the CAP has been a key element in the Franco-German bargain that permitted the creation and development of the EC: Germany agreed to support France's influential agriculture sector in return for French policy that would aid German industrial development. This is clearly an oversimplification. Not only is agriculture politically important in Germany, too, especially for the CDU, which derives important support from farmers (even though agricultural employment makes up only 3.5 percent of the working population, it is concentrated in southwestern Germany and the new East German Länder, where it accounts for 11 percent, see *Economist,* November 3, 1990, p. 76), but also because the CAP plays an important role for most EC countries, in addition to France. *Financial Times,* October 24, 1990; *Le Point,* September 28, 1991, pp. 19–20. Overall, there are three times as many farmers in the EC than in the United States, although only one-third as much land is under cultivation. Environmental concerns have also boosted support for maintaining EC agriculture.

[118]In addition to specific disagreements over agriculture subsidies, many EC countries object that the United States is unfairly singling out agriculture, while refusing to compromise on issues that would benefit European trade.

Finally, in May 1992, the EC Agriculture Ministers reached a compromise (over the objections of Italy) that would cut the guaranteed prices for a number of key commodities (grain by 29 percent over three years, beef by 15 percent over two years, milk by 15 percent over three years, and butter by 5 percent over two years) and convert some EC payments to direct payments to farmers who set aside 15 percent of their land.[119] Nevertheless, this reform still failed to satisfy the United States, and an effort at compromise at the G-7 summit in Munich in July also met with failure. The pressure to reach an agreement on agricultural subsidies grew in autumn 1992 as the United States made good on its threat to impose retaliatory tariffs on EC exports to the United States to compensate for what the United States claimed were GATT-violating EC subsidies for oilseeds.[120] On November 5, 1992, the United States announced $300 million in compensatory tariffs on EC white wine, rapeseed oil, and wheat gluten, to take effect on December 5, and threatened another unspecified $700 million in tariffs on farm and industrial products.[121] Although France pushed its fellow Community members for a hard-line response, the other EC states adopted a more conciliatory tone, and on November 20, the United States and the EC Commission trade negotiators reached agreement on a package to solve both the oilseed controversy and the overall farm trade deadlock in GATT.

Under the agreement, the United States agreed to accept the acreage limits on oilseeds contained in the EC's May 1992 CAP reform (which would cut oilseed acreage by 15 percent in the first year and 10 percent in future years of the agreement) rather than a specific new oilseed limit as the United States had originally sought. The two sides disputed just what impact this agreement would have on actual output (estimates ranged from 8.5 million tons to more than 11 million tons as the likely output). In addition, the EC agreed to cut overall farm exports by 21 percent, lower than the U.S. announced target of 24 percent.[122] French leaders immediately denounced the

[119]To satisfy the United Kingdom and other nations with large farms, most of the preferential treatment for smaller farms was eliminated. "Political Agreement on CAP Reform," Council of Ministers of 18, 19, 20 and 21 May 1992 (mimeo).

[120]Although most agricultural trade falls outside GATT, oilseeds are under GATT jurisdiction as a result of a 1960s EC agreement not to raise oilseed tariffs. The United States argued that EC subsidies violated that agreement, and on two occasions a GATT panel agreed with the U.S. argument. In part as a result of EC subsidies, U.S. oilseed exports to the EC fell from 11.9 million tons in 1982 to 6.4 million in 1990. *Economist,* May 30, 1992, p. 66.

[121]*Financial Times,* November 6, 1992, p. 1.

[122]*Financial Times,* November 21–22, 1992, p. 1; *Wall Street Journal,* November 23, 1992, p. 1.

agreement, but did not say specifically whether France would use its veto (under the Luxembourg Compromise) when the full GATT package was presented to the EC Council.

Although agriculture was a major sticking point, a number of EC-U.S. trade issues remain on issues such as anti-dumping laws, semiconductors, and U.S. film and television program exports. But the prospects for GATT agreement improved considerably with the farm agreement, assuming it is not blocked by the Council.

Even with the CAP reforms, in the short term the cost of the CAP will actually grow slightly, though the shift to direct payments should reduce, if not entirely eliminate, its trade-distorting impact as well as lower food prices for EC consumers.[123]

INDUSTRIAL POLICY AND STATE AID TO INDUSTRY

In contrast to the EC's strongly interventionist approach to agriculture, the Community has for the most part avoided developing an industrial policy. Although the Community includes several highly *dirigiste* states (Italy, France, and Spain), others, notably the United Kingdom, Germany, and Denmark, have firmly set themselves against Community involvement in promoting industry, with the limited exceptions of research support, discussed below. There is evidence to suggest that the Single Market Program has had a broadly deregulatory effect (i.e., breaking down national barriers without constructing equivalent trans-EC regulations).[124] In addition, the Community has used its competition policy to develop Community-wide rules on mergers and acquisitions and to restrict individual states' aid to industry on the grounds that such aid creates unfair competitive advantage.[125] The Community's Industry Ministers have also endorsed a Commission policy paper that opposed sectoral intervention.[126]

This anti-subsidy policy has created considerable tension between the Commission and some states, a problem that has grown under Leon Brittan, the current Competition Commissioner.[127] In a highly

[123] *The Times,* July 2, 1992; *Wall Street Journal,* May 22, 1992, p. A3. See also *Economist,* May 23, 1992, p. 20.

[124] See Woolcock et al., *Britain, Germany and 1992,* p. 5–6.

[125] For a discussion of the EC's competition policy, see Douglas E. Rosenthal, "Competition Policy," in *Europe 1992.*

[126] *Financial Times,* June 17, 1991, p. 12.

[127] See ibid., p. 332–334.

charged case, Brittan took on France's aid to Renault and won a partial victory, when France agreed to pay back FF 6 billion of the alleged FF 8.4 billion in illegal loans. Brittan also challenged the U.K.'s financial sweeteners granted to British Aerospace when it acquired Rover, a British automobile manufacturer. The Commission has also taken on Germany's politically sensitive coal subsidies.[128] But there is division even within the Commission: the Information Technology Directorate has advocated greater intervention to ensure the survival and competitiveness of Europe's computer firms.[129]

The problem of subsidies is particularly acute for state-owned enterprises.[130] To help curtail illegal subsidies, the Commission has ordered member-states to notify the EC of its relations with state-owned firms before aid is paid. Although the Rome Treaty is explicitly neutral on the choice of public versus private sector industry, many free trade advocates argue that state ownership disguises state aid. The subsidy problem is not limited to intra-EC disputes; in several high-visibility cases—most notably the Airbus-Boeing controversy—it has become a source of conflict between the United States and the Community. In the Airbus case, the United States alleges that, through 1990, EC countries have provided $5.6 billion in direct subsidies plus other benefits, such as German government guarantees against losses due to exchange rate fluctations. In response, Europeans charge that the United States indirectly subsidizes Boeing by as much as $22 billion through military and space research and development funds and tax preferences.[131] The United States and the EC Commission reached a

---

[128]*Süddeutsche Zeitung,* June 15, 1991, p. 33. German coal subsidies amount to some DM 10 billion per year.

[129]*Economist,* February 16, 1991, p. 57. France, Germany, Italy, and the Netherlands supported the proposal; the United Kingdom, Ireland, Spain, and Portugal opposed. *Wall Street Journal*, April 30, 1991. *Economist,* June 8, 1991, p. 70.

[130]State aid in the EC averaged an annual ecu 89 billion in 1988–90 (1989 prices), down slightly from 1986–88. *Economist,* August 8, 1992, p. 61 (EC data). For France and Italy, state-owned enterprises account for some one-third of GDP (*Economist,* March 2, 1991, p. 14), while for Europe as a whole, the figure is around 12 percent. *Le Monde,* October 14, 1990. In absolute terms, Germany averaged ecu 26 billion in annual state aid during the period 1988–90 compared with ecu 23 billion for Italy, ecu 16 billion for France, and ecu 8 billion for the United Kingdom. In manufacturing subsidies, Italy topped the list, with nearly ecu 13 billion in aid in 1990 (6 percent of valued added), followed by Germany, France, and Britain. *Economist*, June 8, 1991, p. 17; August 1, 1992, p. 61.

[131]Bruce Stokes, "Deadline Nears in Aircraft Subsidy Rift," *National Journal,* March 28, 1992, pp. 760–761. *Wall Street Journal,* December 15, 1991. A report prepared for the U.S. Department of Commerce put the total direct support for Airbus by 1990 at $8.2 billion, which, if Airbus had to acquire the funds at "commercial rates,"

tentative agreement to settle the dispute on March 31, 1992, but the agreement has proved difficult to sustain in practice.[132]

Subsidies are only one element of industrial policy that divides the Community. Quantitative restrictions on imports, most notably on automobiles, are an important component of national industrial strategies designed to protect European industry from competition. Although the Commission has supported countries, such as the United Kingdom, that have fought to remove quantitative restrictions, the recent agreement to limit Japanese car sales to no more than 16–17 percent of the EC market through 1998 (including Japanese cars made in EC countries) demonstrates the strong support for protecting key sectors. Anti-trust policy, too, has implications for European industrial structure: some in the EC advocate relaxing monopoly restrictions to permit European firms to compete with Japan and the United States in computers and electronics.[133] Similarly, the EC's expanded use of anti-dumping provisions are viewed by some as an element of protectionism.[134]

The conflict between interventionism and a laissez-faire approach to industrial policy came to a head in the Intergovernmental Conference leading up to Maastricht. Belgium tabled a paper on industrial policy, calling for planning, temporary tariff protection for high-technology industries, and less restrictive rules on state aid to industry. Germany, the Netherlands, and the United Kingdom all criticized the Belgian proposal.[135]

The appointment of Edith Cresson as France's Prime Minister in May 1991 raised fears that France would push for a more active EC role in industrial policy, particularly in key sectors such as information technology and aerospace, where many industrialists believe that European firms' survival requires greater support and protection.[136]

---

would be worth $25.9 billion. Gellman Research Associates, Inc., "An Economic and Financial Review of Airbus Industrie," September 4, 1990 (mimeo).

[132]See *European Community News,* No. 9/92, April 1, 1992.

[133]Some in industry have also called for increasing the external tariff on computer chips and consumer electronics.

[134]New EC anti-dumping cases rose from 27 in 1989 to 43 in 1990. *Financial Times,* June 17, 1991, p. 12.

[135]*Financial Times,* February 15, 1991, p. 8.

[136]In a speech to the French National Assembly, Cresson stated: "Europe cannot be just a large market. The Europeans cannot depend on the outside world for certain products which are essential for their technological future or their defense. An urgent effort is needed to ensure a common future in key sectors like cars and electronics. . . . Forty years ago the founding fathers created the European Coal and Steel Community;

Similar fears arose from the publication of an influential book by Konrad Seitz, head of Policy Planning in Germany's Foreign Ministry, who argued that Japan's technological challenge required a more activist European response.[137]

In the end, the anti-interventionists largely prevailed at Maastricht. France again led the effort to expand the EC's ability to aid key industrial sectors and allow majority voting for industrial policy, spurred on by anger at the Commission's October 1991 decision to block France's Aerospatiale and Italy's Alenia from acquiring the Canadian aircraft manufacturer De Havilland.[138] While Chancellor Kohl joined with President Mitterrand in asserting that "industrial policy should be part of Europe's responsibility,"[139] the German Finance and Economics Ministries opposed broad EC powers in this area. The EC leaders ultimately agreed to include a new article in the Treaty, entitled "Industry," setting forth the goals of "speeding up the adjustment of industry to structural changes," "promoting industrial cooperation and small and medium sized firms," and "fostering better exploitation of the industrial potential of policies of innovation, research and technological development."[140] However, the United

---

today it is a true Electronics Community that we need." *Financial Times,* May 23, 1991, p. 1.

[137]Seitz summarized his views in an article in *Der Tagesspiegel,* August 25, 1991 (reprinted in the *German Tribune*, September 8, 1991, p. 5): "Will we wake up in time and join forces with France to become the motive force of a grand European strategy aimed at catching up with the others? The answer to this question will decide Europe's future in the 21st century." See also *Handelsblatt,* November 27, 1991, p. 9 (FBIS-WEU-92-002, January 2, 1992, p. 10). An advisor to Seitz, Achim von Heynitz, an economist at the Stiftung Wissenschaft und Politik in Ebenhausen, Germany, observed: "German policy will clearly be less confident in a liberal, market-led process in the future. Industrial policy will inevitably be on the rise." *National Journal,* May 25, 1991, p. 1228.

[138]The Commission was divided over the case, with Competition Commissioner Leon Brittan opposing the takeover and Industry Commissioner Martin Bangemann in favor. *Financial Times,* February 11, 1992, p. 2.

[139]*Financial Times,* December 2, 1991, p. 17.

[140]Article 130, Maastricht Treaty, pp. 52–53. In a comment after the Maastricht summit, Elisabeth Guigou, French Minister for European Affairs, stated: "In the past, industrial issues were not covered by the Treaty of Rome. They were approached under the heading of competition. In a vast market we must certainly harmonize the rules of competition, but what was lacking—what we fought so hard for and obtained at Maastricht—was a section on industry that enables the Community to establish programs to strengthen competitiveness." Mme. Guigou rejected the term "industrial policy" (which she said "wrongly has a statist and thus pejorative connotation to many of our partners") to characterize France's objective, preferring instead "an industrial strategy for Europe and its enterprises." *Les Echos,* January 9, 1992, p. 4 (FBIS-WEU-92-029, February 12, 1992, p. 27).

Kingdom's opposition, quietly supported by the Netherlands, sufficed to prevent adopting majority voting for industrial policy.[141]

After Maastricht, the debate over the EC's industrial policy shifted to the Community's budget, with President Delors arguing that the Community should focus its efforts on four "endangered sectors"—automobiles, textiles, electronics, and defense industry conversion.[142] Community nations divided over the proposal. In particular, southern EC countries (with few defense firms) joined the United Kingdom in questioning the proposed aid for defense conversion.[143]

It is unlikely that the Community will resolve definitively the debate over the appropriate degrees of EC industrial activism. The election of John Major in the United Kingdom will certainly reinforce the EC's anti-interventionist wing, and the possibility of a center-right victory in next year's French parliamentary elections could mute France's leadership in favor of industrial support. The outcome will depend in part on Europe's overall future economic performance; the recent recession has contributed to increasing calls for protection and state aid to industry.

RESEARCH AND TECHNOLOGY POLICY

Research and technology policy is closely related to the debate over Community industrial policy. But unlike industrial policy, there is a broader consensus among the Twelve for an active EC role.

In the late 1970s and early 1980s, European high-technology firms and governments grew increasingly worried about the vulnerability to U.S. and Japanese competition. They pointed to the small size and fragmented structure of European industry and increasingly pushed for collective action. The SEA formalized the EC's involvement in supporting technology research and development: "to strengthen the scientific basis of European industry and to encourage it to become more competitive at the international level."[144] The Community's research efforts are organized under a multiannual Framework Program, funded from the EC's budget and matched by funds from industry. The Third Framework Program for 1990–94 is funded at ecu 5.7 billion, 40 percent of which is for research in information

[141] *The Times,* January 5, 1992, p. 19.

[142] Ibid.

[143] *Financial Times,* March 23, 1992, p. 4. Most of the aid would be focused on support for research. See below.

[144] SEA, Article 24.

technology. This amounts to some 3 percent of the Community's budget.

The EC's principal activities under the Framework Program are ESPRIT (European Strategic Program for Research in Industrial Technology, funded at some ecu 3.1 billion over the period 1984–94); RACE (Research in Advanced Communications Technology in Europe, ecu 1.1 billion 1987–91); and BRITE (Basic Research in Industrial Technologies for Europe, ecu 125 million over four years).

Like most Community activities, the Framework Program has generated its share of controversy. The Community is split between those who believe that funds should go primarily to leading European technological giants and those who want to support efforts by small- and medium-sized firms. Smaller and poorer EC states in particular are concerned that their less technologically sophisticated firms will be left behind in the Community's effort to develop European champions who can do battle with U.S. and Japanese firms.

Not all European collaborative research comes under the EC umbrella. Eureka, founded in the mid-1980s, partly in response to the U.S. SDI program, involves 19 European countries and focuses more heavily on industrial applications rather than basic research. JESSI (the Joint European Submicron Silicon Initiative program) is the largest Eureka program, budgeted at ecu 4 billion over eight years. The European Space Agency (ESA), which includes nine EC countries plus four EFTA states, is another forum for European research and development collaboration, funding both basic research and applied projects. Euclid is the framework for European collaboration in defense research under the Independent European Program Group (IEPG), which includes all European members of NATO except Iceland.

Maastricht made little change to the provisions on research other than to bring the procedures for adopting the overall Framework Program and specific program activities into line with the new Treaty decisionmaking mechanisms.[145] Rather, the focus shifted to questions of how to implement the proposed increase in research funding, from ecu 2.5 billion ($3 billion) in 1992 to ecu 4.2 billion in 1997, and

[145]The Community will use the new "conciliation" procedure, see Section 4, for adopting the overall Program and broad priority guidelines, with the further requirement that the Council must act unanimously. For specific programs, the Council may act by qualified majority after consulting the Parliament on Commission proposals (a procedure essentially unchanged from the SEA).

whether to focus on generic technologies ("horizontal" approach) or key sectors ("vertical" approach).[146]

COMMON EXTERNAL ECONOMIC POLICY

One of the strongest elements of supranationality in the Community is the conduct of external economic relations. While the Twelve continue to conduct much of their diplomatic activity as individual states (although coordinated through EPC), on matters of trade and tariffs (the Common External Tariff, or CET), the Community acts jointly and is represented in multilateral fora by the Commission either solely (GATT) or in conjunction with individual states (OECD, G-7).[147]

The Community's "commercial policy" is one of the most important areas of friction between the EC and other countries, including the United States. In addition to tariffs, the commercial policy embraces EC activities on unfair competition (anti-dumping) and negotiating voluntary restraints (such as restraints on European steel exports to the United States). Other external activities include aid and duty-free trade access for "southern" countries (such as the Lomé Conventions with a number of African, Caribbean, and Pacific countries),[148] cooperation agreements with Mediterranean states, and the evolving relations between the Community and Eastern Europe.[149]

---

[146]*Financial Times,* April 3, 1992, p. 2; *The Times,* January 5, 1992, p. 19; *Economist,* January 25, 1992, p. 65.

[147]The EC's Common External Policy for trade is based on Articles 110–116 of the Rome Treaty.

[148]Articles 131–136 of the Rome Treaty.

[149]The Community's policy toward Eastern Europe is discussed in Section 7, below.

7. ENLARGING THE COMMUNITY: THE DEBATE OVER BROADENING

Article 237 of the Rome Treaty stipulates that "Any European State may apply to become a member of the Community." The changing European political environment since 1989 has shaken the Cold War assumptions about which countries are "European" and has opened a new, potentially far-reaching debate over expanding the Community's membership. In particular, two categories of states are now pressing for membership: the economically developed EFTA countries[1] and the new democracies of Eastern Europe.[2]

THE EFTA COUNTRIES

Until the late 1980s, the EFTA countries eschewed EC membership for two reasons: a desire to retain some economic independence and the commitment by most of them to political neutrality in the East-West confrontation.[3] The neutral EFTA countries believed they had

---

[1]The members of EFTA are Austria, Finland, Iceland, Norway, Sweden, and Switzerland, joined in September 1991 by Liechtenstein.

[2]Turkey's application for membership, filed in 1987, falls into a separate category. Although the 1963 association agreement between Turkey and the EC provides explicitly for eventual Turkish membership, problems associated with Turkey's relatively low level of economic development, human rights concerns, and Greece's adamant opposition raise significant barriers to positive action by the EC in the foreseeable future. In the words of Dutch Prime Minister Ruud Lubbers: "a country like Czechoslovakia is much closer to Europe, even if it is weak in democracy. Despite all its problems Czechoslovakia belongs to Europe more than Turkey does. Turkey will be integrated with the EC market, but full membership will not be possible." *Cumhuriyet,* November 7, 1991, p. 1 (FBIS-WEU-91-218, November 12, 1991, p. 2). For the present, Turkey and the EC are continuing negotiations on completing a customs union by 1995.

There are two other applications pending; Malta and Cyprus applied in 1990. Morocco has also sought EC membership.

[3]Norway is a special case, since Norway's application for membership had already been approved by the Community, and Norway's membership in NATO means that there is no obstacle in the security field. Rather, domestic political and economic considerations that led Norway's voters to reject membership in 1971 remain the principal issue. Iceland, too, is a member of NATO, but the peculiar nature of Iceland's economy (which is based heavily on the fishing industry) makes it unlikely that Iceland will seek EC membership in the near term. See the comments of Iceland's Foreign Minister Jon Baldvin Hannibalson, *Svenska Dagbladet,* October 21, 1991, p. 6 (FBIS-WEU-91-206, October 24, 1991, p. 21); and Prime Minister David Oddson, *Aftenposten,* October 31, 1991, p. 10 (FBIS-WEU-91-213, November 3, 1991, p. 35).

the best of two worlds—a free trade agreement with the Community that promoted their economic growth while preserving independence in sensitive economic sectors (e.g., fishing and agriculture) and security policy.

With the deepening EC economic integration brought on by the 1992 project, however, their perspective began to change dramatically. The Community's dominant economic weight in Europe increasingly meant that the smaller EFTA bloc was de facto governed by the Community's economic rules, without a say in policy formulation.

The Community also had a interest in building stronger economic ties with EFTA to harness the economic strengths of the EFTA countries to the engine of European growth. But many, especially at the Commission, remained wary of expanding the Community's size. The attempt to reconcile these positions found expression in EC President Delors's January 17, 1989, proposal to create a European Economic Area (EEA)—a "structured partnership" between the EC with "common decisionmaking and administrative bodies."[4] The Strasbourg EC summit in December 1989 authorized the negotiations for creating the EEA. Talks began in July 1990, with the goal of creating the expanded free trade area by January 1, 1993, to coincide with completing the EC's Single Market Program. Negotiations proceeded slowly as a result of EFTA's demand for joint decisionmaking with the EC for the EEA (including judicial review), disagreements over specific economic issues,[5] and demands by the poorer EC members that EFTA states contribute to a regional development fund.[6]

Even before the negotiations were completed in October 1991, many of the EFTA countries had already set their sights on full EC mem-

---

[4]The idea of linking the EC and EFTA dates back at least to 1984, a concept endorsed at a joint conference of EC and EFTA Ministers. *Neue Züricher Zeitung,* February 11–21, 1990, p. 13.

[5]Key stumbling blocks included applying the Community's agriculture and fishing policies and Austrian and Swiss restrictions on heavy truck traffic.

[6]*Financial Times,* November 21, 1991, p. 6.

bership. But they proceeded with the EEA, as a hedge against delays in Community expansion, and because the work of harmonizing their laws with the Community's *acquis* gave them a head start toward completing membership negotiations.[7]

The two sides reached agreement on October 22, 1991.[8] However, the European Court of Justice threw the process into disarray when it issued an opinion on December 13, 1991, stating that the agreement violated the Rome Treaty's provisions guaranteeing the Court's judicial supremacy on EC matters.[9] The two sides agreed to a revised judicial procedure on February 14, 1992, but the new procedures were criticized by the European Parliament's Justice Committee,[10] although the European Court of Justice (ECJ) finally approved the agreement on April 10, 1992.[11] On December 6, Swiss voters rejected the EEA agreement in a referendum, but in principle the remaining EC and EFTA countries are free to continue the ratification process.

Although the EEA was a half-way measure, the EFTA countries initially embraced it, primarily because most felt that it was the only way to retain political neutrality while gaining the benefits of economic integration with the EC. As the Cold War evaporated, however, it swept away the neutrals' last major objection to membership:

---

[7]*Financial Times,* December 8–9, 1990, p. 6. Austrian Economics Minister Wolfgang Schlüssel estimated that "60 percent of Austrian membership in the European Community would be covered by participation in the EES." *Profil,* November 26, 1990, pp. 34–35 (FBIS-WEU-91-008, January 11, 1991, p. 1). A Swiss official put the figure at 80 percent for his country. *Economist,* July 13, 1991, p. 55.

[8]Key concessions that led to the agreement included a limited right for Portugal and Spain to fish in Norwegian and Icelandic waters, an EFTA commitment to make ecu 1.8 billion in low interest loans plus ecu 600 million in grants to underdeveloped EC regions in Spain, Portugal, Greece, Ireland, and Northern Ireland, and a compromise on trucking rights across the Alps. The two sides agreed to defer decision on how to apply the Common Agricultural Policy to EFTA countries. *New York Times,* October 23, 1991, p. 1.

[9]The October 1991 agreement created a joint EC-EFTA panel to resolve disputes under the agreement.

[10]*The Times,* February 15, 1992, p. 8; *Aftenposten,* March 26, 1992 (FBIS-WEU-92-061, March 30, 1992, p. 4).

[11]*Financial Times,* April 13, 1992, p. 3.

the concept of neutrality seemed increasingly less relevant. First Austria (in 1989),[12] then Sweden (in July 1991),[13] Finland (March

[12]In the months following Austria's application, the government stated that it supported the process of political union but indicated that it sought to "secure a certain leeway so that we can continue our policy of neutrality." *Die Presse,* October 11, 1989, p. 1 (FBIS-WEU-89-195, October 11, 1989, p. 1). However, over time, Austria began to show additional flexibility: Chancellor Vranitzky observed in May 1990 that its "policy of neutrality must be adapted to the changing conditions." *Die Presse,* May 10, 1990, p. 2 (FBIS-WEU-90-095, May 16, 1990, p. 1). But Austria's decision to include a special clause on neutrality in its membership application was criticized by the EC's External Affairs Commissioner (*Profil*, October 29, 1990, p. 64 [FBIS-WEU-90-210, October 30, 1990, p. 4]), a view echoed in the EC Commission's report on the Austrian application. *Der Standard,* August 1, 1991, p. 5 (FBIS-WEU-91-148, August 1, 1991 p. 2). In response, the Austrian government announced that "Austria stands ready to meet the obligations which will arise from our accession to the EC," including security policy. *Guardian*, August 1, 1991, p. 6. However, Vranitzky noted a potential problem in the area of defense: "if today the question of participation in an EC army were raised, the answer would certainly be no. If completely new structures aiming at collective security were chosen with the future EC member Austria, however, the question might perhaps no longer be raised in this form." *Kurier*, August 2, 1991, p. 3 (FBIS-WEU-91-150, August 5, 1991, p. 2). In its August 1990 opinion on Austria's application the Commission also highlighted two additional areas of potential difficulty: agriculture and transit.

Austrian officials warmly welcomed the Maastricht Treaty and argued that it posed no new problems for Austrian membership, even in the defense dimension. Foreign Minister Alois Mock, who had earlier suggested that Austria could participate in an EC peacekeeping force (*Der Standard*, August 3, 1991, p. 2 [FBIS-WEU-91-150, August 5, 1991, p. 3]), argued that "For the EC to make the WEU a pillar of its defense policy means that things will become easier for a neutral country because the WEU is an organization outside the EC." *Die Presse*, December 12, 1991, p. 4 (FBIS-WEU-91-239, December 12, 1991, p. 1). Mock subsequently added that the issue of Austria accepting observer status in the WEU or NATO "is currently not relevant." *Kurier*, March 3, 1991, p. 2 (FBIS-WEU-92-042, March 3, 1992, p. 4).

[13]The debate on EC membership among Sweden's political parties turned primarily over its implications for neutrality. While Social Democrat party leader, then Prime Minister, Ingvar Carlsson, declined to rule out EC membership, he argued that Sweden could not join the EC unless Europe moved to a system of collective security or if the EC decided against a common foreign and security policy. *Dagens Nyheter*, May 30, 1990, p. 8 (FBIS-WEU-90-119, June 20, 1990, p. 43). He subsequently limited his objections to the possibility that the EC would embrace military cooperation. *Svenska Dagbadet*, November 14, 1990, p. 13 (FBIS-WEU-90-226, November 23, 1990, p. 57). His principal opponent, Conservative party leader Carl Bildt, dissented, arguing that Sweden should apply to the EC no later than early 1992. *Dagens Nyheter*, July 7, 1990, p. 4 (FBIS-WEU-90-188, September 27, 1990, p. 25). Under the pressure of growing public support (one poll put approval of EC membership at 70 percent [*Dagens Nyheter*, February 16, 1991, p. 9, FBIS-WEU-91-065, April 4, 1991, p. 44]) and growing economic difficulties, the governing Social Democrats agreed to support EC membership, and Sweden filed its formal application with the Community on July 1, 1991. In the wake of the Maastricht agreement, Prime Minister Carl Bildt (who assumed that post in October 1991) indicated that Sweden was prepared to participate in the Common Foreign and Security Policy but intended to remain outside any military alliance system. *Die Welt*, December 23, 1991, p. 7 (FBIS-WEU-91-247, December 24, 1991, p. 18).

1992),[14] and Switzerland (May 1992)[15] applied for full membership. In Norway, public opinion is divided, but the governing Labor party has decided to apply for membership.[16]

---

[14]Historically, proximity to and close economic ties with the Soviet Union led Finland to take a cautious approach toward integration with Western Europe. During the late 1980s, Finland, like other EFTA countries, focused primarily on the EEA negotiations, with a particular emphasis on assuring EFTA countries a meaningful voice in joint legislation, while preserving Finland's neutrality. *Financial Times*, August 17, 1990; September 14, 1990. As Finland begin to free itself of its Cold War relationship with the Soviet Union (including abrogating the military restrictions of the post-World War II Paris Peace Treaty), the issue of EC membership came to the fore, impelled by polls showing a majority supported it. *Hufvudstadsbladet*, September 19, 1990, p. 2 (FBIS-WEU-90-220, November 14, 1990, p. 32). March 1991 elections led to a new center-right coalition government headed by the Center party, whose rural constituency was traditionally unenthusiastic about EC membership, and the new Prime Minister, Esko Aho, initially promoted a go-slow approach. *Dagens Nyheter*, June 11, 1991, p. 18 (FBIS-WEU-91-116, June 17, 1991, p. 27). But delays in the EEA negotiations, coupled with a recession brought about in part by the collapse of Finland's trade with the former Soviet Union and fears that Finland would be left behind the first wave of new EC members, led to growing support for membership. *Wall Street Journal*, February 13, 1992, p. A12. In February 1992, the Cabinet approved applying to the EC, and on March 20, after the Finnish Parliament endorsed EC membership, the Finnish government presented its formal application. Unlike Austria's application, Finland's does not specifically mention the issue of neutrality, but in a statement made at the time of application, the Finnish Prime Minister reiterated that "Finland must adhere to its traditional neutrality policy after joining the EC, because this guarantees security on the northeastern European border." Helsinki Radio Network, March 20, 1992 (FBIS-WEU-92-056, March 20, 1992). Finland's Foreign Minister, Paavo Vayrynen, subsequently stated: "We have never hidden our intention to maintain our neutrality . . . the essence [of which] can be be characterized by two elements. We do not belong to any military alliance and we have an independent defense system." Austria ORF Television Network, March 27, 1992 (FBIS-WEU-92-061, March 30, 1992).

[15]Swiss policy toward Europe evolved rapidly in the aftermath of the Cold War and growing interest among EFTA countries in EC membership. In the early stages of the EEA negotiations, Switzerland seemed among the most recalcitrant participants, out of fear of jeopardizing its jealously guarded independence in both economic and political affairs (Swiss voters had, as recently as 1987, blocked Swiss membership in the UN) as well as its commitment to direct democracy and decentralized federalism. But by October 1991, the Swiss Federal Council had come to accept not only the EEA but full membership: Swiss President Rene Felber stated: "The option of joining [the EC] is no longer an option, but the goal of Swiss foreign policy." Agence France Press, October 22, 1991 (FBIS-WEU-91-204, October 22, 1991, p. 27). It is unclear how the Swiss no vote on the EEA agreement will affect its application for full EC membership.

[16]Norway's political parties are deeply divided over the future of Norway's relationship with the Community. In October 1990 former Prime Minister Jan Syse resigned when his three-party governing coalition government split over what concessions the government would make in the EEA negotiations, particularly in Norway's laws restricting foreign ownership of domestic industries and natural resources. Agence France Presse, October 29, 1990 (FBIS-WEU-90-209, October 29, 1990, p. 33); *Guardian*, January 1, 1991, p. 26. He was succeeded by Labor's Gro Harlem Brundtland, whose government supported greater flexibility in the EEA negotiations. But the new government initially tread cautiously on the issue of EC membership, in light of the division within Labor's own ranks and the lack of a clear

Public opinion in the EC states, at least prior to the Maastricht Treaty, strongly supported accession of the EFTA countries; for Sweden, Norway, Austria, Switzerland, and Finland support was between 85–89 percent.[17] In the EFTA applicant states, public opinion is mixed, and the Danish rejection of the Maastricht Treaty increased opposition to EC membership, especially among Denmark's Nordic neighbors. But all of the applicant governments have vowed to press on.

NEW DEMOCRATIC COUNTRIES OF CENTRAL AND EASTERN EUROPE

For the newly democratic countries of Central and Eastern Europe, developing ties with the EC has become a central part of their economic and political strategy.[18] They desperately need access to EC markets and investment, particularly in light of the collapsing trade among the former Council for Mutual Economic Assistance (CMEA) nations and the need to reduce dependence on the former USSR republics for raw materials. Austerity measures have reduced domestic demand, putting an additional premium on exports to Western markets. This is particularly important for traditional East European export sectors—agriculture, steel, and textiles—which are critical for maintaining employment during the economic transition.[19] They have observed the dramatic growth experienced by the Community's newest members, Spain and Portugal, after accession to the EC as well as the substantial economic assistance poorer EC members receive from the Community's structural funds, and they eagerly seek to share in the wealth.

---

favorable majority in the Parliament (Storting). Sweden's EC application (followed by Finland) increased the pressure on Norway to apply quickly in order to assure that the EC would consider Norway in the first wave of applications. The Norwegian parliament approved applying for EC membership in November 1992.

Public opinion in Norway is nearly equally split over EC membership. In a March 1992 poll, 40 percent favored applying and 36 percent opposed. *Aftenposten* , March 16, 1992, p. 7 (FBIS-WEU-92-058, March 25, 1992, p. 39).

[17] *Los Angeles Times,* July 16, 1991, p. H4.

[18] EC-Eastern European relations were extremely circumscribed until 1986, when the USSR first agreed to the idea of economic relations not only between CMEA and the EC but also with individual COMECON states. A series of bilateral agreements were signed between 1988 and 1990, with all European COMECON countries forming the background to the negotiations on the so-called "Europe Agreements." See Commission of the European Communities, "EC-Eastern Europe Relations-GX Background Brief," November 6, 1991 (mimeo).

[19] Josef C. Brada, "The European Community and Czechoslovakia, Hungary, and Poland," *Report on Eastern Europe,* December 6, 1991, pp. 27–32.

The EC tie is at least as tempting politically. Membership in Europe was an important factor in stabilizing the democracies in Greece, Spain, and Portugal, and Central/East European leaders hope for a similar effect.[20] They fear isolation in a *cordon sanitaire* between prosperous, secure Western Europe and an increasingly unstable region to the East.

East European countries initially focused on gaining economic assistance from the West, including the Community, through the G-24 "Phare" program,[21] and through trade and cooperation agreements.[22] But they continued to press for closer association with the EC, and on January 17, 1990, President Delors outlined a plan for a new form of "association agreement" (later called "Europe Agreements") that "would make it possible, if those countries so desired, to include a veritable body for dialogue and political and economic consultations in the institutional framework of those agreements."[23] The Commission set out its plan for negotiating the agreements in September 1990, and negotiations began at the end of December.[24] The Commission had hoped to finesse the issue of future EC membership in the agreements[25] but, under heavy prodding from the East Europeans, accepted in April 1991 that the agreement

[20]The new democracies have sought "Western" ties through virtually every available avenue, including membership in the Council of Europe, association with NATO and the WEU, and promoting a more active role for the CSCE.

[21]The G-24 consists of the EC and EFTA countries, the United States, Canada, Japan, Australia, New Zealand, and Turkey. In 1992, the EC plans to spend $1.2 billion on economic assistance under Phare compared with $940 million in 1991 and $600 million in 1990.

[22]Thus, for example, Czechoslovakia signed a trade agreement with the EC on May 7, 1990, which was followed by agreements with most other East European countries in the spring and summer of 1990. *Guardian*, May 8, 1990; European Commission, "Association Agreements with the Countries of Central and Eastern Europe," September 7, 1990, Europe Documents N. 1646/47.

[23]*Le Monde*, January 18, 1990, p. 4.

[24]European Commission, "Association Agreements with the Countries of Central and Eastern Europe," September 7, 1990, Europe Documents N. 1646/47. The plan focused on Poland, Hungary, and Czechoslovakia, while deferring opening talks with Yugoslavia, Bulgaria, and Romania. The Commission indicated its intention to limit ties with the USSR to trade and cooperation agreements for the time being. After the Soviet Union's dissolution, the Community turned toward individual trade and cooperation agreements with the republics. Agence France Presse, January 9, 1992 (FBIS-WEU-92-007, January 10, 1992, p. 3).

[25]The Commission proposal noted that "Several governments have referred to their interest in eventual membership for their countries in the Community. This, however, is not among the objectives of the association agreements." Commissioner Andriessen even proposed a kind of "à la carte" affiliate membership for East European countries, allowing voting participation on some but not on all aspects of Community affairs. *Financial Times*, April 25, 1991, p. 2; *Independent*, April 20, 1991, p. 12.

would specify membership as a "final objective," though not an "automatic consequence," of the association agreements.[26]

In September 1991, in the wake of the failed coup in the Soviet Union, the Commission sought to accelerate the association negotiations stalled over disagreements on access for East European agriculture, textiles, steel, and coal. Most EC countries were prepared to compromise on national concerns (Belgium and Ireland on beef and sheep, Portugal on textiles), but France refused to support raising the beef quota.[27] Under pressure from fellow EC nations, France at last relented, and on November 22, 1991, Poland, Czechoslovakia, and Hungary initialed association agreements with EC.[28] The agreements, which went into effect on an interim basis on March 1, 1992, provided for gradually lifting trade barriers over five to ten years, with some restrictions remaining on "sensitive" sectors (primarily agriculture, coal, steel, and textiles). The Community reserved the right to implement additional protection in emergency situations.[29] The agreements are "asymmetrical"; providing that the EC will act first to liberalize its trade barriers, the East Europeans will follow later.[30] The agreements acknowledge that Poland, Czechoslovakia, and Hungary aim for EC membership but do not commit the EC.[31]

---

[26]Agence France Presse, April 15, 1991 (FBIS-WEU-91-073, April 16, 1991, p. 2).

[27]The Commission proposed increasing the quota by 10 percent a year over the period 1992–96 from its base of some 11,000 tons. See *Financial Times,* September 6, 1991, p. 14.

[28]The agreements were formally signed on December 16, 1991. The *London Times,* December 17, 1991, p. 11. As of spring 1992, the Commission had not released the actual texts of the individual agreements but has made available a draft English text of the basic agreement signed in December 1991 with Poland from which the references in this section are drawn.

[29]See, e.g., Article 21 of the Agreement with Poland: "Notwithstanding other provisions of this Agreement . . . if, given the particular sensitivity of the agricultural markets, imports of products originating in one Party, which are the subject of concessions . . . cause serious disturbance to the markets in the other Party, both Parties shall enter into consultations immediately to find an appropriate solution. Pending such solution, the Party concerned may take the measures it deems necessary."

[30]In practice, the three East European countries have already eliminated most tariff and quota restrictions on EC products. *Financial Times,* December 2, 1991, p. 15.

[31]The preamble states: "Recognizing the fact that the final objective of Poland is to become a member of the Community and that this association, in the view of the Parties, will help to achieve this objective." The break-up of Czechoslovakia into two independent republics could complicate their relationship with the EC. Czech Prime Minister Vaclav Klaus has indicated that he hopes the economically more prosperous Czech Republic might accelerate its EC membership, but the Community is noncommittal.

THE DEBATE PRECEDING MAASTRICHT

In the months preceding the Maastricht summit, Community members were divided in their reaction to expanded membership and differed over the relative priority to give broadening versus deepening the Community. Advocates of deeper political integration argued that the main decisions on political and economic union must precede Community expansion. They reasoned that it would be harder to build a political union in a larger Community with more diverse interests and perspectives and that new members should not be allowed to slow down the process of integration. They worried that adding the neutrals, in particular, would inhibit adopting a security and defense component to the EC. France was a leading voice for deferring action on new applications until the process of political union is well underway.[32]

By contrast, countries that favor a looser, confederal EC tended to support more rapid expansion, both to increase the size of the Single Market and to slow down political integration. The United Kingdom and Denmark argued that new entrants such as Austria and Sweden were ideal candidates: they would be net financial contributors to the Community, easing the burden on the current more wealthy states, and they would share an inclination to oppose extending Community competence to defense.[33]

Germany stood between the two camps. It was an ardent advocate of a stronger, more integrated Community. At the same time, it occupies a unique position in the center of Europe, with a strong stake in the stability and prosperity of its neighbors to the East and South. For this reason, Germany supported reasonably rapid expansion both to the EFTA countries and the new democracies.[34]

---

[32]In October 1989, President Mitterrand suggested that "perhaps we should give the Twelve time to breathe" before expanding the Community. *Le Monde,* October 27, 1989, p. 3. He later observed, "I believe it would be wise to improve the cohesion of the Twelve before going further." *Le Monde,* June 20, 1990, p. 1. As for the East Europeans, Mitterrand suggested that they would not be ready for membership for "decades and decades." *Le Monde,* June 14, 1991, p. 4.

[33]Mrs. Thatcher was one of the earliest and strongest advocates of expanding the Community to the East. In a speech in Prague on September 18, 1990, she stated that "The European Community should declare unequivocally that it is ready to accept all countries of Eastern Europe as members, if they want to join, when their economies are strong enough and when democracy has taken root." *Independent,* September 22, 1990, p. 11.

[34]As early as October 1989, as the revolutions in Eastern Europe began to unfold, Foreign Minister Genscher stated that the Community should be open to East European countries. In response, President Delors suggested that those countries

Other EC members had a particular interest in specific applications. For example, Italy and Germany supported their neighbor Austria, while Denmark was eager to expand the Scandinavian presence in the Community.[35] In contrast, the poorer members of the Community feared extending membership to the new East European democracies, concerned that they would sap investment and Community financial support away from the needs of current beneficiaries. Many countries worried about the impact of tariff-free trade with Eastern Europe in sensitive sectors: Greece and Portugal for textiles, Spain for steel, and Britain for clothing.[36] Overall, in the EC states, over 70 percent support eventual membership for Poland, Czechoslovakia, and Hungary.[37]

The Commission itself adopted the position of those who believed that deepening should precede broadening. The EEA initiative was the Commission's attempt to forestall EFTA countries' applications for full membership. Similarly, the Commission's push for new association agreements with the Central/East European countries was designed to delay their membership application.

THE IMPACT OF MAASTRICHT ON ENLARGEMENT

By the time the EC leaders gathered at Maastricht, the pressure for expanding the Community had become virtually irresistible. With the completion of the Maastricht Treaty, even the deepeners softened their resistance. To some extent they were simply bowing to the inevitable, but they could point to the agreements on Economic and Monetary Union and the Common Foreign and Security Policy as evidence that key steps toward deepening were firmly in place. Enlargement now occupies a central place on the EC's agenda.

Although the Commission had previously suggested that membership negotiations with current applicants might begin in 1992 following the Maastricht Treaty's signing, problems with the Treaty's ratification raised questions over how to proceed. At the Lisbon EC summit, the 12 leaders decided that negotiations should begin initially with

---

should orient themselves to EFTA. *Die Welt,* October 4, 1989, p. 1 (FBIS-WEU-89-191, October 4, 1989, p. 9).

[35]In March 1990, Danish Foreign Minister Ellemann-Jensen wrote: "The proper future place for the Nordic countries is in the EC where jointly they have an opportunity to affect Europe's development." *Aftenposten,* March 26, 1990, p. 2 (FBIS-WEU-90-070, April 11, 1990, p. 2).

[36]*Wall Street Journal,* July 25, 1991; *Washington Post,* March 24, 1990, p. A26. *Economist,* January 6, 1990, p. 50.

[37]*Los Angeles Times,* July 16, 1991, p. H4.

the EFTA country applicants but only after Maastricht's ratification and an agreement on a new five-year EC budget. The leaders stated that the EC could accommodate the EFTA applicants within the existing "institutional arrangements" but that further enlargement would require institutional reform.[38] Even France supported this approach, hoping the enthusiasm of the Scandinavian applicants, Sweden and Finland, would help sway Danish voters to a more favorable view of Maastricht and the EC.[39] At the Edinburgh summit, the EC leaders agreed to open negotiations with Austria, Sweden, and Finland in early 1993, to be followed by Norway.

Even though formal negotiations were delayed, the Commission staff work on the EFTA applications went forward: the Commission has already completed its report on Austria's,[40] Sweden's,[41] and Finland's applications.[42] Assuming the publics in the applicant countries do not change their minds, the stage is set for adding three to five new members by around 1996.[43] But the turmoil surrounding Maastricht's ratification could lead to additional delay.

Further enlargement is more problematic. A draft Commission proposal, developed before the Lisbon summit, suggested that expansion might follow three tracks: The EFTA countries in the mid-1990s; Poland, Czechoslovakia, and Hungary around the turn of the century, and "others" (Turkey, Cyprus, Malta) around the same time as the Central Europeans.[44] But this timetable is based on a number of

---

[38]*European Community News,* No. 23/92, June 29, 1992, p. 1.

[39]In the immediate aftermath of the Danish vote, polls in Sweden showed a significant increase in opposition to joining the EC compared with polls earlier in the spring, which indicated that opinion was evenly divided. Support in Norway and Finland also appeared to decline. *The Times,* June 5, 1992; *Economist,* August 8, 1992, p. 40.

[40]The Commission report found that, on economic grounds, the EC should respond positively to Austria's application. Only agriculture and transportation need substantial adjustment. On the political side, the report noted the need to reconcile Austria's neutrality with the EC's evolving foreign and security policy. *Der Standard,* August 1, 1991 (FBIS-WEU-91-148, p. 2).

[41]The Commission reported that there were no insurmountable problems to accepting Sweden's application but noted difficulties in the areas of agriculture, state alcohol monopolies, and aid to the Arctic region. The report also recommended that Sweden give "specific and binding assurances" on its commitment to the planned Common Foreign and Security Policy. *Guardian,* August 1, 1992.

[42]The report on Finland mirrored the Commission's findings on Sweden.

[43]*The Times,* June 26, 1992.

[44]*Arbeiderbladet,* February 10, 1992, p. 8 (FBIS-WEU-92-029, February 12, 1992, p. 3). For the Central Europeans, EC Vice President Martin Bangemann has said that admission by 2000 is "realistic." *Kurier,* January 1, 1991 (FBIS-WEU-91-001, January 2, 1991, p. 1). In a recent speech, however, Chancellor Kohl said that their full

uncertainties, including the course of EC integration during this period, the degree of consensus on institutional reform, and political and economic progress in the applicant countries. It is possible that the controversy over Maastricht may improve the prospects for adding new members since it may slow down the pace of integration and thus reduce the possible gap between new applicants and existing members. At the same time, the most committed integrationists, already concerned about the impact of less enthusiastic countries such as Denmark, may dig in their heels harder against new members who are unlikely to share their commitment to a strong Union. Adding new full or associate members requires unanimous approval of the Council as well as an absolute majority of the European Parliament.

Even for the likely new members from EFTA, there remain substantial unresolved questions concerning their relationship to the Community's foreign, security, and defense dimensions. It is possible that the growing tendency toward a multiple-speed Europe (including full, observer, and associate members within the WEU), coupled with the Danish no, and the possible emergence of the Franco-German Corps as a *noyau dur* within the broader EC for European defense will facilitate the membership of the former neutrals without the requirement that they join fully in the EC's security dimension. As for the Central Europeans, their desire for strong security links to the West means that they are likely to agree to participate in the EC's security activities, at least so long as they are not forced to choose between EC ties and links to the United States, either directly or through NATO.

---

membership was unlikely "until well into the next decade." "European Challenges for Our Economy, Society and Politics," *Bulletin,* No. 121, November 11, 1992.

PART 3

THE IMPLICATIONS OF EUROPEAN INTEGRATION FOR EUROPE AND FOR TRANSATLANTIC RELATIONS

8. IMPLICATIONS OF EUROPEAN INTEGRATION FOR EUROPE

On one level, the Maastricht Treaty can be seen as an intricate jumble of horse trading, compromise, and ambiguity among 12 states with differing views and interests across the four principal dimensions of the long-running EC debate. But woven into the thread of more than 300 pages of Treaty text, some general themes emerged from Maastricht that are likely to guide the Community's future development, whether or not the Treaty is ratified by all 12 Community members.

1. *The Franco-German partnership continues as the locomotive of Community construction and will remain an effective engine for European construction to the extent that France's and Germany's objectives coincide*. The broad outlines of the Maastricht agreement emerged from the core Franco-German bargain. On the economic front, France was eager for the Community to move toward EMU, because (as a result of the EMS) its macroeconomic policies were largely dictated by the decisions of the Bundesbank, over which France had little influence. EMU offered the possibility of collective macroeconomic decisionmaking, giving France (and other EC states) a voice in policymaking. On security policy, France hoped to push the development of a European identity to underscore Europe's independence from the United States, to enhance French influence, and to anchor the foreign policy of a newly unified Germany. Germany, in turn, wanted to see further development of the political union; in particular, measures to strengthen the communitarian institutions. Germany agreed to support EMU (at the cost of giving up national control over the deutschemark) in return for France's willingness to accept a European Central Bank free from political influence and firmly committed to anti-inflationary policies; France in turn agreed to support some strengthening of the Community institutions. The two countries jointly pushed for expanding the Community's role in security policy.

Throughout the process leading up to Maastricht, Franco-German initiatives embodying this approach served to animate the Community's negotiations. The Kohl-Mitterrand letter of April 1990 (proposing to add an Intergovernmental Conference on political union to the already agreed-to conference on EMU), their joint proposals on the eve of convening the two conferences in December 1990 (proposing a timetable for EMU and suggesting linking the WEU and EC for defense), and the Franco-German security initiative in October 1991 (further elaborating their concept of a European defense) all helped propel the negotiations forward. The key areas of Franco-German agreement formed the cornerstone of the final Treaty, and the need to maintain Franco-German cooperation (or at least prevent Germany from "going it alone") was a key theme for Treaty supporters in the French referendum.

France and Germany did not see eye-to-eye in all matters. France preferred a more intergovernmental approach than Germany, which led to conflict over the Treaty's basic structure (France supported the pillar approach; Germany was more favorable to the "tree" model). In particular, France successfully supported an intergovernmental structure for both security and crime/immigration measures over Germany's opposition. Germany was especially eager to include immigration in the communitarian part of Community decisionmaking and wanted to strengthen substantially the role of the European Parliament, positions resisted by France (among others). After the Maastricht summit, France and Germany continued to work in tandem: the La Rochelle agreement concerning the formation of the Franco-German Corps, Kohl's dramatic French television appearance on the eve of the French referendum supporting Mitterrand's drive for ratification, the quick Kohl-Mitterrand summit immediately after the vote, and the Bundesbank's determined defense of the franc.

2. *Germany will exert increasing influence in Community affairs.* If the Franco-German partnership is the locomotive of EC integration, it seems increasingly apparent that Germany will be the conductor for several reasons. First, Germany's size and economic clout give it *primus inter pares* status within the Community for both economic and political issues (witness Germany's strong insistence that the proposed European Central Bank mirror the Bundesbank and Germany's forceful actions leading the EC to recognize Slovenia and Croatia at the end of 1991). If, as seems likely, the Community expands in the coming years, Germany's influence will grow even greater; many of the EFTA and Central European countries have close economic, political, and, in some cases, cultural and historical ties to Germany. To the extent that Germany comes to embrace a more activist international role (including a willingness to extend the operations of the Bundeswehr beyond its current NATO responsibilities), it is likely to exert additional influence in the security dimension, an area now dominated by France and the United

Kingdom, with their nuclear arsenals and permanent membership on the UN Security Council.

Many in France fear that Germany's growing assertiveness will unbalance the Franco-German relationship and thwart France's aspirations to use the Community as a vehicle to project French influence. In Britain, former Cabinet Minister Nicholas Ridley caused a sensation by suggesting that moves to deepen the Community were evidence of Germany's desire to dominate its partners (an assertion that cost Ridley his job but which mirrored sentiments held by many others in the United Kingdom). With characteristic directness, Mrs. Thatcher recently observed: "Germany's preponderance within the Community is such that no major decision can really be taken against German wishes. In these circumstances, the Community augments German power, rather than containing it."[1]

Maastricht itself was only a limited success for Germany: its views mostly carried sway on the details of EMU, but Chancellor Kohl was largely unsuccessful in his crusade for new power for the European Parliament and for including immigration within the Rome Treaty framework. German efforts to achieve expanded representation in the European Parliament (to reflect the addition of the citizens of the former GDR) met with an ambiguous response from Community leaders,[2] but Kohl's persistence paid off a year later at Edinburgh, where the EC leaders agreed to add 18 new German MEPs.[3]

Chancellor Kohl's personal commitment to pursue Thomas Mann's vision ("a European Germany, not a German Europe") not only led

---

[1] *The Times,* May 16, 1992, p. 4.

[2] Prior to Maastricht, President Mitterrand stated that the number of Parliamentarians was not based on proportional representation but on equality of the larger states and reiterated: "I think the principle is correct." *Frankfurter Allgemeine Zeitung,* November 16, 1991, p. 3. At Maastricht the EC leaders adopted a declaration providing: "The Member States agree to examine the questions relating to the number of members of the Commission and the number of members of the European Parliament no later than at the end of 1992, with the view to reach agreement which will permit the establishment of the necessary legal basis for fixing the number of members of the European Parliament in good time for the 1994 elections. The decisions will be taken in the light, *inter alia,* of the need to establish the overall size of the European Parliament in an enlarged Community." "Declaration On the Number of Members of the Commission and of the European Parliament," Maastricht Treaty, p. 227. Germany has also campaigned for expanding the use of Germany as an official EC language.

[3] Under the Edinburgh agreement, France, Italy, the Netherlands, and the United Kingdom will have six additional MEPs each, Spain four, Belgium, Greece, and Portugal each one additional MEP, while Denmark, Ireland, and Luxembourg are unchanged.

Germany to advocate further integration at Maastricht but also enhanced its willingness to compromise. With the drama of Germany's unexpectedly quick unification in mind, German leaders were anxious to demonstrate that unification did not presage a more "go it alone" (*alleingang*) policy. But German willingness to compromise its objectives in the interest of European unity may decline in the future: many segments of the press and some political leaders have vocally criticized what they viewed as Kohl's capitulation at Maastricht, and the pressure to defend what is perceived as Germany's legitimate interests is likely to grow over time. The perception that the German government and the Bundesbank were unwilling to take adequate steps to bail out the ERM in the frantic weeks before the French referendum presages further conflict between domestic political pressures and the demands of preserving unity in the future.[4]

The dynamic surrounding the EC's recognition of Slovenia and Croatia, where France agreed to follow Germany's lead despite serious policy reservations, may be a model for the future—greater French flexibility to accommodate German assertiveness. The alternative is an Alliance—perhaps led by France and the United Kingdom—"against" Germany in the EC, a sure recipe for disrupting the course of European integration.

3. *The most important unresolved issue—the timing and extent of enlargement—casts a broad shadow over the future of European integration.* The debate leading up to Maastricht was often characterized as a choice between "deepening" (expanding the range of the Community's activities) and "broadening" (extending the Community's geographical scope). Deepening advocates, led by France and many of the Community's smaller and poorer countries, argued that it was essential to transform the EC into a true "union," with responsibility for the full range of activities normally associated with sovereignty, including foreign and security policy and defense, while the Community remained at the relatively manageable size of the Twelve. Expanding membership before taking basic decisions on these issues would make subsequent consensus far more difficult, if not impossible, to achieve. Proponents of deepening also believed that potential new entrants should understand that their decision to

---

[4]On September 14, the Bundesbank cut slightly its key Lombard rate in a move designed to ease pressure on the pound (the move was accompanied by a devaluation of the Italian lira). The Bundesbank's rate cut was criticized by the United Kingdom and others as too small to remove the pressure on the pound—yet in Germany, the Bundesbank was criticized for caving in to political pressures.

join the Community meant taking part in a tightly knit structure, not just a loose confederation of sovereign states. In particular, deepeners were concerned that the likely new members, especially the Cold War neutral EFTA countries, would only accept a Community foreign and defense policy if it was a condition of membership rather than something they could choose to block once they became members.

Broadening supporters believed that the EC would derive substantial political and economic benefits from moving promptly to enlarge the Community. From their perspective, including the EFTA countries as members would improve the Community's economic performance and competitiveness and provide a new group of relatively wealthy nations to help bear the costs of the Community's activities. Broadening to include the countries of Central and Eastern Europe would help bring political stability and economic prosperity to that region, which in turn would help Western Europe by reducing potential sources of conflict in Europe and opening new markets for Community goods and services. Although broadeners understood that this would create a reciprocal obligation to open EC markets to East European imports, they tended to favor free trade philosophically and saw that open trade was preferable to direct government assistance in stabilizing East European economies. Because broadening advocates on the whole were skeptical at best about developing a Common Foreign and Security Policy (at least one based on majority voting), the prospect that new members would be less enthusiastic about this aspect of Community affairs (the EFTA countries because of their neutrality, the Eastern Europeans because of their Atlanticist orientation) troubled them little: in fact, for some it was a positive attraction of broadening.

To a considerable extent, the pace of events in Europe largely overtook this debate before the EC leaders reached their final decision at Maastricht. Although deepening advocates had pushed for creating a European Economic Area (EEA) as an alternative to EFTA countries joining the EC, their efforts produced the opposite effect. Most EFTA countries became convinced that they would be subject to EC rules whether or not they joined the Community: if they wanted a full say in the critical economic and political decisions that would govern their fate, they had to accept the need to become full members. Second, the USSR's rapid disintegration and the former Warsaw Pact countries' desperate search for political and economic links to the Community caused East European countries to accelerate their efforts to join the Community. Although France continued to resist, the prospect that the new democracies would fail without close EC ties forced most Community members to accept, with varying degrees of enthusiasm, broad association agreements and liberalized trade regimes (signed in December 1991) with the most advanced of the former Warsaw Pact countries (Poland, Czechoslovakia, and Hungary), with the growing prospect of full membership for at least those three around the turn of the century.

Thus, by the time of Maastricht, the Community, including its leading deepener, President Delors, accepted that the EC must begin the slippery path of enlargement. While Maastricht contained some important elements of deepening, key questions that the deepeners hoped to resolve before enlargement (including reform of the Community's decisionmaking procedures and an irrevocable commitment to a Common Foreign and Defense Policy) remained open. Prior to the Danish vote, President Delors hoped to accelerate the move toward further institutional reforms with the goal of completing the work before any enlargement. But at the Lisbon summit in June 1992, the EC leaders decided to go forward with the EFTA countries' applications on the basis of existing institutions (as modified by Maastricht), although they agreed that actual negotiations on the applications should await the Treaty's ratification and a new five-year budget deal. At Edinburgh, following the agreement on the EC budget and the "Danish problem," the EC leaders agreed to begin negotiations with Austria, Finland, and Sweden, to be followed quickly by Norway. The Community still plans a new Intergovernmental Conference on institutional reform in 1996 before any subsequent wave of enlargement, but it now seems likely that future reform will require the support of as many as 17 members rather than the current 12. The major barrier to expansion now may be the divided popular sentiment in the applicant countries, where opposition to EC membership grew after the Danish vote, rather than the willingness of the Twelve to enlarge.

4. *Economics remains the focus of European integration and the area of greatest consensus, although movement to a single currency for all EC members is in doubt.* The most decisive step taken at Maastricht was the agreement on EMU—to a large extent the natural outgrowth of the Single Market Program and the EMS. The Maastricht ratification debate focused to a considerable extent on the Treaty's effort to include an element of irreversibility in the process and timetable. Given the deep reservations in Germany and the doubts created by the currency panic in the run-up to the French referendum, modification of the Treaty's EMU provision seems

likely.[5] But there remains a substantial chance that at least a subset of the Community will eventually adopt a single currency, despite the doubts expressed by some economists, financiers, and segments of the public.

More important, the turmoil over EMU has not significantly lessened the commitment to the Single Market Program. Although publicized disputes over EC rules that might ban Camembert or regulate tractor seats continued to capture headlines, the work of building a Single Market marches on. The Community also took additional steps in the economic dimension at Maastricht. The Community extended its jurisdiction over employment issues, consumer protection, and trans-European networks. By contrast, in the more "political" aspects of European policy (internal security, immigration, foreign and defense policy), the disagreements were more widespread, and the basic intergovernmental approach was, to a greater or lesser degree, left intact.

5. *While economic protectionism remains a concern, Maastricht reinforced the likelihood that the Community on the whole will pursue a non-interventionist and relatively free trade approach.* At Maastricht, the EC leaders resisted efforts to develop an industrial policy for the Community, insisting that all decisions in this area remain subject to unanimous approval. Given the strong objections of many EC states (as well as key EC Commissioners, such as Competition Commissioner Leon Brittan) to interventionism, requiring unanimity means for the most part that there is little prospect for a vigorous EC industrial policy.

This does not mean that the Community will remain entirely on the sidelines in promoting industrial competitiveness. To some extent this will depend on the overall level of European prosperity and the degree to which key sectors (information technology, aerospace, automobiles) become more competitive as a result of integration and scale economies arising out of the Single Market. In any event, the Community is likely to continue an active research and technology program.

---

[5]In response to public and parliamentary criticism of the EMU agreement, Chancellor Kohl has promised the Bundestag an opportunity to approve bringing the deutschemark into the single currency before the decision is implemented. Although the Bundestag vote will not be legally binding on the Chancellor, the agreement de facto reserves for Germany rights that the Treaty formally grants only to the United Kingdom and Denmark.

The strategies of Europe's principal technology competitors, the United States and Japan, will have a major impact not only on European industrial policy but also on the openness of Europe's market. The indicators are not all sunny. The recent extension of voluntary restraints on Japanese automobiles and conflicts with the United States over Airbus, agricultural subsidies, banking services, and broadcast programming show that the instinct for protection is ingrained. A world of three competing but somewhat insulated trading blocs is not inconceivable, as the EC expands and the North American Free Trade Agreement (NAFTA) is completed. The size of the growing European economic sphere will tempt some to close the barn door. But key countries remain committed to relatively free trade (Germany, the United Kingdom, and the Netherlands), suggesting that the more dire fears of a Fortress Europe are misplaced.[6] The EC is heavily dependent on the multilateral trading system (in 1989, 19.5 percent of its external trade was from imports and exports, compared with 16 percent in the U.S. and 17 percent in Japan) and stands to lose much if it becomes less open.[7]

Agriculture is another, and important, matter. Since the status quo already features massive subsidies and strong elements of protectionism, the EC will have to reach some consensus to produce reform in favor of freer trade. But even here the prospects are somewhat promising. The proposed CAP reform announced in May of 1992 and the tentative agreement on agricultural subsidies in November, in response to both the rising cost of CAP and international pressures arising from the GATT Uruguay round, represent a clear, although not complete, step toward freer trade in agriculture. Enlargement on the whole will produce an additional impetus to reform since, without changes in the CAP, new members could dramatically swell CAP's cost. There will be some countervailing pressures from the likely new members to retain elements of protection since many of these nations now have highly protected agricultural sectors, but the overall direction of developments seems modestly hopeful.

---

[6]A recent GATT report on EC compliance found a number of continued problems, particularly in the use of bilateral trade arrangements, but concluded that claims of a Fortress Europe were unfounded. It warned, however, that EC institutions may lack the authority to resist national pressures for protectionism in key sectors. *Economist,* June 8, 1991, p. 20.

[7]According to a study by the Bank of England based on 1988 data, the EC has the largest share of the world's non-intra-bloc trade (24.3 percent compared with 22.9 percent for East Asia and 16.1 percent for the United States). *The Times*, August 20, 1990.

The Social Market will prove more difficult to achieve. Deep national differences in political philosophy and continued economic discrepancies will make it difficult to impose anything more than highest common factor regulations even among the 11 countries that signed the social policy agreement. Workers' protection is more likely to come about through national political forces, as rising standards of living in most of the poorer countries lead naturally to improved social welfare schemes. Increased labor mobility will accelerate this process, although linguistic and cultural considerations will assure that the European labor market remains more fragmented than the business sectors.

6. The EC will expand its ties with Japan, but these will remain overshadowed by the U.S.-European relationship. Over the years the EC has maintained a mostly one-dimensional relationship with Japan, centered on economic ties and competition. Unlike the U.S.-EC relationship, where common cultural ties and shared security interests help smooth out trade and economic friction, the EC-Japan relationship has been infected with suspicion and mistrust.[8] The EC-Japan agenda was dominated by trade disputes, ranging from EC complaints over lack of access to the Japanese market to concerns about EC barriers to Japanese products (designed to protect against the perceived Japanese threat to European manufacturing and high technology). Japan's trade surplus with the EC, which eased in the late 1980s, widened again in the early 1990s, primarily as a result of declining EC exports to Japan.[9] In addition, some Europeans began to worry that, as the United States toughened its trade stance toward Japan, Japan would turn its attention to the European market. This fear was reinforced by bilateral U.S.-Japan agreements, which Europeans felt could harm EC-Japan trade.[10]

More recently, EC-Japan ties have deepened. In 1991, the EC and Japan issued a Joint Declaration, modeled to some extent on the U.S.-

---

[8]The EC's Ambassador to Japan characterized the EC-Japanese relationship as "inadequate, distant, even indifferent" on the eve of Jacques Delors's May 1991 visit to Tokyo. *Economist*, May 25, 1991, p. 41.

[9] The EC's trade deficit reached $16.3 billion in fiscal year 1990. This was partially offset by Europe's surplus in services (approximately $10 billion) for a current account deficit of $6.2 billion. Commission of the European Communities, "A Consistent and Global Approach: A Review of the Community's Relations with Japan," (Communication to the Council) Com (92)219 final, Brussels, May 21, 1992 (mimeo), p. 4.

[10]The EC has expressed particular concern about U.S.-Japan agreements on semiconductors and auto parts. "This trend is unacceptable in the context of the new relationship symbolized by the Hague Declaration, as it leads to discrimination between trading partners and the distortion of trade." See ibid., p. 9.

EC Declaration of November 1990, which introduced a previously lacking political and foreign policy dimension to the bilateral relationship. In a follow-up report, the Commission called for a "strengthened political dialogue, which must show a qualitative difference from the arrangements currently in force." The Commission suggested that the new dialogue embrace foreign policy, science and technology, social affairs, the environment, and development assistance.[11] Some firms began to nurture cooperative industrial links, such as the strategic alliance between Daimler-Benz and Mitsubishi.

Despite these improvements, the relationship remains troubled. Disputes over automobiles (temporarily quieted by voluntary Japanese export restraints)[12] and electronics are likely to continue in the future.[13] Although some EC countries (notably Britain) have welcomed Japanese investment for its job-creating potential, others, especially France, have worried that Japan intends to dominate or even destroy Europe's high-technology industry.[14] Some have even advocated a U.S.-EC alliance to counter the Japanese threat.[15] Although Japan is taking an increased interest in European security matters (recently Japan became an observer in the CSCE), the strategic links between Europe and Japan remain weak and certainly do not threaten to rival the importance of the U.S.-EC (or, for that matter, the U.S.-Japan) relationship.

7. *A truly "communitarian" foreign and security policy and a defense role for the Community remain a highly uncertain prospect.* The Community's future involvement in foreign and security policy was

---

[11]Ibid., p. 3.

[12]*Financial Times*, April 24, 1992, p. 6; *Wall Street Journal*, April 27, 1992, p. 13.

[13]Bruce Stokes, "Staking Out Europe," *National Journal*, May 25, 1991, pp. 1224–1227.

[14]According to Alain Gomez, CEO of France's preeminent electronics firm, Thomson: "Without radical change, Japanese pressure will prove fatal in the fields of computers, televisions, and semiconductors, well before the end of the decade. The only good solution is to turn Europe into a protected area . . . [t]o make up for the undue advantage the Japanese have acquired through their thirty years of unfair practices." *Le Monde*, April 20, 1991, p. 28. This sentiment found a powerful champion in former French Prime Minister Edith Cresson, whose tenure was characterized by repeated attacks on Japanese business practices and intentions.

[15]See, e.g., Henri Conze, "Prospects for Armament Industry," Paris, August 22, 1990, p. 9 (mimeo): "facing the Japanese techno-nationalism, in certain strategic sectors, only a common approach between Europe and the United States, based on the existence of two comparable markets, will enable us to save an independent technological and industrial capacity." Former Head of the German Foreign Ministry's Planning staff, Konrad Seitz, has echoed similar fears about Japanese domination.

one of the most hotly contested issues at Maastricht. In the end, both sides claimed victory. Those who advocated a stronger Community role point to several features in support of their success: the decision to adopt CFSP, the Community's acceptance that CFSP "shall include the eventual framing of a common defence policy," language linking the EC and WEU and establishing an independent WEU planning staff, and the offer of WEU membership to all EC states. Those who opposed a stronger Community role noted that Maastricht granted extremely limited majority voting under CFSP and deferred the issue of a "common defence" to the future. They also pointed to the agreement to continue the WEU's ties to NATO.

The ambiguity of Maastricht's language reflected underlying uncertainties about the Community's future role. The Yugoslavia crisis played an important part in underscoring the two sides' differing perspectives. For those in favor of a more integrated approach to security policy, the limitations in the EC's response to Yugoslavia proved the need to strengthen the Community's foreign policy and defense capabilities. For those opposed, the Yugoslavia experience demonstrated the improbability of reconciling diverse views among Community members into a single, effective policy.

Whether a Community approach to foreign and security policy (including defense) emerges will depend largely on whether the underlying strategic interests among Community members converge. Yugoslavia has already demonstrated that, even in "European" foreign policy, there are differences in approach (Germany's more supportive attitude toward Slovenia and Croatia's independence; France and Spain's inclination to try to preserve the Yugoslav federation). More broadly, there is reason to believe that Germany may follow its own course in dealing with Eastern Europe; geographical proximity, historical ties, and growing economic involvement will all give Germany a different "take" on Eastern Europe. Equally important are potential divergences on the former Soviet Union: to date the major European powers have all followed a similar tack, but Germany's complex relationship with Russia is unique.

For out-of-area foreign policy challenges, the Gulf War experience shows some of the limits of foreign policy cooperation—the EC showed a greater ability to achieve consensus on economic measures (sanctions and embargoes) and greater diversity on the more complex and nuanced aspects of diplomacy (witness the French peace proposal). In any event, the decision to follow the agreed "common" foreign and security policy will be voluntary; there is little prospect of sanctions to enforce compliance.

Defense is the most problematic element of integration. Despite France's strong push for a European defense identity, there is little concrete indication of how France sees defense cooperation in practice. The proposed Franco-German Corps could represent a real commitment to defense integration or, like its predecessor the Franco-German brigade, merely a political symbol. It seems fair to question how far France is willing to subordinate its hard won independence in defense in favor of greater common action.[16]

Germany's attitude will prove critical. As Germany's policy became more "normal" and the reassuring bond of NATO military integration becomes more attenuated, two choices will emerge—a more independent Bundeswehr or new links with other European countries. If the Russian threat revives, Germany may seek assurances from its neighbors through a European security identity. But if the climate is more benign and France and the United Kingdom continue to insist on their independence in matters of defense (including nuclear policy), Germany could decide to develop its own more independent capabilities for national defense and even power projection. Yet it is the very prospect of German independence that may lead France, in particular, to do what it has thus far been unwilling to do—share decisionmaking with Germany and its other neighbors on defense. This grand bargain is possible, but serious obstacles lie in its path.

Ironically, the end of the Cold War, which helped bring the issue of European defense integration to the fore (by raising the specter of U.S. withdrawal from Europe), may also prove the effort's undoing. Just what are Europeans going to do with a European security identity? This will of course depend on the nature of security challenges in the future. But it is unlikely that the Europeans will be

---

[16]For example, in 1990 French Foreign Minister Dumas observed: "our doctrine of (nuclear) dissuasion could not easily be adapted to collective decisionmaking." *Financial Times,* December 15, 1990. But more recently Defense Minister Joxe suggested that, in the context of European integration, France could already envisage consultation on the multilateral use of nuclear weapons and the expansion of the French nuclear guarantee. "Statement of the Defense Minister at the Opening of the Colloquium," A New Strategic Debate, September 29, 1992 (mimeo). The temptation to maintain France's independence is strong; President Mitterrand observed: "As far as concerns the permanent seat that France has on the Security Council—that is not up for discussion. It surprises me that some take as their point of departure that France should give up this seat. There cannot of course be any suggestion of that." *NRC Handelsblad,* March 4, 1991 (FBIS WEU-91-047, March 11, 1991, p. 15).

prepared politically or militarily to confront a revived Russian military challenge on their own. This could either lead to Europeans seeking renewed U.S. involvement or possibly result in acrimonious divisions within the EC if some Europeans prefer to compromise with a strong, potentially aggressive neighbor to the East.

As for instability in Eastern or Southeastern Europe, the European response to Yugoslavia's civil war demonstrates that Europe is likely to have little taste for military intervention (other than for peacekeeping/observers).

Out-of-Europe threats that would require a military response seem even less amenable to collective European action. The Gulf crisis is a rare example of unanimity of views, yet even there, many European nations were reluctant to commit military forces. Problems in North Africa and the Middle East could well arise, but the Mediterranean states of Europe may not share the same approach as nations more removed from the conflict.

Europeans are likely to move toward a more integrated approach to defense acquisition as a result both of industry's trend toward intra-European consolidation and government efforts to promote collaboration and common procurement procedures. The decision to explore folding the Independent European Program Group (IEPG) into the WEU is a step in that direction. But national preference will remain, especially for the larger states, which view a measure of national self-sufficiency as necessary on the grounds of national security and technological competitiveness.

For the future of a European defense policy, the timing and scope of enlargement may hold the key. Unless the Community can generate greater consensus on enhancing the Community's security role in the near future, the task will be much more daunting in a larger, more diverse Community. But the ultimate outcome of this debate will turn on factors external to the Community, including the pace and extent of U.S. military withdrawal from Europe, the scale of instability in the countries of the former Warsaw Pact, the Balkans and the Mahgreb/Middle East, and pressures on European defense budgets. Internal factors too will be important: Germany's willingness to play a larger global role (including the use of Bundeswehr forces under a European/WEU flag), France's willingness to subordinate its traditionally independent security policy (including perhaps its nuclear deterrent) to collective European decisionmaking, and the United Kingdom's willingness to re-orient its strategic posture away from its ties to the United States and toward its European partners. The future is too uncertain to prognosticate with any certainty, but it is fair to say that Maastricht did not finally resolve the issue. The WEU's agreement in June 1992 to begin to create a European operational capability seems promising on paper but has yet to be tested in any significant way.

8. *Equity issues between richer and poorer EC states are likely to plague Community consensus.* Despite the relatively faster growth of most of the Community's less affluent members in recent years, there remains a substantial gap between the haves and the have-nots (Spain, Portugal, Greece, Ireland). Present economic trends do not suggest that this disparity will close dramatically in the near future. Implementing EMU could harden the line between the two groups: either they will become members of the system, subject to the ECB's stringently anti-inflationary policy and Community fiscal discipline (which will impede their ability to use macroeconomic policy to stimulate growth) or they will be left out of EMU altogether. At Maastricht, the Community refused to accept Spain's proposal for an automatic compensation mechanism (transferring resources from richer to poorer countries). The leaders did agree to provide assistance to the poorer countries for transportation improvements and environmental costs, but the larger Community states rejected President Delors's call for expanding the share of Community GDP available for common action. The cohesion issue was one of the most contentious problems in the run-up to the December 1992 Edinburgh summit.

The prospect that the EFTA countries may soon join the Community will have a mixed impact. On the one hand, this will mean several more relatively affluent members to help share the financial burden of helping less developed countries; on the other, the political and economic outlook of these likely new members will mirror most closely the concerns and objectives of the EC's more developed nations, rather than creating new supporters within the Community for redistributive measures. Further down the road, adding the Central East European states, the Baltic nations, republics of the former Yugoslavia, or (much less likely) Turkey and the former Soviet republics would help shift the balance back.

9. *There is a growing tendency toward a "multiple-speed" Europe.* The Maastricht agreement contains three decisions, which, taken together, suggest that EC leaders are willing to contemplate a "multiple-speed" Europe; that is, varying membership for different Community activities. For EMU, only those states that meet the convergence criteria will be eligible for membership: under the scheme adopted at Maastricht, as few as two countries could go

forward with EMU. On "social" policy (employment and workers' rights), rather than accept a British veto, the other 11 countries agreed to go forward on their own. Finally, on defense, the Community leaders decided to establish a link between the EC and the WEU, even though two EC members (Ireland and Denmark) have thus far opted not to join the WEU.

This is not the first time that a subset of the EC membership has agreed to work together without the full participation of all EC countries. The Schengen Agreement on eliminating border controls began with only five EC states (France, Germany, and the Benelux countries) and now extends to nine (with the addition of Italy, Spain, Portugal, and Greece). But the Community has long resisted codifying the idea of "variable geometry," a barrier that was clearly broken at Maastricht. If the rest of the Community ratifies Maastricht and Denmark continues to balk, a grand two-speed Europe might result—the Twelve of the Rome Treaty and the Eleven of Maastricht. The Edinburgh solution, a broad set of "opt-outs" for Denmark, is less dramatic but reinforces the sense of an "à la carte" approach to membership in the Community. The breakdown of the ERM in the run-up to the French referendum has strengthened calls for a two-speed approach, although EC Finance Ministers formally rejected that proposal.[17]

Embracing the concept of variable geometry has important consequences for the process of enlargement. In particular, it suggests that the Community might be prepared to accept new members without requiring them to participate fully in all aspects of security and defense policy. Some in France now speak of a "hard core" ("noyau dur") of EC members (embracing at a minimum, France, Germany, Italy, and the Benelux states, with the possible addition of Spain and Portugal) that would participate in all facets of Community activities, with other members joining or not, as they so choose. This would allow the most committed integrationist nations to proceed with deepening the Community, but it also risks weakening the Community's cohesion.

10. The process of integration is threatened by deep public dissatisfaction with mainstream European political parties. During the Maastricht ratification debate, virtually all major political parties supported the Treaty (albeit with reservations), but that support has had little impact in generating popular enthusiasm. This phenomenon was especially striking during the Danish ratification

[17] *Los Angeles Times,* September 27, 1992, p. D1.

campaign, when political leaders across the often divisive Danish political spectrum united behind the Treaty but failed to persuade a skeptical public.

More generally, mainstream political leaders throughout Europe supported the Treaty. In France, the leaders of the three main parties, Socialist, UDF, and RPR, supported ratification, leaving opposition to party dissidents (Chevènement among the Socialists, Seguin and others for the RPR) and the far right and left. In the United Kingdom, John Major held fast for ratification, and newly elected opposition leader John Smith put down a revolt in his own party. Yet throughout Europe, the public remained unconvinced. If anything, political leaders' support for the Treaty has increased anti-Treaty sentiment, as opponents successfully harnessed public dissatisfaction with incumbents and other traditional politicians to the cause of "no." This was particularly evident in France, where anti-Mitterrand and anti-Socialist feelings swelled the number of Treaty opponents.

This revolt against the leaders was but one manifestation of growing popular disenchantment with mainstream parties that goes beyond merely rejecting the party in power. In Germany, fringe parties, rather than the opposition SDP have benefitted from declining support for Chancellor Kohl. Similarly, in France, it is the National Front and the ecologist parties that profit from the Socialist's political collapse to a much greater extent than the traditional center-right opposition. In Italy, disgust with politics as usual is fueling support for regional parties such as the Lombard League and anti-political movements such as Mario Segni's crusade for electoral reform and the Sicily-based La Rete (the Network).

While there is considerable diversity among these non-mainstream parties, many share a nationalist orientation and a suspicion of government sturctures. This orientation ties in with anti-centralist, anti-Brussels sentiments and is especially resistant to the "top down" construction of Europe that has typically characterized the path of European integration since the days of Schuman, Adenauer, and Monnet. Although, as we will see below, there remains considerable public support for the idea of Europe, there is growing resistance to the idea of a politician's Europe. This makes the task of integration more difficult, since national and Community leaders will have to re-establish public confidence in the integration process and in the responsiveness of the Community's institutions if integration is to move forward in the future.

11. *The nation-state still retains considerable vitality in Europe.* One of the most important subtexts underlying the negotiations leading up to Maastricht was the future of the nation-state. The cause of the deepeners was, at one level, an effort to transform the nation from the preeminent political actor on the international stage to one among many political jurisdictions (Community, nation, region, municipality). This effort found its greatest expression in support for a proposed "tree" structure for Community decisionmaking: a single Treaty structure for all aspects of Community decisionmaking that would move toward stronger communitarian institutions and expanded majority voting. Symbolically, the debate turned on whether the EC leaders would accept, in Treaty language, the idea of a "federal goal" for the Community.

The defenders of the nation-state preferred the "pillars" approach, which would preserve the intergovernmental character of many important (primarily non-economic) decisions. Their rallying cry was "subsidiarity": leaving decisionmaking at the lowest practical level, which meant, for the most part, at the level of the nation.

On the rhetorical level, the defenders of the nation-state prevailed: the EC leaders dropped the proposal to include explicit reference to a "federal goal" in favor of the more ambiguous "new stage in the Process creating an ever closer union among the peoples of Europe." The Treaty explicitly agreed to "respect the principle of subsidiarity," defined as permitting Community action "only if, and insofar as, these objectives can be better achieved by the Community than by the Member States acting separately." The pillar approach predominated.

Events since the Treaty's signing have only served to confirm the strong attraction of the nation and the mistrust of the more distant Brussels. Although the French and Danish opponents of the Treaty wove together many strands of disaffection, their appeal contained a strong element of anti-centralism, a sentiment found throughout the Community states. The effort to save Maastricht is now centering in part around giving practical content and credibility to subsidiarity as a constraint on centralization.

The dream of a "unitary" Community thus seems remote: governments will seek to preserve significant national control over sensitive areas of foreign and security policy, police, and legal systems while ceding more in economic affairs. Greater convergence is likely on immigration; continued policy divergence seems untenable in the longer run. Radical reform is even more remote; there seems little prospect of an elected President of Europe or full legislative empowerment of the European Parliament. Absent greater homogenization on the human level, there is simply too much diversity to permit a truly "European" government to emerge. The Community will remain, as most accept, a unique form of government, blending nation-states and common decisionmaking features.

In the future, the role of the nation-state compared with the Community will turn on both the process of enlargement and the degree to which European publics begin to look to Brussels, rather than their national capitals, as the locus of decisionmaking. Prior to Maastricht, surveys by *Eurobarometer* for the European Commission showed growing support for the Community and the process of integration. That support slipped after Maastricht.[18] In March 1992, the survey found that 30 percent of all EC residents were "very much for" efforts to unify Western Europe, down from 33 percent in October 1991, while another 46 percent were "for—to some extent," unchanged from October 1991. Sixty-five percent believed that membership in the EC "was a good thing"—down 4 percent from October 1991. Fifty-three percent believed that their country has benefitted from EC membership, also down slightly from October 1991.[19]

Although many Europeans (49 percent) often, or sometimes, think of themselves as "European" (as well as Belgian, Danish, etc.), an equal number (48 percent) "never" do. Not surprisingly, the highest number of those who "never" think of themselves as European are in the United Kingdom (69 percent) and Ireland (64 percent). They are followed by the Netherlands (60 percent), Denmark (53 percent), and

---

[18]The post-Maastricht survey was conducted between March 17 and April 10, 1992, published as *Eurobarometer No. 37* (Commission of the European Communities, June 1992). The pre-Maastricht survey was conducted between October 15 and November 21, 1991, published as *Eurobarometer No. 36* (Commission of the European Communities, December 1991). Historical trends can be found in a companion volume, *Eurobarometer Trends 1974–1990* (Commission of the European Communities, March 1991).

[19]The Portuguese (82 percent) and the Irish (81 percent) expressed the greatest sense of benefit from Community membership; followed by the Netherlands and Greece (73 percent), Luxembourg (72 percent), and Denmark (67 percent). In France, 50 percent, and in Germany, 48 percent, felt their country has benefitted from Community membership; the United Kingdom (45 percent) and Spain (44 percent) shared the least sense of benefit. The figure for Spain represents an 11 percent drop post-Maastricht.

Germany (51 percent).[20] The most "European" are in Greece, Luxembourg, and Spain (61 percent think of themselves as European often, or sometimes).

Initially, Maastricht had little impact on support for EMU and a Community role in foreign and defense policy; but over time, impelled by the Danish vote, support appeared to be deteriorating dramatically. Popular support for integration will almost surely rebound as the focus moves away from ratifying the Maastricht Treaty; the idea of Europe is stronger than its specific embodiment. But this debate demonstrated the fragility and volatility of support for specific European initiatives. In the immediate aftermath of Maastricht, there was widespread support for most aspects of the proposed EMU and EPU. 54 percent favored a single currency, and 55 percent favored a single Central Bank.[21] 55 percent wanted to see the EC responsible for foreign policy, and 65 percent favored EC responsibility for a common policy in security and defense, while 17 percent opposed.[22]

THE COMMUNITY IN THE YEAR 2000

Thus a portrait of the Community at 2000: larger by two to five states; more integrated in its economic activities, with some (but not all) countries sharing a single currency; more institutionalized foreign policy cooperation but retaining a strong intergovernmental flavor;

[20]The figure for Germany is affected to some extent by including residents of the former GDR (58 percent never thought of themselves as European); the comparable figure for West Germany is 49 percent. These figures are from the October 1991 survey. In the spring of 1992, the Commission changed the question, asking about the "near future" rather than the present; this formulation resulted in 38 percent saying they saw themselves as their nationality only, 48 percent nationality and European, 7 percent European and nationality, and 4 percent European only.

[21]Denmark and the United Kingdom were the only countries where less than a plurality favored a single currency. Greatest support for the single currency was found in Italy (69 percent), France (64 percent), and Belgium (62 percent); 45 percent of all Germans favored a single currency (43 percent of West Germans).

[22]In Denmark (34 percent), the UK (42 percent), and Ireland (43 percent), less than a majority favored a foreign policy role for the EC; a majority in all other states favored it. Similarly, only 33 percent in Denmark and 49 percent in Ireland favored a security/defense role. U.K. attitudes on a security/defense role for the EC changed dramatically between autumn 1990 and autumn 1991 (before and after the Gulf War). Before the war, 56 percent favored a security/defense role; by spring, support had dropped to 33 percent; in the autumn it was back to 50 percent. Greatest support for an EC defense role was found in the Netherlands (76 percent), Italy (75 percent), and Belgium (70 percent), followed by Germany (67 percent), France and Spain (66 percent), Greece and Luxembourg (65 percent).

and still flirting with, but not acting on, real defense integration. In other words, a Community that continues to follow the course of its first 40 years, ever closer, but not union.

9. IMPLICATIONS FOR U.S.-EC RELATIONS

ECONOMIC IMPLICATIONS

If, as this Report suggests, Europe's future is toward only modest integration over the next decade, the course of U.S.-European relations is likely to change, but not radically. Overall, there will be shifts in the balance of power as Europe comes to speak somewhat more frequently with one voice in economic and political affairs. Yet the prospects for generally positive relations remain good.

U.S.-European economic relations are central to the economic prosperity of both the United States and the EC nations. Taken as a whole, the EC is the United States' largest trade partner, with both imports and exports approaching $100 billion a year, 21 percent of total U.S. trade (24 percent of exports, 18 percent of imports).[1] Europe is also a key partner in the international financial system, through institutions such as the G-7, the IMF, and the World Bank.

European integration will have significant consequences for the evolution of this relationship, although the ultimate direction depends on a number of other factors, including the overall world economic situation and unpredictable economic events (such as the possibility of a new energy crisis brought on by events in the Middle East). Three broad conclusions stand out.

1. *U.S. leverage over European economic policy decisions will decline, especially in macroeconomic policy if the EC actually moves to EMU.*

One of the more significant changes will come in macroeconomic relations. EMU would increase Europe's clout on the international stage. The ecu will become one of the (if not the) world's leading reserve currencies,[2] the G-7 would de facto become the

---

[1]According to the U.S. International Trade Commission, U.S. exports to the EC-12 countries in 1991 amounted to $97.6 billion, ahead of Canada ($78.7 billion), and Japan ($46.1 billion). For imports, the EC ranked third ($85.1 billion) behind Canada ($90.9 billion), and Japan ($90.5 billion). *U.S.I.T.C. Fourth Follow-Up Report*, pp. 1–7, 8.

[2]Today the ecu, although nominally only an accounting unit, is already the world's third largest reserve currency (behind the dollar and the deutschemark). As of 1991, the combined ERM currencies (including the ecu) account for 37 percent of all foreign exchange reserves (compared with 51 percent for the dollar). Forty-six percent of international bonds were denominated in ERM currencies (v. 37 percent dollar denominated).

G-4,[3] and the United States would almost certainly lose some of its already waning influence over European monetary policy, as the need to achieve internal consensus among the EC members makes it harder for the EC to thereafter modify course in response to the urgings of Europe's trading partners.[4] As the European economy grows and diversifies, it will be less influenced by U.S. economic conditions, and therefore there is a growing risk of divergent economic policy interests.[5] The current dispute between the United States and Germany over Germany's high interest rates (driven by the Bundesbank's desire to prevent inflation from German deficit spending on reconstructing the East) could be an unhappy model for the future. Political pressures within the Community may take some of the edge off the Bundesbank's current highly conservative approach; however, to date at least that impact has been modest.

But there are corresponding advantages for the United States. David Mulford, U.S. Treasury Under Secretary has observed: "Having only three main currencies . . . the yen, the dollar, and the ecu . . . could allow progress towards improving the world monetary system. The simplicity of one European currency would give us a chance to strengthen policy coordination and discipline."[6] Over time, EMU could lead to broader arrangements to coordinate monetary policies (perhaps to include mechanisms to regulate exchange rate fluctuations) among the three principal global currencies. The

---

[3]From the perspective of the smaller EC states, the G-7 ought to become the G-4 *de jure,* with Europe represented by Commission and/or the EC Presidency (the President of the EC Commission already attends G-7 meetings in addition to the French, German, Italian, and British heads of government). According to Dutch Minister Van den Broek, "an EC Economic and Monetary Union is not possible unless the same member countries that now continue to participate in the economic G-7 relinquish their place to the Community." *NRC Handelsblad,* June 12, 1990 (FBIS-WEU-90-140, July 20, 1990, p. 2). Similar issues will arise with respect to multilateral financial institutions, such as IMF and the World Bank, although technically membership in these organizations is open only to "countries." This could lead to a dramatic development: a single EC membership would give the Community the largest stake in the IMF and World Bank. (The EC accounts for 29.1 percent of the IMF quotas; the United States and Japan combined account for 24.2 percent.) By their own rules, the two organizations would then be required to transfer their headquarters to Europe. *Financial Times,* January 21, 1991, p. 15.

[4]To the extent that an independent European Central Bank follows a policy strictly tied to price stability, the United States will have even less opportunity to influence European macroeconomic policy.

[5]See, e.g., "American Economy Now Has Less Impact Abroad, Foreigners Say," *Wall Street Journal,* November 7, 1990, p. A1.

[6]*Economist,* July 7, 1990, p. 25. Indeed, some, such as Jeffrey E. Garten, Managing Director of the Blackstone Group, have argued that such policy coordination will become even more necessary in a world with rival reserve currencies to the dollar. See Bruce Stokes, "Fading Greenback," *National Journal,* December 14, 1991, p. 3015.

efficacy of that coordination may depend on how much consensus there is behind a primary policy goal—price stability—particularly if the European Central Bank achieves real independence.[7]

2. *Europe will not become broadly protectionist, but serious disputes will develop or continue in a number of key sectors.*

The Single Market Program will have a mixed impact on the United States and on U.S. firms. On the one hand, the completed market will be more accessible to U.S. exporters, who will no longer have to deal with a bewildering array of differing national standards and regulations. This will prove an even greater benefit to U.S. firms operating in Europe (so long as they meet EC tests for local content).[8] Moreover, to the extent that EC 1992 enhances European growth, European demand for U.S. imports may increase. On the other hand, increased European efficiency from the Single Market Program could generate new competition for U.S. firms, both in the European market and for exports. There is a lively debate over whether the main impact of 1992 is trade diversion at the expense of non-EC producers or trade creation, which will benefit producers both within and outside the EC.[9]

---

[7]There are some potential direct costs and benefits to the United States and U.S. firms from EMU. For example, the reduced use of the dollar in favor of the ecu could lead to a loss of seigniorage and higher U.S. debt service costs. EC economists estimate the EC seigniorage gain from EMU at $35 billion and $200 billion from reduced reserve holdings. *The ECU Report,* pp. 119, 124. It could also lead to a slightly devalued dollar, which could improve U.S. competitiveness but risk higher inflation in the form of higher import costs. While U.S. firms trading with or doing business in Europe will experience gains from reduced currency risks and transactions costs, U.S. financial firms that derive revenues from exchange operations will lose profitable operations. Increased invoicing in ecus could also impose costs on U.S. firms. See *U.S.I.T.C. Fourth Follow-Up Report,* pp. 4–8, and sources cited therein. A devalued dollar could increase European pressures for protectionism. See Richard N. Cooper, "Will An EC Currency Harm Outsiders?" *Orbis,* Fall 1992, pp. 517–528. On balance Cooper concluded that the risk of EMU to other nations such as the United States is greater during the transition than a "settled" EMU.

[8]See Stephen Woolcock, "U.S. Views on 1992," *National Institute Economic Review,* Vol. 134, November 1990, pp. 86–92. As a general rule, the EC accepts the GATT definition of country of origin: the place where the "last substantial transformation" takes place. But for many items, such as radios, televisions, ball bearings, and semiconductors, the EC has added special restrictions that make it more difficult for products to qualify as EC products for the purpose of tariff-free trade within the Community. There are similar problems in EC definitions of origin and local content for the application of preferential tariff and anti-dumping rules.

[9]One study has found that the Single Market Program would lead to a short-term decline of 2.4 percent in U.S. exports to the EC, but in the longer term, EC growth would also lead to increased trade with the United States. On the whole, the study found that EC-1992 was unlikely to have a major impact on aggregate U.S. employment, although individual sectors could experience a greater impact. R. Shelburne and G. Schoepfle, "The European Community 1992 Program and U.S.

Common EC standards could still result in excluding U.S. products: the recent controversy over hormone-fed beef is a case in point.[10] On the whole, standard setting in the Community should not prove a major problem, since the Community has adopted mutual recognition as a general principle. But questions remain whether Europeans will accept U.S. health and safety certification on the basis of mutual recognition.[11]

Mutual recognition rules have caused particular problems in the banking and financial services sector.[12] The U.S.-European dispute was partially resolved when the EC agreed to accept "national treatment" (EC banks would be treated the same as U.S. banks in the United States and vice versa). But the EC insisted that the United States guarantee "effective access" under the regime, opening the door for future disputes over whether EC banks were receiving their fair share of the U.S. market. There is a danger that requiring guarantees of effective access in this and other sectors could be the first step toward a regime of sector-by-sector managed trade, a risk that could grow if the current Uruguay round fails.[13]

Workers," *Monthly Labor Review* (November 1990), reported in *U.S.I.T.C. Fourth Follow-Up Report,* p. 2–4.

[10]Prior to adopting a Community-wide standard barring imports of hormone-treated meat (effective July 1, 1989), each EC nation had its own rules, which allowed access of BGH-fed beef to some markets.

[11]Thus, for example, the United States argues that the EC should accept U.S.D.A. inspections under the principle of "equivalency"—that U.S. procedures, while differing in detail from EC-prescribed inspections, produce equivalent degrees of safety. To date, the system used by the EC in effect requires that each individual U.S. plant pass muster before the EC will accept its products.

The U.S. Chamber of Commerce has identified a number of additional concerns in the area of standards, testing, and certification, including the possibility that EC standards will discriminate against non-EC products, that delays in informing non-EC nationals about new or proposed EC standards will put them at a disadvantage in product development, and that foreign products will not have the same access to EC testing labs as their EC counterparts. U.S. Chamber of Commerce, *Europe 1992: A Practical Guide for U.S. Business,* November 1991. For a detailed discussion of standards issues and their implications for the United States, see *U.S.I.T.C. Fourth Follow-Up Report,* Ch. 5.

[12]The EC initially sought "mutual reciprocity" with the United States (banks licensed to operate in the EC would be allowed to offer their services anywhere in the United States in return for allowing U.S. banks to operate in the unified EC market). But the United States objected that this would result in the EC banks receiving more favorable treatment in the United States than U.S. banks themselves, which have to meet diverse state regulations to operate in the various states.

[13]This approach departs from the basic GATT norm, which calls for "overall reciprocity" in liberalizing trade relations. On the banking and securities sectors generally, see Carter H. Golembe and David S. Holland, "Banking and Securities," in *Europe 1992,* Ch. 2; and Stephen Woolcock, *Trading Partners or Trading Blows: Market Access in EC-U.S. Relations* (New York: Council on Foreign Relations Press,

The mix of benefits and costs to the United States from the Single Market would change if Europe responded to an enlarged barrier-free European trade zone by increasing barriers against external imports (higher tariffs, decreased quotas, and non-tariff barriers). As the Single Market undermines existing national quotas and other trade barriers, there is a risk that they will be transferred to the Community level. Some analysts have seen the EC's increased use of anti-dumping remedies as a sign of growing non-tariff barriers, although the EC in turn complains that U.S. firms are using anti-dumping and countervailing duty actions to harass European producers.[14] New barriers could also be erected to protect sensitive industries: some Europeans have already called for higher tariffs on computer chips and consumer electronics. The decision to extend voluntary restraints on Japanese cars, in effect transferring national quotas to the Community level, shows that Europe is not immune to protectionist sentiment in the post-1992 environment.

To the extent that the Community moves toward a more activist industrial policy (including support for research and development), the sentiment for protection may grow. The EC and member-states are not likely to make major investments in Community-wide research and development only to see those firms eliminated by foreign competition. The determined European defense of its support for Airbus is a clear case in point, although the recent U.S.-European agreement is evidence that the two sides can make progress even on difficult, high-visibility disputes. The United States has also complained that the EC's regional assistance program represents an unfair subsidy to European firms.

Public procurement is another area of likely conflict. The new EC directive on public procurement in the GATT-excepted sectors (water, energy, transportation, and telecommunications) explicitly permits discrimination against non-EC bidders. Agriculture, too, will remain a problem, not only in the broad controversy over reforming CAP but also in the periodic flare-up of commodity-specific disputes, such as the U.S. threat to impose retaliatory tariffs under Section 301 of the

1992), Chs. 3 and 4. The problem of different treatment in the United States and the EC could lessen over time as a result of regulatory convergence.

[14]See "Andriessen Claims U.S. Harassment of Normal Trade Flow in Steel," *European Community News,* No. 24/92, July 1, 1992.

U.S. Trade Act against EC products as compensation for GATT-violative oilseed subsidies.[15]

But as the preceding section indicates, Europe has much to lose from protectionism, and on the whole, a Fortress Europe is unlikely to develop.

3. *European growth, spurred on by the Single Market and EMU, will produce conflicts with the United States over interest and exchange rates and access to capital.*

In recent years, there has been a marked movement of foreign investment away from the United States and toward Europe. In 1987, U.S. securities accounted for 51 percent of all Japanese purchases of foreign securities, the EC only 42 percent. By 1990, this relationship had dramatically reversed: 61 percent of Japanese investments were in the EC, 16 percent in U.S. securities. In 1990, for the first time in over a decade, total foreign direct investment in the EC exceeded such investment in the United States.[16] If, as some believe, European growth outpaces the United States in the coming years (helped by the Single Market Program and EMU), this trend will continue,[17] and at a time when some have raised concerns over a "capital crunch," this could raise the cost of capital to U.S. firms and to the U.S. Treasury for debt financing. Higher interest rates in the United States in turn would lead to an overpriced dollar, harming U.S. exports and raising U.S. unemployment.[18] In addition, as European capital markets grow in importance, the regulatory and policy setting dominance of the United States in this area will continue to decline.

---

[15]*Financial Times,* June 19, 1992, p. 3.

[16]*U.S.I.T.C. Fourth Follow-Up Report,* pp. 1–14.

[17]A DRI/McGraw Hill estimate forecast an annual average increase of 8.3 percent in EC capital demand from 1990–95, which would produce a tripling of Europe's capital demand over the period 1985–95. Bruce Stokes, "Trans-Atlantic Shocks," *National Journal,* April 21, 1990, p. 955. See also, *National Journal,* March 14, 1992, p. 628. Although the EC real GDP grew only by an estimated 1.1 percent in 1992, EC forecasts predict growth of 1.0 to 1.5 percent in 1993. *Süddeutsche Zeitung,* December 3, 1992, p. 25.

[18]See, e.g., *National Journal,* April 21, 1990, p. 952.

But European growth has a positive side (in addition to increasing the potential export market for U.S. goods)[19]—generating additional capital to meet U.S. needs. The EC countries were the largest investors in the United States in 1990, investing some $230 billion (versus $83 billion for Japan), 57 percent of all foreign direct investment in the United States.[20]

FOREIGN POLICY AND SECURITY IMPLICATIONS

Conflicts between the United States and its European allies over Europe's role in foreign and security policy are nothing new. For more than 40 years, the Alliance has engaged in a continuing process of sorting out roles and responsibilities and the sharing of burdens.

The current debate over establishing an EC Common Foreign and Security Policy and a European defense identity marks a new phase in this process. The U.S. administration has broadly accepted the idea of a new security partnership with Europe, with particular focus on U.S.-EC relations.[21] But the devil is in the details.

U.S. policy has focused on six goals in defining the new relationship:

- Maintain NATO's primacy as the forum for discussion and action for matters within the scope of the North Atlantic Treaty;
- Assure the "transparency" of European foreign policy and security deliberations;
- Broaden the NATO mission to include liaison with the former Warsaw Pact countries and the possibility of acting as the peacekeeping arm of the CSCE;
- Strengthen the European pillar of transatlantic security within NATO (and its integrated military structure) for "in-area" actions, but support an independent WEU-based European capability for out-of-area military activities so long as there is no duplication with NATO;
- Continue stationing combat-capable U.S. troops in Europe; and

---

[19]In 1990 and 1991, the United States had a trade surplus with the EC ($2.3 billion in 1990 and $12.5 billion in 1991), fueled by growth in the dollar value of exports and a decline in imports. *U.S.I.T.C. Fourth Follow-Up Report,* pp. 1–7.

[20]The United States in turn invested $173 billion in the EC in 1990, 41 percent of all U.S. direct investment abroad. Ibid.

[21]See the Bush and Baker statements in Section 2, above, and the Transatlantic Declaration.

- Shift financial burdens by expanding aspects of Europe's role in global affairs, with particular emphasis on Eastern Europe and the former Soviet Union.

For most EC members, these objectives are, in principle, consistent with their own concepts of developing a security and foreign policy identity. Even France, which is most zealous in favor of developing a distinctive European defense identity and capability (including in-area activities) as part of completing the European Union and thus opposes expanding NATO's role, accepts the importance of maintaining NATO and a U.S. troop presence in Europe.[22] But the United States continues to fear that moving toward CFSP and a defense role for the EC will lead at a minimum to a "European caucus" within NATO and, at worst, to a loss of the U.S. "seat at the table" and a growing distance between the United States and Europe in foreign and security matters.

Whether these fears will come to fruition will depend on the scope and timing of European foreign policy and defense integration as well as the evolution of European nations' attitudes toward global and regional problems (individually and collectively). The outcome will also depend on the United States' own future foreign policy orientation and objectives. There is a synergy between the two. A more isolationist U.S. policy will generate additional pressure for European integration to fill the vacuum created by a diminished U.S. political and military presence. Conversely, transatlantic frictions that come from the integrative process, especially if integration efforts are seen as hostile to U.S. interests, could drive the United States further toward a unilateralist or isolationist posture.

For the most part, maintaining close ties and a cooperative relationship between the United States and Europe will turn on the continued perception of shared interests and objectives, rather than the organizational structure through which Europe arranges its affairs. Shared interests have knit the Alliance together through difficult times in the past and have helped contain differences in policy approaches. These interests may diverge to a greater extent in the future, now that the central importance of deterring a Soviet attack on Western Europe has disappeared and as new, more diverse security challenges arise. If Europe's future conflicts resemble Yugoslavia and if the United States declares that these conflicts do

---

[22]See Daniel Vernet, "France in a New Europe," *The National Interest,* Fall 1992, pp. 36–37; Philip Gordon, *French Security Policy After the Cold War: Continuity, Change, and Implications for the United States*, RAND, R-4229-A, 1992.

not involve important U.S. national interests, the transatlantic framework will begin to fray. Similarly, if Europe becomes preoccupied with its own problems at the expense of broader global issues, the United States will have less stake in closer collaboration with its European allies. It is difficult to predict whether a more integrated Europe will become more Eurocentric or, as its power grows, whether it will assume greater global responsibilities. The EC has always had a strong interest in North/South issues, but primarily with an economic focus. Whether Europe will develop a stronger interest in non-European security problems is uncertain. But the common commitment to democracy, economic growth, and human rights assures that, on many important international issues, Europe and the United States will see reasonably eye-to-eye.

Yet structures can have some impact. In particular, growing European foreign policy and security integration will have five important consequences.

1. An expanded EC foreign policy and defense role will reduce but not eliminate NATO's importance as a forum for transatlantic dialogue.

The changing nature of European security threats and the diminishing risk of East-West confrontation will, in themselves, lead to a less dominant role for NATO, especially in its military dimension. European integration will contribute to that process. To the extent that the EC successfully moves toward a Common Foreign and Security Policy, the transatlantic dialogue will increasingly involve two rather than 16 actors. The new procedures for EC-U.S. consultation under the Transatlantic Declaration are a step in that direction and will become more central if EPC is further institutionalized in the Maastricht Treaty's framework for CFSP and in a broader, more operational role for the WEU. Europeans will strive to assure that they do not present foreign policy decisions as *faits accomplis* to the United States, but the difficult process of generating consensus within the Community inevitably means that Europeans will need to consult closely and continuously among themselves in a structured process that holds the United States at some distance.

This trend will grow as the Community expands to embrace more non-NATO members and there is less overlap between NATO's European membership and the EC.[23] The NACC, which was designed

---

[23]There is, of course, the prospect of simultaneously expanding NATO's membership. While several East European countries have expressed interest in joining NATO, the neutral EFTA countries are less likely to follow this course.

to enhance NATO's relevance to the changing European security context, could accelerate this trend by convincing West Europeans of the need to have a distinctive Western European voice in the broader deliberations. NATO, in its consultative role, will become one of many channels for the United States to discuss common problems with its Allies, but it will cease to hold the undisputed place as *primus inter pares.*

2. European foreign policy will become less disposed to accommodate the American view.

Historically, the United States and the EC countries have had divergent views on a number of foreign policy issues. In the Middle East, for example, the EC has followed a course that is more supportive of the Palestinians. Differences also surfaced over policy toward Vietnam and Central America. But on many key issues, especially involving East-West relations, the United States has generally been able to count on EC members' support, if not collectively, then at least from key individual European allies. Integration could increase the prospects for common European positions that conflict with the United States. In the words of Belgian diplomat Jean de Ruyt: "More and more the Americans will have to recognize that they cannot impose an attitude on the Europeans and that they cannot play one country off against another."[24]

First, an integrated approach may slow the speed of European reaction and enhance the leverage of the more recalcitrant actors in the EC. The record here is mixed: on the one hand, the EC responded promptly with economic and diplomatic measures in the wake of the Iraqi invasion of Kuwait and the outbreak of fighting in Yugoslavia. Arrayed against this is the difficulty of organizing a European military response to the Gulf crisis and past debacles such as the nearly three-week delay in developing a common approach to the Soviet invasion of Afghanistan. Germany's insistence on recognizing Slovenia and Croatia and the Greek veto over recognizing Macedonia under its current name show how powerful one determined member can be in shaping or blocking the common policy.

Second, the likely expansion of the EC will make it even more difficult to achieve consensus; yet the pressure to preserve a common front will make it harder for individual states to back the United States. A larger EC membership will lead to more cumbersome and time-consuming decisionmaking, and many of the likely new

---

[24]*National Journal,* August 18, 1990, p. 2000.

members, lacking the long transatlantic association with the United States through NATO, may have a more divergent and less activist approach to foreign and security policy than current EC members.[25] But it is important not to overstate this danger: while some of the potential new members (Austria,[26] Sweden, Finland, Switzerland) are Cold War neutrals, others are staunch NATO members (Norway and Turkey), and the Central/East European states, particularly Poland, Czechoslovakia, and Hungary, have strongly supported many U.S. policy initiatives (the Gulf is a notable example).

Finally, when there is consensus among Europeans, Europe is likely to stand more firmly for its views. Initially, the United States and Europe are most likely to clash over non-security-related aspects of foreign policy; the conflict over global CO_2 emissions and biodiversity at the 1992 Rio Environmental Summit and disputes over aid to Eastern Europe and the former Soviet Union are cases in point. Over time, however, these disagreements could extend to more core security questions.

Although it may be more difficult for the United States to secure European support in the future, this does not mean that Europe will oppose U.S. initiatives. Rather, integration could lead to indecision rather than an assertive independence. How "independent" Europe becomes will turn to a considerable degree on the extent to which effective European leaders emerge and their relationship to the United States. It will also depend on the development of new U.S.-EC consultation procedures, discussed below.[27]

3. The importance of "special relationships" will diminish but will not be eliminated completely.

A growing European commitment to develop common positions will make it more difficult for the United States to rely on its various

---

[25]Even within the current EC, there are members who stand somewhat outside the broad consensus on many foreign policy matters, especially neutral Ireland and Greece.

[26]The Austrian role in the Yugoslav crisis demonstrates that even where nations have distinctive interests that, in isolation, might lead to a different foreign policy response, the weight of the common view can have an important impact. Thus Austria, with its close geographic and historical ties to Slovenia and Croatia, might well have recognized the breakaway republics in the early stages of the conflict had it not been concerned about the impact of its actions on its prospects for EC membership.

[27]Lily Gardner Feldman has identified three possible futures for Europe as an international actor: "assertive Europe" (incremental improvements on current foreign policy cooperation), "decisive Europe" (a major global actor), and "diffident Europe" (a hesitant and purposeless actor). "The EC in the International Arena: A New Activism," in *Europe and the United States, Competition and Cooperation in the 1990s*, Committee on Foreign Affairs, U.S. House of Representatives, 1992, pp. 141–161.

"special relationships" to achieve its foreign policy objectives, since the U.S. ability to develop "à la carte" cooperation with individual Europeans will diminish. To take but one example, the United States might well have faced more difficulty in obtaining British approval for using U.K. bases during the attack on Libya in 1986 if the EC had developed a more integrated approach to foreign and security policy.[28]

But special relationships will not erode entirely, in large measure because individual EC countries will retain distinctive interests and perspectives, which in some cases will bring them closer to the United States than their fellow EC members. The European nuclear powers will continue to have a unique perspective on issues of arms control that they will not fully subordinate to the European Union in the foreseeable future. They are also likely to continue to hold individual seats in the Security Council, where their actions will be affected, but not fully constrained, by the CFSP.[29] Some countries will maintain special interests in aspects of global policy (France in Africa, Spain in Latin America, the Mediterranean states in the Middle East and Mahgreb), which could form the basis of U.S.-European policy concertation outside the ambit of the EC-U.S. relationship, as can be seen in the case of the U.S.-led UN operation in Somalia in December 1992. Even though increased integration will reduce the likelihood that individual EC nations will depart from a broad European foreign policy consensus, the fundamental importance of security issues virtually guarantees that EC nations will reserve that option. More important, bilateral relationships will continue to provide the United States with an avenue to affect EC decisionmaking. But this will affect which bilateral relationships are most important, a point discussed further, below.

---

[28]The U.K. role in the Libya bombing caused considerable friction within the EC. At the time that the United States was preparing to launch F-111 raids from Britain (April 14, 1986), the EC Foreign Ministers were meeting in the Netherlands to work out a common diplomatic approach to the allegations of Libyan complicity in the Berlin nightclub terrorist attack. Many in the EC felt that Foreign Secretary Howe deliberately withheld information from (or even lied to) his colleagues during the EPC meeting, a charge denied by Howe. See Pijpers et al., eds., *European Political Cooperation in the 1980s,* pp. 181–184.

[29]There was some discussion in the EPU negotiations over an "EC" seat on the UN Security Council, but neither France nor the United Kingdom seem willing to go in that direction at this time. Based on past experience, the two will show more independence on the Security Council than in the General Assembly, where the EC has attempted to coordinate EC members' positions through EPC, although the SEA commits the two European UN Security Council members "to take full account of positions agreed in European Political Cooperation." Article 30(7). In Germany, there is a growing political willingness to discuss a German seat on the Security Council; Foreign Minister Klaus Kinkel raised the issue in his fall 1992 speech to the UN General Assembly, although Chancellor Kohl has stated that it is not a "priority."

4. Europe will become increasingly independent on foreign policy matters that directly touch on European interests but will continue to look to the United States for leadership in many important aspects of global affairs.

In many ways, Yugoslavia and the Gulf crisis represent the two paradigm cases for the future respective roles of the United States and Europe. In the case of Yugoslavia, after the fighting began in June 1991, the EC quickly led the diplomatic efforts to resolve the crisis, while the United States was content to follow. This is attributable to a number of factors. First, Yugoslavia's European neighbors felt more directly affected. Second, the United States had limited political and economic influence over Yugoslavia. Third, few (either in Europe or the United States) favored military intervention or NATO involvement, which would have enhanced the importance of the U.S. role. Finally, the EC's economic leverage seemed the most suitable tool for response. This pattern is likely to hold for European conflicts in the future, especially internal ethnic disputes, although the United States may play a larger role where there are important U.S. ties.[30] But the Yugoslav crisis also showed that there are divergent opinions within the EC itself on fundamental geostrategic questions, which will continue to cause problems even under streamlined and more integrated EC procedures. The fact that the United States had to step in to galvanize UN action as the Bosnia crisis escalated in May 1992 demonstrates that the United States will still have opportunities to play a major role if, in future European crises, the EC is paralyzed by internal divisions.

By contrast, the Gulf War showed some of the limits of the European role in more remote crises. While the EC was able to act quickly to impose economic sanctions, many EC nations were hesitant about committing military forces. The lack of an established mechanism or standing European intervention forces contributed to Europe's difficulties, a problem that a more integrated CFSP and robust WEU could partially remedy. But divergent approaches and the anti-interventionary bias of many European countries suggest that European leadership outside of Europe will be limited, and forceful U.S. policies will be necessary to goad Europeans into action.

Policy toward republics of the former USSR is the most complex case. Throughout the Cold War, Europeans have tended to follow the U.S.

---

[30]For a more detailed assessment of the implications of the Yugoslavian crisis for European security institutions, see Steinberg, *The Role of European Institutions in Security After the Cold War.*

lead in East-West relations because of the importance of maintaining the U.S. security commitment to Europe. Even during this period of confrontation, however, significant differences of opinion between the United States and many Europeans emerged. On the whole the European approach was less confrontational and more inclined to seek political accommodation.

In recent years, Europe has become even more assertive in articulating a distinct policy toward the USSR and, more recently, the former Soviet republics. Europeans on the whole have pushed heavily for expanding economic assistance in the face of U.S. reluctance. Germany negotiated important aspects of German unification bilaterally with the USSR. The EC is expanding its bilateral contacts. The risk that the USSR's implosion will unleash ethnic conflict on Europe's borders and a flood of refugees and immigrants has a more direct impact on Europe than on the United States.

So long as Russia remains a powerful nuclear-armed nation with global interests, Europeans will accept a major U.S. voice in Western policy toward the former USSR. Continued political uncertainties in Russia serve to remind Europeans of the potential risks to their security. But European integration will mean that the European voice will become more influential, especially if Europe continues to foot a major share of the bill for reconstructing Eastern Europe and the former Soviet republics.

5. Europe will make some progress toward an independent defense capability distinct from NATO. But most EC members will remain committed to a (reformed) NATO-integrated military command, and NATO will remain the primary forum, both for consultation on major security questions and for implementing decisions requiring the use of military forces, for some time to come.

Since the Rome 1991 NATO summit and the Maastricht agreement, West Europeans have begun to take some concrete steps toward constructing an operational European defense identity, primarily through the WEU and the proposed Franco-German (European) Corps. To date, most of these efforts focus on enunciating principles (organization and missions) and creating nascent planning capabilities, although the WEU has deployed a small force in the Adriatic Sea to assist in monitoring the UN embargo against Serbia. While France and Germany insist that the Franco-German Corps could provide the nucleus of a future European army, their European partners show little enthusiasm, at least at this time.

Financial limitations provide a powerful impetus toward creating European coordination in order to maintain military effectiveness in the face of declining resources. But these same limits also constrain Europe's ability to develop the new capabilities needed to mount large-scale military operations without U.S. involvement, such as force projection and space surveillance, command control, and communications. This, coupled with the shrinking size of European armies and the legal and political barriers against using conscripts in out-of-area operations, means that it will be difficult for Europe to conduct significant military activities outside of Europe on its own. For European operations, at least of a modest scale, the potential for an independent European role is greater. But on a political level, there is reason to believe that Europeans on the whole will continue to prefer some continued U.S. involvement even in purely European military contingencies.

The transatlantic link serves not only to protect against the residual (or potentially resurgent) threat from nuclear-armed Russia but also acts as a kind of blanket insurance against a broad range of unforeseen developments in the future. U.S. involvement through NATO helps take the edge off potential intra-European feuds and thus indirectly helps facilitate other aspects of European integration. Although many think of NATO as a means for the United States to influence Europe, NATO consultations also provide Europeans with an opportunity to influence U.S. policy.

Meanwhile, NATO has taken steps to assure its relevance to the new European political environment, moving forward with its own military reorganization that focuses on greater mobility, more multinational formations, and an enhanced European role in the command structure, including a British Deputy Supreme Allied Commander, Europe (SACEUR) and a German Chief of Staff at Supreme Headquarters, Allied Powers Europe (SHAPE), as well as British command over the new Rapid Reaction Corps (RRC). Although there have been serious disagreements between Germany and the United Kingdom over the RRC, all the participants have strongly urged the United States to make a significant contribution to the force, demonstrating a strong interest in an active U.S. role. The creation of NACC in 1991, NATO's decision at the Oslo 1992 summit to make its forces available (at least in principle) for CSCE peacekeeping operations, and the NATO naval deployment in the Adriatic to monitor the UN embargo against Serbia demonstrate that the Allies want to maintain NATO's continued political and military relevance to European security.

Thus, given the likely limitations of the evolving independent European defense capability and the considerable benefits that NATO (including its military component) offers to West Europeans, particularly as NATO reforms enhance its relevance and "European-ness," Europeans are likely to support NATO's continuation as an important element of the European security landscape. From the European point of view (with perhaps the partial exception of France), a meaningful NATO and a stronger European defense identity are complementary rather than in conflict. And even France may be prepared to play a bigger politico-military role in NATO, with suitable reforms to NATO's structure.[31]

POLICY RECOMMENDATIONS FOR THE UNITED STATES

1. The United States should continue its long-standing policy of supporting European integration.

European integration will have political and economic costs and risks for the United States, as the preceding discussion has shown. Nonetheless, the United States is best served by supporting the integration process, a policy followed by every President since Truman, though with varying degrees of enthusiasm.

European integration is likely to serve a number of key U.S. interests:

- A politically integrated Europe will enhance European political stability;
- An integrated European market can help promote world economic growth and financial stability; and
- A more concerted European foreign and security policy (including an independent defense capability) can offer an alternative to U.S. involvement when the United States prefers not to become directly involved and may provide the United States with an effective international partner to share the burdens of global security.

In any event, supporting integration is in the U.S. interest because a more refractory policy will almost certainly prove counterproductive. Opposing the process will not seriously change the general direction of integration, which is primarily determined by forces internal to Europe, but will sacrifice U.S. influence over the specific form and substance. EC members who want to ensure that integration

[31]See the address by Defense Minister Joxe, Section 5, n. 75, supra: "Why not imagine that France could participate more tomorrow than today in [NATO's] politico-military discussions?"

proceeds in a way that is compatible with U.S. interests will be handicapped in the intra-European dialogue if they are seen as allies of an obstructionist United States. In short, the real alternatives for the United States are not supporting or blocking integration; instead, the choice is to shape the process through constructive participation, or to stand by as a carping outsider while Europeans tend to their own affairs.

2. The United States should champion the cause of a broader European Community.

The United States has an important stake in seeing the EC expand. Extending EC membership to Central and Eastern Europe's developing democracies is critical to promoting their economic growth, easing the transition to free markets, solidifying democratic governments, containing ethnic conflicts and separatist movements, and providing a measure of enhanced security. While the United States could achieve some of the objectives by supporting an enlarged NATO, the EC is the only organization that offers the critical economic and political benefits.

The United States also has a stake in EC/WEU membership for the two NATO members not now in the EC (Norway and Turkey) to ensure that the interests of these two key flank allies are not neglected as the EC develops a security dimension.

An enlarged EC also poses potential risks for the United States. For example, an enlarged Community could prove less cohesive, which would have costs as well as benefits for the United States; because a less cohesive Community would make a less useful interlocutor for the United States as well as a less effective competitor for policy leadership. And a less cohesive Community risks reviving intra-European feuds that could, in the worse case, lead to renationalized policies and even outright conflicts. Enlarging the EC also carries with it a greater risk that Europe will view itself as more self-sufficient economically (and thus less dependent on open global trade). But the EFTA countries' trade and economic policies are already highly integrated with the EC, so a de facto trade bloc already exists, and U.S. trade relations with potential new EC members are limited, so the potential trade diversion at best will be small.

Many Europeans insist that there is no conflict between broadening and deepening the Community. But the priority given to the two processes will have an impact not only on whether the Community plays a more active political and security role but on the potential benefits that the Community can offer to the region and the world at large.

There is much truth to the claim that the EC needs to put in place a more effective structure to maintain the momentum of integration. The decision to put off action on new applications until after the Maastricht Treaty is ratified and the five-year budget is in place was well-founded. For the East European countries, membership can only come at the end of a process that is now beginning with new association agreements to ensure that neither the countries themselves nor the EC is unduly taxed by adding poorer nations with fragile political and economic structures. But it is important that this reasonable delay not become an extended excuse for excluding qualified applicants from the Community. The EC took a calculated gamble by admitting Greece, Spain, and Portugal under uncertain conditions. While the U.S. influence is limited, the United States should urge that the EC be at least as forthcoming with applicants such as Poland, Hungary, the Czech and Slovak Republics, and, in the most difficult case, Turkey.[32]

3. The United States should support NATO reforms that promote the complementarity of NATO and the EC/WEU.

Although the movement toward a European defense identity is likely to be slow and limited, the United States has a stake in the orderly development of European capabilities for three reasons: to enhance the European contribution to NATO (relieving some of the U.S. burden), to provide a more effective partner for joint security operations outside of NATO, and to create an option for military response in situations where the United States itself chooses not to act (most likely in Eastern Europe, conceivably in the Mahgreb).

The objections to an independent European defense identity are threefold:

- It will undermine political support for NATO;
- It will lead to duplication of resources and confusion of responsibilities, to the detriment of both European and U.S. security;

[32]Secretary Baker, in his June 18, 1991, speech in Berlin, gave voice to this general sentiment, although he was extremely circumspect on the issue of EC membership: "In the near term, perhaps the EC's greatest external challenge is to reach out to the East. . . . Whether by example, supportive policies, association, ties with other regional groups, or even if some day Europeans so decide—through further integration, the EC can help these market democracies establish a home in a large community of common values."

- Europeans might become embroiled in a conflict without consulting the United States, then look to the United States for support if the problem proves more difficult than anticipated.

These concerns are legitimate, but not insurmountable, and can be addressed in a way that still allows the United States to reap the benefit of a more capable European security partner. To achieve this goal, it is important that NATO's evolution accommodate the development of European operational and military capability, a position supported, at least in principle, in the NATO Rome Communiqué. NATO force structure should be designed to permit Europeans to act effectively both with and without the United States. Dual-hatting arrangements and flexible "mix and match" force packages will facilitate this approach. In particular, the structure should permit easier coordination with French military forces, which will remain outside NATO. At the same time, the United States should urge Europeans to develop their own independent capabilities in a way that does not produce unnecessary duplication, sap scarce defense resources, or undermine NATO's own role in guaranteeing the security of all member-states. A complementary approach to defense responsibilities is the best way to assure, over the long run, NATO's continued viability as a durable transatlantic security link.

One key element of this approach is to support the development of contingency planning capability by the WEU. This will prove valuable for joint U.S.-European operations out-of-area as well as any independent European effort.

A more difficult question concerns the development of the proposed Franco-German Corps. It is undeniably true that some French proponents of the Corps see it as a substitute for, not complement to, NATO. But, insofar as *French* forces are concerned, assigning them to the Corps puts them no further away from NATO than existing arrangements and may, as German officials have argued, actually improve their links to NATO. For the German forces in the Corps, the issue is more complex, given their dual assignments to the Corps and to NATO. But the conflict is more apparent than real; since the German forces likely to be assigned to the Corps will be drawn from forces assigned to NATO's Main Defense Forces, their probable wartime missions in the event of an attack against NATO territory would be comparable under either guise. In any event, it is highly unlikely that NATO will need to deploy its Main Defense Forces in the near future. By focusing less on the motivations of the Corps' protagonists and more on the practical arrangements to assure complementarity and coordination, it should be possible to achieve a suitable arrangement that meets France's and Germany's political objectives without detracting from the Alliance's political solidarity or the effectiveness of its military forces. The recent agreement between NATO and France and Germany on the Franco-German Corps' relationship to NATO structures and missions is promising.

Fears than an enhanced European capability will cause Europe to go it alone in a way that prejudices U.S. interests seem misplaced. In the end, it remains unlikely that Europe will initiate significant military operations without consulting the United States; on the contrary, Europe will most likely need U.S. political and military support, or even leadership, to undertake such actions. As a practical matter, the United States will be in on the take-offs as well as the landings and often piloting the aircraft. The greater danger is that if European integration fails, there will be no one to occupy the co-pilot's seat.

4. The United States should focus its bilateral diplomacy on nations who are the most influential in the European Community.

Over the past 40 years, the United States has had two dominant bilateral relationships in Europe: U.S.-U.K. and U.S.-Germany. The relationship with Germany will continue to grow in importance as the role of the EC grows, since Germany will play a key role in most aspects of Community policy.

The future importance of the Anglo-American relationship will depend in large measure on the extent to which the United Kingdom accepts an integral role in the EC's development. Under Prime Minister Thatcher, the United Kingdom was often isolated in EC deliberations and its influence was therefore limited. Prime Minister Major seems determined to play a more involved role, but there remain serious questions of political support at home: both Conservatives and Labour are still lukewarm at best to Europe. If the United Kingdom becomes more involved in setting EC policy, both in economic and security affairs, the United Kingdom has the potential to be an important avenue of access for the United States to the Community, based on our long relationship of trust and similar viewpoints on many global political and economic issues. If not, the "special relationship" will continue to have value, but its importance will decline.

The third key player is France. The Franco-American relationship has experienced almost constant difficulties in the last three decades, and disagreements over security policy (particularly a defense role for the EC) and trade and industrial policy issues remain high. Yet

France is central to setting future EC policy, and U.S. influence will grow if the U.S. maintains an effective dialogue with both sides of the Franco-German axis. This is a difficult task, because the problems in the Franco-American relationship stem from real differences in strategic perspective, but it should be a high American priority.

5. The United States should strengthen its bilateral relationship with the EC in economic and security policy.

The new U.S.-EC consultation procedures agreed to in the Transatlantic Declaration mark an important step in elevating the bilateral U.S.-EC relationship. But meetings at the top by themselves are insufficient. It is important to build ongoing processes of interaction.

In security policy, this means closer links with EPC (and as it evolves, the Common Foreign and Security Policy). Europeans will resist making the United States a full member of the EPC's elaborate information exchange and consultation system (COREU), which keeps key EC foreign policy decisionmakers in constant touch—on the whole, they do not want a powerful 13th member of EPC. But the United States should explore new institutional links with the EPC process: this is the most effective guarantee against an insulated European caucus that considers U.S. views only after an EC consensus is reached. The United States should develop similar links with the WEU as its coordinating and planning role grows.

In the economic area, the most important new link to forge is with the emerging EC macroeconomic policy process. The United States has a unique opportunity to offer its views on both the bilateral and international financial aspects of designing a single European currency and central monetary institutions. The G-7 format can play a role, as well as existing links among central bank leaders, but more intense involvement is needed. This will prove complex before the EC creates the formal institutions, but the United States cannot afford to wait for a *fait accompli* before it enters into discussions, given the profound impact that EMU would have. EMU would herald a new era in the international financial system and require many adjustments; the United States can help assure that EMU is constructed in a way that meets the needs of a new international financial order and the economic interests of the United States.

In trade relations, too, there is need for improvement. Relations between the U.S. Trade Representative and the respective EC Commissioners and Directors General are too often suspicious and confrontational and occur too late in the process of EC policy formulation. While most of the work on Single Market Program directives is now complete, there is still considerable scope for dialogue on implementation, and as the Community's jurisdiction grows into new areas with EPU, there will be many substantive areas for discussion.

Research and development offers a particularly promising avenue for greater U.S.-European cooperation: U.S. firms have been interested in participating in European collaborative efforts such as JESSI and ESPRIT; Europeans in turn want access to U.S. efforts. Although there will be resistance from forces within the EC who view EC research and development as a way to strengthen Europe's economic hand against the U.S., many others support U.S.-EC collaboration as an effective means of meeting Japanese competition. The United States should explore with the EC new opportunities for transatlantic research collaboration in both civil and defense sectors.

CONCLUSION

The end of the Cold War marks a turning point in U.S.-European relations. For 45 years the pattern of our relations was clear: we knew who our friends were, and why we needed each other, and the importance of our common security and political interests buffered the many frictions we encountered along the way.

Today, both sides of the Atlantic are in the midst of profound internal debates over future interests and orientations. On one level, these internal debates seem isolated from each other and inward looking; Western Europe struggles over whether and how to broaden and deepen the Community while the United States debates how best to address long-neglected domestic needs. Yet the outcome of these debates will profoundly shape relations with each other in the years to come in obvious ways, such as the choice between protection or more open trade, and in more subtle ones, such as the definition of our future security interests.

For many Europeans, the end of the Cold War is an opportunity for Europe to cast off an old relationship of dependence in favor of new assertiveness. For many Americans, it is a time to expect Europeans to carry a greater share of the regional and global security burden and to demand more reciprocal treatment in economic affairs, especially trade. In some cases, this leads each side to mistrust the other's motives and objectives. For example, U.S. proposals concerning European security arrangements are treated with suspicion by some Europeans who fear continued U.S. dominance, just as some Americans resent Europeans' complaints about trends in U.S. trade policy. Yet it is surely appropriate for two long-standing and deeply interdependent allies to consult each other on the potential costs and benefits of proposed courses of action. Otherwise, there is risk of setting off an ever downward spiral of complaint and counter-complaint that could slowly but surely erode this crucial alliance. The U.S.-European relationship is hardy but not indestructible, and it can be destroyed by neglect as well as by intent. The proposals suggested here represent an approach that focuses on building a new framework of consultation and cooperation that will keep the relationship vibrant into the next century.

BIBLIOGRAPHY

"The Alliance's New Strategic Concept," Press Communiqué S-1(91)85, November 7, 1991 (mimeo).

Asmus, R. D., "Germany and America: Partners in Leadership?" *Survival,* November/December 1991.

Bonvicini, G., "Mechanisms and Procedures of EPC," in *European Political Cooperation in the 1980s,* edited by A. Pijpers et al., Martinus Nijhoff, 1988.

Brada, J. C., "The European Community and Czechoslovakia, Hungary, and Poland," *Report on Eastern Europe,* December 6, 1991.

"Budgetary Policies in Stage I of EMU," *European Economy,* No. 46, EC Commission, 1990.

Cecchini, P. (English edition, J. Robinson, ed.), *The European Challenge, 1992: The Benefits of a Single Market*, EC Commission, 1988.

Colchester, N., and D. Buchan, *Europower,* The Economist Books Limited (New York: Random House, 1990).

Commission of the European Communities, "A Consistent and Global Approach: A Review of the Community's Relations with Japan" (Communication to the Council), COM (92)219 final, Brussels: May 21, 1992 (mimeo).

Commission of the European Communities, "EC-Eastern Europe Relations—GX Background Brief," November 6, 1991 (mimeo).

Commission of the European Communities, "The Economics of 1992," in *European Economy,* No. 35, March 1988.

Commission of the European Communities, *Eurobarometer No. 36,* June 1992.

Commission of the European Communities, *Eurobarometer No. 37,* June 1992.

Commission of the European Communities, *Eurobarometer Trends 1974–1990,* March 1991.

Commission of the European Communities, "One Market, One Money," *European Economy,* No. 44, October 1990.

Commission of the European Communities, "The System of Own Resources," COM (92)81 final, Brussels: March 10, 1992.

Commission of the European Community, *Steps to European Unity,* Luxembourg Office for Official Publications of the European Community, 1987.

Cooper, C., J. Steinberg, and M. Shires, *The Evolution of the European Economy: Implications for Transatlantic Relations,* Santa Monica, Calif.: RAND, N-3432-FF, 1992.

Cooper, R. N., "Will an EC Currency Harm Outsiders?" *Orbis,* Fall 1992.

Corner, D. C., and I. Tonks, "The Impact of the Internationalisation of World Stock Markets on the Integration of EC Securities Markets," in *European Integration and Industry*, edited by M. Macmillan, D. G. Mayer, and P. van Veen, Tilburg: Tilburg University Press, 1987.

Council of Ministers of 18, "Political Agreement on CAP Reform," 18, 19, 20, and 21 May 1992 (mimeo).

Crouch, C., and D. Marquand, eds., *The Politics of 1992*, Blackwell, 1990.

Debouzy, O., *The Debate on the American Presence and Role in Europe,* European Strategy Group, January 1991.

Declaration on European Security and Defence, Policy Statement 62/91, October 4, 1991.

Duchêne, F., "Less or More Than Europe? European Integration in Retrospect," *The Politics of 1992,* edited by C. Crouch and D. Marquand, Blackwell, 1990.

Emerson, M., and C. Huhne, *The ECU Report,* London: Pan Books, 1991.

European Commission, *Annual Economic Report 1991/1992,* 1991.

European Commission, "Association Agreements with the Countries of Central and Eastern Europe," September 7, 1990, Europe Documents N. 1646/47.

European Commission, "Budgetary Policies in Stage I of EMU," *European Economy*, No. 46.

European Commission, *Forecast for 1992/1993*, 1991.

European Council, "Presidency Conclusions—Maastricht 9 and 10 December 1991," SN 271/1/91 (Maastricht, December 11, 1991).

Feldman, L. G., "The EC in the International Arena: A New Activism," in *Europe and the United States, Competition and Cooperation in the 1990s,* Committee on Foreign Affairs, U.S. House of Representatives, 1992.

Final Communiqué Ministerial Meeting of the North Atlantic Council, Oslo, Norway, June 4, 1992.

Fitzmaurice, J., "An Analysis of the EC's Cooperation Procedure," *Journal of Common Market Studies,* June 1988.

Froment-Maurice, H., and P. Ludlow, "Towards a European Foreign Policy," in *Governing Europe,* Center for European Policy Studies, Paper No. 45, 1990.

Froot, K. A., and K. Rogoff, "The EMS, the EMU and the Transition to a Common Currency," NBER Working Paper No. 3684, April 1991, summarized in *The Effects of Greater Economic Integration Within the European Community on the United States: Fourth Follow-Up Report,* USITC Publication 2501, April 1992.

Gellman Research Associates, Inc., "An Economic and Financial Review of Airbus Industrie," September 4, 1990 (mimeo).

Ginsberg, R., *Foreign Policy Actions of the European Community,* Adamantine Press, 1989.

Gordon, P., *French Security Policy After the Cold War: Continuity, Change, and Implications for the United States,* Santa Monica, Calif.: RAND, R-4229-A, 1992.

Hufbauer, G. C., ed., *Europe 1992*, Washington, D.C.: The Brookings Institution, 1990.

Kaiser, K., C. Merlini, T. de Montbrial, E. Wellenstein, and W. Wallace, *The European Community: Progress or Decline?* Royal Institute of International Affairs, 1983.

Laird, R., *The Europeanization of the Alliance,* Boulder, Colo.: Westview Press, 1991.

Ludlow, P., *Beyond 1992*, CEPS, 1989.

Maresca, J. J., *To Helsinki,* Duke University Press, 1985.

Menon, A., A. Forster, and W. Wallace, "A Common European Defence?" *Survival,* Autumn 1992.

Moravcik, A., "Negotiating the Single European Act: National Interests and Conventional Statecraft in the European Community," in *International Organizations*, Winter 1991.

Nutall, Simon, "Where the Commission Comes In," in *European Political Cooperation in the 1980s,* edited by A. Pijpers et al., Martinus Nijhoff, 1988.

Pettersen, W. E., ed., *Beyond the Intergovernmental Conferences,* Europa Institute, 1991.

Pijpers, A., et al., eds., *European Political Cooperation in the 1980s,* Martinus Nijhoff, 1988.

Rifkind, Rt. Hon. M., "A Decade of Change in European Security," Centre for Defence Studies, Kings College, London: May 14, 1992 (mimeo).

Rome Declaration on Peace and Cooperation, November 7–8, 1991, *NATO Communiqués 1991*, Brussels: NATO Office of Information and Press, n.d.

Rosenthal, D. E., "Competition Policy," in *Europe 1992,* edited by G. C. Hufbauer, Washington, D.C.: The Brookings Institution, 1990.

Rummel, R., "Speaking With One Voice—and Beyond," *European Political Cooperation in the 1980s,* edited by A. Pijpers et al., Martinus Nijhoff, 1988.

Salmon, T. C., "Testing Time for European Political Cooperation: The Gulf and Yugoslavia 1990–1992," in *International Affairs*, Vol. 68, No. 2, 1992.

Shelburne, R., and G. Schoepfle, "The European Community 1992 Program and U.S. Workers," *Monthly Labor Review*, November 1990.

Smeets, H. D., "Does Germany Dominate the EMS?" *Journal of Common Market Studies,* September 1990.

Steinberg, J. B., *The Role of European Institutions in Security After the Cold War: Some Lessons from Yugoslavia,* Santa Monica, Calif.: RAND, N-3445-FF, 1992.

Steinberg, J. B., *The Transformation of the European Defense Industry,* Santa Monica, Calif.: RAND, R-4141-ACQ, 1992.

Stokes, B., "Deadline Nears in Aircraft Subsidy Rift," *National Journal,* March 28, 1992.

Vernet, D., "France in a New Europe," *The National Interest,* Fall 1992.

Wallace, W., *The Transformation of Western Europe,* New York: Royal Institute of International Affairs/Council on Foreign Relations Press, 1990.

Western European Council of Ministers, "Petersberg Declaration," Bonn: June 19, 1992 (mimeo).

Woolcock, S., et al., *Britain, Germany and 1992: The Limits of Deregulation*, New York: Council on Foreign Relations Press, 1991.

Woolcock, S., *Trading Partners or Trading Blows: Market Access in EC-U.S. Relations*, New York: Council on Foreign Relations Press, 1992.

Woolcock, S., "U.S. Views on 1992," *National Institute Economic Review,* Vol. 134, November, 1990.